Winnipeg 19
The strikers' own history of the
Winnipeg General Strike

Edited and with an introduction
by Norman Penner

James Lewis & Samuel
Toronto
1973

Published with the assistance of the Social Science Research Council, using funds provided by the Canada Council.

ISBN 0-88862-037-3 (cloth)
ISBN 0-88862-038-1 (paper)

Cover design by Chrigter Themptander
Design by Lynn Campbell

James Lewis & Samuel, Publishers
Egerton Ryerson Memorial Building
35 Britain Street
Toronto
Canada

Printed and bound in Canada

Contents

The Winnipeg General Strike is the proudest achievement of the Canadian working class. It is immortal.

This book is dedicated to the memory of Jacob Penner (1880-1965), who wrote the passage above, who participated in the events described in these pages, and who spent most of his life helping to build the Winnipeg labour movement.

Acknowledgements

My grateful thanks are extended to the following: my friends, Sam and Dianne Cristall, whose library yielded the book that is the main reason for this collection; Daniel Drache of Atkinson College, York University, who first suggested the project; Joan Brown and Ruth Griffin, most efficient secretaries at Glendon College, York University, who made it possible to meet impossible deadlines; I. M. Abella, associate professor of History at Glendon, for his helpful comments; and David Millar, doing graduate work at York, for his collection of photographs of the Winnipeg General Strike from which we selected, with his advice, the photos used here.

NP

CITY HALL

VICTORIA PARK

MAIN

RED RIVER

PORTAGE AVENUE

MAIN STREET

EATON'S

DOWNTOWN WINNIPEG, 1919

MANITOBA LEGISLATIVE BUILDINGS

ASSINIBOINE RIVER

Introduction

In the Canadian labour movement's long and continuing history of struggle to establish its trade-union rights, no episode was more spectacular, explosive or meaningful than the Winnipeg General Strike of 1919. It was, in the words of one writer, "the first and only time in Canadian history that a major city was split clearly into two opposing classes."[1] But it went beyond the city of Winnipeg. It involved the federal state, which threw its whole weight behind the business interests of Winnipeg, and aroused deep and bitter feelings in the ranks of labour all over the country. Its impact was far wider than the immediate economic issues of the strike. In the end, the six weeks that shook Winnipeg also shook the politics of Canada, and the legacy of the strike is more to be seen in its political consequences than in any other of its many aspects.

This epic event continues to challenge Canadian historians, who are finding generally that there is a rich and largely neglected mine of material in the history of Canadian labour. The present collection is intended as a contribution to that study, and as a hopeful attempt to widen the circle of interest beyond the scholars.

The general strike grew out of two ordinary strikes which began on May 1st and 2nd, 1919, one involving the building-trades unions, and the other, metal-trades workers at three metal shops.

Although these strikes were separate, their demands were quite similar. The Builders' Exchange said that, while it was prepared to deal with individual construction craft unions, it would not recognize the Building Trades Council which was co-ordinating the demands of all the separate unions. The Metal Trades Contractors also refused to bargain with the Metal Trades Council. As a result, the issue became quite clearly the right of the workers to bargain collectively through union structures of their own choice.

On May 6, the two groups of unions informed the Winnipeg Trades and Labour Council of the employers' refusal. It was thereupon agreed that the membership of all the affiliated unions of the TLC would be polled on their willingness to engage in a general sympathetic strike in support of the building-trades unions and the metal workers.

1. Kenneth McNaught, *A Prophet in Politics* (Toronto, 1963), p. 99.

On May 13, the results of the balloting showed 8,667 for and 645 against a general strike.

The strike was called for May 15. Within two hours of its commencement, the whole industrial and commercial life of Winnipeg ground to a halt. Thousands of workers — men, women, boys and girls — who were not members of any union joined the strike. The police, who also voted to strike, were asked by the strikers to keep to their jobs of protecting law and order. The essential services such as milk deliveries, waterworks and fire protection were maintained at a minimum level, "by authority of the Strike Committee." Soldiers just returned from the war declared their full support for the strike. At its high point, the strike involved as many as 35,000 workers out of a total population of 175,000, although the Trades and Labour Council comprised only 12,000 unionized members prior to May 15.

The strike quickly became a confrontation between the strikers and a committee representing the business interests of Winnipeg, the Citizens' Committee of 1,000. This committee had the complete support of the federal government, and made it clear that there would be no bargaining of any kind unless the general strike was called off.

The Citizens' Committee launched a massive propaganda war against the strike. Among other things, it called for the deportation of aliens on strike. It sought and obtained amendments to the Immigration Act which permitted such deportations to take place without trial.

The strikers, for their part, organized a series of demonstrations to show their strength and to protest the arrest on June 17 of their leaders. A "silent parade" held on June 21[1] was attacked by special police armed with baseball bats, and by the mounted police and units of the militia and regular armed forces with small-arms fire.[2] One person was killed and dozens were injured.

The arrest of the main leaders, the intransigence of the federal government, the power of the Citizens' Committee and, finally, the use of armed force, made it impossible to continue the strike; accordingly, it was called off by the Strike Committee on June 25, 1919.

The Winnipeg General Strike has been given widely differing interpretations, ranging from the original accusation by the federal government of the day that it was a conspiracy to seize power by revolutionary means, to the more accepted version of today, that it was one of the major battles that Canadian labour has had to wage to establish its trade-union rights. This is the view that emerged out of the first

1. It should be noted that this parade and several others that took place earlier were organized by the returned soldiers and not by the Strike Committee. The committee discouraged parades, concentrating on meetings in various parks in the city.
2. For full details, see the "Address of Peter Heenan," p.239.

— and still the only — major study of the strike, *The Winnipeg General Strike* by D. C. Masters (Toronto, 1950), and most historians who have written subsequently on various aspects of the strike generally accept his interpretation.

But this does not exhaust the subject by any means, and the number of short pieces that have been published since Masters's book whet the appetite for another major treatment, more sympathetic to the strikers' cause and covering a wider canvas. The trouble with a great deal of historical writing on the Canadian labour movement is that it tends to be confined to specific trade-union questions, and seldom examines the impact the working class has had on the general political development and political culture of Canada. Yet this is the aspect of the Winnipeg General Strike that really needs more study; for it was, as one writer has said, "a watershed of some consequence in the evolution of Canada."[1]

The present collection should help in this respect. The main document, a detailed account of the strike as seen by the strikers themselves, has been largely ignored by scholars. Even Masters, who in most respects appears to have been thorough and painstaking in researching the strike, does not refer to it at all.

Yet this document is of enormous value, and not only as a source of information about the events of the strike and the views of the strikers. Its publication was itself an event in the significant Canada-wide movement that followed the strike to organize and finance the defence of the arrested leaders and to secure their release after imprisonment.

This activity was initiated by the Winnipeg Defence Committee, which replaced the Strike Committee after the strike had been called off. Strike leaders while out on bail, and those who were acquitted, toured the country continuously for almost a year, addressing public gatherings and trade-union locals and soliciting funds for the defence. Well over $60,000 was collected to pay legal costs and to subsidize the families of the arrested men. After the trials had been concluded on April 6, 1920, a convention was called by the Defence Committee on April 11 to decide on further steps. Over six hundred delegates attended. They decided to appeal the verdict of the Canadian courts to the Privy Council in London; to pay $35 a week for the duration of the men's imprisonment to their families; and to step up efforts to place the labour movement's position before the general public.[2]

At the beginning of May 1920, the Winnipeg Defence Committee

1. H. C. Pentland, "Fifty Years After," *Canadian Dimension* 6, no. 2 (July 1969): 14.
2. The Privy Council ruled that, as the trials and sentences related to offences under the Criminal Code, the Supreme Court of Canada was the court of last appeal.

announced in a circular letter the availability of four pamphlets, which it described as "very Interesting and Educative Literature," about the recent trials and the events of the strike: *Dixon's Address to the Jury in Defence of Freedom of Speech, Russell Trial and Labour's Rights, W. A. Pritchard's Address to the Jury* and *The Winnipeg General Sympathetic Strike.* The latter two were new publications, the others having appeared earlier.

The circular described the fourth document in particularly glowing terms:

> About three hundred pages of the most interesting reading ever published. No worker should be without a copy.
> THE TRUTH — THE WHOLE TRUTH — AND NOTHING BUT THE TRUTH

The RCMP did not share this opinion. In a letter to his commissioner in Ottawa, the superintendent of the Manitoba command reported on the publication of the history, sent him six copies, and gave his critical assessment as follows:

> The contents are a more or less garbled account of the proceedings in Winnipeg last year, at the time of the general strike, according to the version of the Defence Committee.
> I would draw your attention to pages 152-158 inclusive, dealing with the alleged actions of the RNWMP in arresting the strike leaders.[1]

The commissioner acknowledged receipt of the copies and asked for six more.[2]

The strikers' history appeared just as Manitoba was approaching a provincial election in which the labour movement sought to make the strike the main issue. There is no doubt that this book, along with the other activity generated by the Defence Committee, contributed to the victory that labour registered in electing eleven members to the legislature, four of them strike leaders in Winnipeg, three of whom were still in penitentiary. This victory had been foreshadowed in the civic elections the previous November when labour increased its representation from five to seven aldermen, and the same kind of support was further demonstrated the following year when J. S. Woodsworth, an arrested strike leader who had been acquitted, was elected to the House of Commons from Winnipeg Centre.

The activity of the Defence Committee and the response it received throughout Canada expressed a spirit of defiance and strength, with

1. Public Archives of Canada, RCMP files HV-1, vol. 10, letter from Superintendent R. S. Knight, May 3, 1920. Pages referred to are   in this book.
2. *Ibid.* May 12, 1920. (Between the time of the strike and this exchange of letters a year later, the Royal North-West Mounted Police had become the the Royal Canadian Mounted Police.)

little or no evidence that the labour movement regarded the general strike as a failure.

The statement of the Strike Committee in calling off the strike had been confident and prophetic. Labour, it said, had made a magnificent fight, and must now prepare for the next fight, which would be in the political field. It called for immediate preparation by the labour movement to contest the next elections for the city council, provincial legislature, and what it called "the House of a thousand scandals in Ottawa," to increase labour representation in all these bodies. The employers must realize by now that "workers are no longer timid, ignorant slaves ... They are going to have more say in the Government."[1]

This same spirit of defiance and confidence permeates the strikers' history. Their account begins before the strike, to include a report of three meetings which the Crown, in its bill of particulars against the arrested strike leaders, had alleged to be part of the "seditious conspiracy" to take over Winnipeg by means of a general strike. These were: a meeting in the Walker Theatre, Winnipeg, December 1918; a second at Winnipeg's Majestic Theatre, January 1919; and, most important, the Western Labour Conference in Calgary in March 1919, where 250 delegates representing the official trade-union bodies of Western Canada voted unanimously to launch a new type of industrial union to be called the One Big Union (OBU).

While these meetings were not directly linked to the strike, they do provide a graphic record of the mood of discontent and protest that gripped the working class, especially in Western Canada, in the aftermath of the First World War. This discontent had been building up during the war and was due primarily to economic conditions connected with a war-time economy, principally those of wild inflation and low wages. But labour also nursed grievances over the imposition of conscription, which it had bitterly opposed. And it had been very much affected by a series of sensational scandals which showed that huge profits were being made by corporations and individuals supplying the armed services. These grievances were joined at the end of the war by the protests of the farmers over high tariffs and the prospect of falling wheat prices, and those of the returned soldiers, who had come home to find that they were superfluous to industry.[2]

This wide and growing unrest was aggravated by the policies of the Union government, and particularly by its minister of the Interior

1. Statement quoted in the Toronto *Star*, June 27, 1919.
2. S. D. Clark in this foreword to Masters's book sees both the agrarian revolt that was gathering momentum in Western Canada at the war's end and the upsurge of labour unrest there as common "expressions of protest against eastern dominance" (p. vii).

and acting minister of Justice, the Honourable Arthur Meighen. He was singularly unsympathetic to the suffering and hardships of the people. He mistook effects for causes, blamed the unrest on agitators and, by seeking to suppress the movements of protest, became himself a cause of further discontent.

W. A. Pritchard's address to the jury conveys labour's particular hostility to this man. Pritchard accused Meighen of being responsible for the infamous Wartime Elections Act, the amendments to the Immigration Act and of being "the head and trunk" of the efforts to break the strike.[1] This view of Meighen was shared by many contemporaries. He was, said Ernest Lapointe, Liberal MP, in the Commons debate of the strike on June 2, 1919, "the apostle of arbitrary enactments and despotic legislation."[2] "His name," said *Le Devoir,* "is coupled to the most arbitrary and hateful measures passed by a tory-unionist government during the war."[3] As minister of the Interior he played a key role in the widespread use of orders in council, by which certain Canadian publications, imported literature and political organizations were banned, and numbers of aliens arrested.[4]

The meetings in Winnipeg and Calgary also reflected the impact of the Bolshevik Revolution of 1917 on the labour movement in Canada. Little was known about the theories of Lenin, whose works had not yet been translated, but there was a widespread feeling that Soviet Russia was a workers' government that should be supported, and this feeling was shared by most labour leaders in Western Canada. They were angry at the action of the Canadian government in sending an expeditionary force to take part in military operations aimed at crushing what they considered to be the first workers' state in history, and they regarded this intervention as one more proof that the Union government was anti-labour.

The Calgary conference showed, in addition, that Western Canadian labour had its own grievances against the eastern leadership that dominated the Trades and Labour Congress of Canada, to which all their unions were affiliated. They felt that the eastern leadership was too conservative, too friendly with the Union government, too oblivious to the needs and feelings of the locals in Western Canada and too much in the hands of the international officers. There was also a

1. See "Pritchard's Address to the Jury," p 247-8. The Wartime Elections Act disenfranchised naturalized citizens who had come from enemy alien countries, and enfranchised grandmothers, mothers, wives and sweethearts of enlisted men. These changes made the victory of the Union government and its conscription measure inevitable. The amendments to the Immigration Act permitted the deportation without trial of "subversive" aliens, including British subjects.
2. Quoted in Roger Graham, *Arthur Meighen* (Toronto, 1960), vol. 1, p. 239.
3. *Ibid.*, p. 299.
4. See "The Winnipeg General Sympathetic Strike," pp. 6-8.

feeling that the craft structure of the trade-union movement was an obstacle to further progress and ought to give way to industry-wide unions.

But before the program adopted at the Calgary conference for a new type of union structure could be acted upon, the general strike broke out and plans to launch the One Big Union movement had to be suspended until after the strike.

There is no doubt that the mood of the Winnipeg and Western labour movement, as portrayed in the first pages of the strikers' history, had a great deal to do with the militant and radical character of the general strike. But the strike itself was a trade-union struggle for very specific economic demands which are detailed in this book. It was led by people representing all political tendencies in the Winnipeg Trades and Labour Council, from Liberals and Conservatives to single taxers, to radical and revolutionary socialists. Only one of the fifteen-member Central Strike Committee, R. B. Russell, was an official of the incipient OBU. And the strike was called by the Trades and Labour Council only after all its affiliates had voted overwhelmingly to support the walkout of the metal-trades and building-trades locals. What followed the calling of the sympathetic strike is graphically portrayed in the diary-like account of their struggle that the strikers have left us.

A number of events which occurred during the first week set the stage for the bitter confrontation that was to follow. As soon as the strike was called and the directing committee established, the Citizens' Committee of 1,000 announced its existence. Ostensibly organized to maintain public services (which the strikers had guaranteed to maintain), the committee quickly became *de facto* an agency of the federal government, even by-passing the Winnipeg city council and the Manitoba government whenever these bodies showed any weakness or hesitation in their dealings with the strikers.

A. J. Andrews, KC, one of the principal members of this committee, was appointed by Meighen as a special deputy minister of Justice, with powers to carry out arrests and initiate deportation proceedings. He and three other leading members of the committee became the Crown prosecutors in the state trials that followed the strike. They were in constant touch with General Kitchen,[1] officer commanding in Manitoba military district, and with the superintendent of the Manitoba command of the RCMP. This committee forced the city council to dismiss the entire Winnipeg police force of 240 men

1. In the strikers' history, this name is spelled Ketchen, while in *Hansard*, 1926, it is Kitchen as above.

which was sympathetic to the strikers, and it recruited a special police
force of two thousand men to replace the regulars. It also got the
chief of police dismissed and replaced by a man more to its liking.

It carried out a massive propaganda drive against the strike, and
it raised one million dollars for its purposes, according to the strikers'
account. The committee also acted to keep all employers in line,
lest any in a moment of weakness might want to negotiate with the
unions individually. The extent of Andrews's power is demonstrated
by a letter reproduced in the history, in which he orders the company
printing the strikers' daily bulletin to cease publication forthwith (p.
207). [1]

The special and extraordinary relationship between the Committee
of 1,000 and the federal government took shape within the first week
of the strike, when Meighen and the minister of Labour, Senator
Gideon Robertson, arrived in Winnipeg with several members of the
committee on the train with them. From that point on, the strike
assumed the character of a class confrontation, with the federal government's weight and authority clearly on the side of the Winnipeg
business elite. When compared with the real power enjoyed by the
Committee of 1,000, which had taken on many of the attributes of
a parallel government, the charge that the Strike Committee actually
ran the city seems ludicrous.

The reader will note in the strikers' history that the Strike Committee
urged the police not to join the strike but to remain on duty, which
they did until dismissed by the city council. The charge that has
been most often made, that the ''authority to work'' cards issued
by the Strike Committee represented assumption of power by the
Strike Committee, is shown in the strikers' account to be false. It
was in fact the proposal of the manager of the Crescent Creamery
(p. 50) that such cards be issued to enable milk deliveries to be
made, and this proposal was accepted by the strikers. Moreover, when
the mayor later asked the strikers to discontinue these cards, the Strike
Committee agreed and withdrew them. The Strike Committee even
sought to discourage the holding of demonstrations in order to avoid
the slightest appearance of provocation. The fateful June 21 parade
of returned veterans and their families in support of the arrested strike
leaders was billed and carried through as a ''silent parade,'' with
no banners, songs, slogans or speeches. Violence erupted only when
the ''special police'' and the mounted police charged the unarmed
marchers.

The intransigence of Meighen and Robertson during the strike

---

1. Apparently the bulletin did cease, but only for one day. It reappeared under a
   different name and presumably with a different printer.

is fully documented in the strikers' account. It was later underscored in the Heenan disclosures to the House of Commons in June 1926, which are also reproduced in this collection. The arrest and detention of the strike leaders (notwithstanding Meighen's own doubts as to the legality of such measures); his orders to carry out deportations before they had been duly ratified; the surreptitious shipment of arms to Winnipeg "without anybody being the wiser"; the refusal to allow the employers to settle the strike lest this be interpreted as a victory for the workers — all these measures support Heenan's conclusion that Robertson and Meighen "were more interested in breaking the strike than in settling the strike."

But it also lends credence to the charge Pritchard made in his address to the jury, which J. S. Woodsworth repeated in the House of Commons in 1926:

> There was then what might almost be described as a conspiracy against labour.[1]

The question is, why did supposedly reasonable men act in this way? Did they really believe that the general strike was an attempt to seize power?

Meighen's fear of Bolshevism was undoubtedly genuine. A month before the Winnipeg events, he had participated in a Cabinet telegram to Prime Minister Borden in Versailles, reporting that "Bolshevism" and "socialism" were "rampant" in Vancouver, Calgary and Winnipeg, and urging Borden to have the British government station a cruiser off Vancouver as this "would have a steadying influence."[2] Meighen had become alarmed at the widespread sympathy for the Russian Revolution that had developed in the ranks of labour, and he was undoubtedly much influenced by the revolutionary rhetoric that had issued from the Western Labour Conference in March of that year. Meighen never got over his fear of socialism, which he considered to be synonymous with Bolshevism, or even of what he called in 1943 "semi-socialism."[3] But in 1919, the fear which he shared with most of the Cabinet bordered on hysteria.

Still, Meighen was able to separate the purely trade-union questions from the political context in which they seemed to appear. He was absolutely convinced, for instance, that it would be wrong to allow a number of unions in a given industry to bargain collectively as though they were one union. He was unyielding in his stand against the right of public-service employees, like the postal workers, to join

1. House of Commons *Debates*, 1926, vol. 4, p. 4118.
2. See Graham, *Arthur Meighen*, vol. 1, p. 231.
3. Arthur Meighen, Lecture on "Socialism" in *Unrevised and Unrepented* (Toronto, 1949).

a sympathetic strike, and he was implacably opposed to the whole idea of sympathetic strikes. The idea that a worker would need authorization from the Strike Committee to perform essential services, constituted in his mind the revolutionary usurpation of power.

Another important factor that conditioned Meighen's attitude to the strike undoubtedly was his close relationship with the Winnipeg business community against whom the strike was directed, and whose reaction largely determined the bitterness and length of the struggle. The Manitoba establishment was, and probably still is, the most obdurate in Canada, and Meighen was its man in the Cabinet.

In his authoritative history of Manitoba, W. L. Morton traces the origins of the province's establishment out of the influx of settlers and "aggressive" businessmen who came to Manitoba, mostly from Ontario, in the wake of the defeat of the Riel Rebellions. By the turn of the century, according to Morton, they had succeeded in making Manitoba a unilingual Protestant province contrary to the original Manitoba Act.[1] According to Thomas Peterson, this class controlled "economic and political power" in Manitoba until 1969.[2]

Murray Donnelly singles out two of the prominent ideological leaders of this elite: Clifford Sifton, owner of the Manitoba *Free Press* and J. W. Dafoe, his editor. He says of Sifton, "A man more unsympathetic to the cause of the working man never lived." Dafoe, he says, "had a blind spot on the question of leftist activity . . . He had educated himself well on many subjects, but he never came to understand that there was a difference between British socialism and Marxist communism, and he condemned proponents of both with brutal vigour."[3]

It turns out that these men had another blind spot, according to Donnelly. They felt uneasy about the large "foreign element" in Winnipeg (whose immigration to help settle the Canadian West Clifford Sifton, as minister of the Interior in the Laurier Cabinet, had encouraged). They came to feel threatened by these people, and "when the strike occurred they fell victim of unreasonable fears."[4]

They lent themselves to an anti-alien campaign which does them no credit. Huge ads appeared in the three Winnipeg dailies calling on the government to deport "the undesirable alien and land him back in the bilgewaters of European Civilization from whence he sprung and to which he properly belongs."[5] And, as pointed out

1. W. L. Morton, *Manitoba: A History* (Toronto, 1957), p. 245.
2. T. Peterson in M. Robin, ed., *Canadian Provincial Politics* (Scarborough, 1972), p. 69.
3. Murray Donnelly, *Dafoe of the Free Press* (Toronto, 1968), p. 102.
4. *Ibid.*, p. 105.
5. Ad in Winnipeg *Telegram*, June 6, 1919.

in the strikers' account, the very day that this ad appeared Meighen was piloting through the House of Commons and Senate the infamous amendments to the Immigration Act referred to above. The same racism that the Manitoba elite had displayed against Franco-Manitobans surfaced again, this time as a reaction against working-class immigrants.

Senator Gideon Robertson, whose name appears frequently in the strikers' history, was the first trade unionist ever to become a minister of Labour. He had reasons of his own for acting the way he did. He feared that a victory for the strike would be a big boost to the OBU, which he saw as a threat to the international unions of which he was an official. And he shared the views of conservative trade-union leaders in eastern Canada who felt that labour's cause was always jeopardized by militant actions. His strong bias against the OBU was again evident after the strike, when he used his post in the government to force mine workers in Drumheller to desert the OBU and re-affiliate to the international unions.[1]

The OBU never fulfilled the promise it seemed to hold when it was first projected in March 1919. The defeat of the Winnipeg strike less than four months later was a serious blow from which the organization never really recovered. The collusion of government and international unions was too much for the OBU to withstand, even in a number of places where it did win sizeable affiliations once it got started.

Yet the attempt to build the OBU was a significant moment in the history of Canadian labour. The industrial unionism which it espoused took hold in Canada twenty years later, when the great organizing drive conducted by the CIO in the United States spilled over into Ontario and Quebec. Ironically, the success of industrial unionism in Canada was at the expense of Canadian trade-union autonomy,[2] but it was achieved in the face of a combination of conservative trade-union bureaucracy and government similar to that which the OBU had faced.

The character of the Winnipeg General Strike was influenced by the fact that many of its leaders were British immigrants who had brought with them militant, democratic and socialist traditions from the British labour movement. Industrial unionism had already taken place in Britain by the end of the nineteenth century, and this development provided the spur that was needed there to bring about labour's political indepen-

---

1. Charles Lipton, *The Trade Union Movement in Canada 1827-1959* (Montreal, 1966), p. 221.
2. See I. M. Abella, *Communism, Nationalism and Canadian Labour* (Toronto, 1973).

dence through the formation of the Labour Party. That party at its inception was a mixture of diverse ideologies — socialist, Marxian, Fabian, radical liberal and labourist.

It is not surprising that these various trends were represented among the British working-class immigrants who came to Canada prior to World War I, among whom were Heaps, Pritchard, Dixon, Johns, Russell and Queen, all principals in the strike and trials of 1919–20. Men like these found Canadian society at a different stage of development, with toryism much more the political culture than democratic liberalism. The working class here was largely unorganized and politically subordinate to the Liberals and Conservatives. The immigrants' desire to win what they considered from their British experience to be elementary is expressed in many of the pages of the history we are publishing, and also in the proceedings of the state trials which followed the strike.

The particulars of the charges and the individuals concerned in these trials are given in "The Winnipeg General Sympathetic Strike," but its account stops prior to the jury trials which began in December 1919 and ended in April 1920. Ten principal figures of the strike were involved. Three — Woodsworth, Dixon and Heaps — were acquitted; five — Pritchard, Ivens, Armstrong, Johns and Queen — were sentenced to one year. Russell got two years, and Bray six months.

Four of them — Queen, Heaps, Dixon and Pritchard — defended themselves, and their addresses to the jury were considered to be outstanding. The Toronto *Star* of February 16, 1920, called Dixon's speech "the most eloquent ever heard in a Manitoba Court, in the opinion of lawyers and court officials, veterans of scores of trials." Pritchard's speech was likewise praised by the press. It took two days, from 10 a.m. to 10 p.m. each day, to deliver. The Winnipeg *Tribune* of March 23, 1920, called Pritchard "the most brilliant of the galaxy of star orators who have so far addressed the jury, displaying a knowledge of other cultural arts that would astound the average individual whose mental picture of a labour leader is a horny-handed, unread, ungrammatical toiler." On March 25 the *Tribune* described the tense and dramatic atmosphere in the courtroom as Pritchard wound up his address:

Speaking with gripping intensity, Pritchard seemed to hold the entire court through the sheer force of his personality and the power of his logic. Although a master orator, he threw tricks of the orator's trade to one side with his brief, and speaking as man to man to the jury, bared his soul to the light of British justice as exemplified by the twelve men sitting as his peers.

It was obviously difficult for us to choose between publishing extracts from Pritchard's address or Dixon's or both, though the latter option was easier to eliminate because of space limitations. We chose to print an abridged version of Pritchard's speech because it deals with material not already covered in the strikers' history.

Pritchard, unlike Dixon, was not directly involved in the Winnipeg General Strike. A resident of Vancouver, a leading socialist and trade unionist there, and as one who was quite prominent at the Western Labour Conference, he had been invited to address meetings in Winnipeg during the strike. He was actually arrested in Calgary on his way back to Vancouver. He interpreted his arrest as an attack on socialism as well as on the general rights of labour, and he made that the burden of his address:

I have to defend the history of two great movements, the labour and socialist movements.

His speech is therefore to be seen as a social document of additional interest; it records the development up to that time of socialist thought in Western Canada, and it contains a vigorous exposition of a working-class counter-culture.

The trials of the strike leaders kept alive the whole public impact of the strike, as did the work of the Defence Committee after the trials. The press across Canada printed lengthy reports daily as the trials progressed. Public meetings, parades, conferences and the circulation of defence literature contributed greatly to the immediate and long-term political consequences of the strike.

On the one hand, the strike gave a strong impetus towards independent labour political action and the eventual formation of a social-democratic party in Canada. It was the Winnipeg General Strike that sent Woodsworth (and later Heaps) to the House of Commons, where he became the figure around whom this movement crystallized. In fact, the majority of the main leaders of the strike joined the Co-operative Commonwealth Federation when it was formed in 1932 and 1933.

But the strike also strengthened the forces of reformism inside the Liberal Party. It gave a boost to Mackenzie King's campaign for the leadership of the party at the national convention in Ottawa in August 1919. He had only the year before published his book, *Industry and Humanity*, in which he warned that, unless the capitalists adopted a more conciliatory approach to their employees, serious unrest leading to explosive confrontations would be inevitable. He had served a number of years under Laurier as deputy minister and minister of Labour, and seemed to many the candidate most conscious of labour's potential role politically.[1] As prime minister he paid a great deal of attention to the labour group in Parliament, trying to woo them to his ranks and trying also to head off the formation of a Canadian labour party.

There is no doubt that the public impact of the strike and its aftermath played a significant part in the resounding defeat that the Conservative Party, led since July of 1920 by Meighen, suffered in the 1921 general elections. It lost every one of its seats in Western Canada, including Meighen's, and was reduced to a corporal's guard of fifty members in the House of Commons.

The main direct impact of the strike was naturally in Winnipeg. The class confrontation that split the city created a division that has lasted up to the present. Winnipeg labour since then has been able to elect a significant number of representatives to all three levels of government, culminating in the NDP provincial victory of 1969 when 17 out of its 27 members came from Winnipeg constituencies. It is of more than passing interest that some among the 17 were descendants of people who participated in the general strike.

The revolutionary socialist wing of the strike split afterwards over the future of the OBU. Russell could not agree with the stand of the newly formed Workers' (later Communist) Party, which called in 1921 for the dissolution of the OBU and the return of its militants to the international unions. Russell kept on as full-time director of the few OBU locals that survived in Winnipeg until 1957, when they merged with the Canadian Labour Congress. The Communist Party, always a small party, has ever since the strike maintained its strongest political base in Winnipeg, regularly electing representatives to the civic bodies and even at one point to the provincial legislature.

But, in spite of charges that it was a revolutionary plot, the impact of the Winnipeg General Strike led away from revolutionary ideology and strengthened reformism. It did this because Canadian capitalism, contrary to predictions from the left, was not at the end of its tether,

1. Mackenzie King anticipated before the convention that his identification with labour matters might give him an advantage over the other contenders for the leadership. On June 23, 1919, he wrote to his brother saying, "It is possible that the labour unrest of the West may cause some of the Party to be disposed towards my leadership . . ." (Quoted in F. A. McGregor, *The Fall and Rise of Mackenzie King: 1911-1919* [Toronto, 1962], p. 335.) Doubtless King had this in mind when he devoted a major portion of his campaign speech at the convention to labour. McGregor states that King had "substantial support" from "many elements in the labour movement" (p. 339). H. S. Ferns and B. Ostry in their remarkable and somewhat neglected book, *The Age of Mackenzie King* (London & Toronto, 1955), confirm the role that the labour question played in King's victory at the convention: "His supposedly progressive and sympathetic attitude towards labour, his promise of jobs in the bureaucracy for labour leaders and his verbal radicalism attracted others to his cause" (p. 322).

but only at the end of one phase. It still had ahead of it a great capacity for growth, and because of that was able to switch substantial support from toryism to liberal democracy.

The Winnipeg General Strike did not win the battle for collective bargaining; that issue has had to be fought and won many times in the later history of Canadian labour. But it did enhance the position of labour economically and, above all, politically.

It is in that sense that we take this epic event to be "a watershed in the evolution of Canada."

NORMAN PENNER

Glendon College, York University
Toronto
December 1972

Chronology of Main Events
of the Winnipeg General Strike

May 1	After three months of negotiations with the Winnipeg Builders' Exchange, all the unions grouped together under the Building Trades Council go on strike.
May 2	A strike is called by the Metal Trades Council of workers at three of the main metal-contracting shops.
May 6	Building Trades Council and Metal Trades Council inform Winnipeg Trades and Labour Council of refusal of the employers to bargain with them. TLC unanimously decides to poll all affiliated unions on a general sympathetic strike.
May 13	Report of strike vote: 8,667 for and 645 against. A general Strike Committee of 300 is set up, made up of 3 delegates from each union. An executive Central Strike Committee of 15 is to be elected later.
May 15	— General strike commences at 11 a.m. Within two hours the whole productive life of the city grinds to a halt as thousands of unorganized workers join the union members in walking off their jobs.
	— A mass meeting of the three main organizations of returned soldiers declares full support to the strike.
May 16	Winnipeg Citizens' Committee of 1,000 is announced. Its aim is to fight the strike.
May 17	The Strike Committee asks for a meeting with city council to discuss maintenance of essential services. At this meeting officers of dairies suggest that the Strike Committee issue work authorization cards to permit milk deliveries and some other services to continue.
May 22	Hon. Arthur Meighen, acting minister of Justice, and Senator Gideon Robertson, minister of Labour, arrive by train in Winnipeg, accompanied by several prominent members of the Citizens' Committee who joined them in Fort William. They engage in a busy round of discussions but ignore the Strike Committee.
May 25	— Senator Robertson issues an ultimatum to the postal employees, giving them until 10 a.m. the following day to return to work and sign an undertaking to sever all

connections with the Winnipeg Trades and Labour Council, on pain of dismissal.

— Provincial and civic governments issue similar ultimatums, the provincial order being directed mainly at telephone girls because the telephone system is provincially owned, and they are therefore employees of the government.

— Mass meeting of 5,000 strikers in Victoria Park rejects all ultimatums.

May 30   City police are given twenty-four hours to sign a contract that prohibits membership in any union whatever. The police refuse, at the same time pledging to uphold law and order.

June 1   Ten thousand returned soldiers march to provincial legislative buildings to express their solidarity with the strike, demand provincial legislation to enforce collective bargaining and call upon the premier to withdraw his ultimatum to the telephone girls. After meeting the premier, they march to city hall and present similar demands.

June 3   Winnipeg daily papers begin carrying ads sponsored by the Citizens' Committee calling for the deportation of "aliens" who support the strike.

June 6   Government in Ottawa introduces amendments to Immigration Act permitting deportation without trial of anyone not born in Canada who is accused of sedition.

June 8   J. S. Woodsworth returns to Winnipeg after a number of years as a longshoreman in Vancouver, and addresses a meeting of 10,000 under auspices of the Labour Church.

June 9   Entire police force is dismissed for refusing to sign the undertaking demanded of them, and Citizens' Committee begins recruitment of "specials."

June 16   Metal-trades employers publish what they consider to be a compromise proposal to settle the strike. That very evening, however, and into the early hours of the next day, the RNWMP carries out a series of raids on labour halls and on homes of strike leaders, arresting ten people and transporting them to the Stony Mountain penitentiary twenty miles north of Winnipeg.

June 18   Announcement made that the arrested leaders would be held for deportation proceedings in line with the new Immigration Act and that bail would therefore be refused.

June 21   — As a result of a storm of protest from all over the country, bail is granted six of the ten prisoners.

— Silent parade called to protest the arrest of the strike

leaders is attacked by special police and RNWMP using baseball bats and small-arms fire. One man is killed, and thirty others injured.

June 23   Woodsworth arrested for taking over as editor of the *Western Labour News,* the strikers' voice, since its regular editor, W. Ivens, was arrested among the first ten.

June 25   — Fred J. Dixon, Labour member of the provincial legislature, takes over as editor and he, too, is arrested.

— The Strike Committee announces that the strike is to be terminated and calls upon labour to get ready for the next round of the struggle — in the political arena — to send a large group of labour representatives to all levels of government.

June 26   The Winnipeg General Sympathetic Strike is over at 11 a.m.

Opposite: The original title page of the strikers' history.

In reproducing this document here, the original typography and style have been retained as much as possible. Only the pagination differs from the original.

"SAVING THE WORLD FROM DEMOCRACY"

THE
Winnipeg General Sympathetic Strike

MAY-JUNE, 1919

TRIAL BY JURY DESTROYED BY STAMPEDE FORTY-FIVE
MINUTE LEGISLATION — WORKERS ARRESTED AND
RUSHED TO PENITENTIARY TO SMASH STRIKE —
LEADING LAWYERS, MEMBERS OF EMPLOYERS'
COMMITTEE OF 1000 — ENGAGED BY FEDERAL
GOVERNMENT TO PROSECUTE WORKERS.

———

Strike – Arrests – Trials – Penitentiary

———

Prepared by the Defense Committee, 220 Bannatyne Ave., composed of
Delegates from the various Labor Organizations in
Winnipeg, Manitoba

———

PRICE FIFTY CENTS

— Manitoba Archives
On the steps of the Winnipeg Labour Temple, late in 1919. As well
as the original Strike Committee which co-ordinated labour activities
between May 15 and June 25, 1919, this photograph shows lawyers
and other members of the Defence Committee who helped write and
publish the strikers' history.

HISTORY
OF
WINNIPEG GENERAL STRIKE
1919

SYNOPSIS OF EVENTS

Leading up to the **Walker Theatre meeting**, the **Calgary Convention**, the **Formation of the O. B. U.**, the **Winnipeg General Strike** — May and June, 1919 — and the prosecutions arising out of the same.

Eight men, Russell, Johns, Pritchard, Armstrong, Heaps, Queen, Bray, and Ivens, are now before the Assize Court of Manitoba, charged by the Government with seditious conspiracy to overthrow the state, etc.*

These men were arrested, together with five non-English speaking men, on June 17th, last, when the general strike was at its height. The real purpose of the arrests was to smash the strike then in existence.

The **Crown alleges** that they were arrested because they were seditiously planning a revolution and that the strike was an attempt to establish a soviet form of government.

The Crown is **attempting to prove** that meetings held in Winnipeg in December, 1918, to protest against orders in council, to demand the withdrawal of troops from Russia, and the release of political prisoners; the various meetings of the Labor Church in Winnipeg; a meeting planned by the Socialist Party of Canada — but prevented by rioting soldiers; a convention of representatives from the Trades Unions of Western Canada, held in Calgary in March, 1919; the Winnipeg general sympathetic strike of May and June, 1919, and the formation of an industrial organization in place of the craft organizations, under the name of the One Big Union, are all connected parts of one big conspiracy.

The facts are that the Labor Church was formed by the Rev. W. Ivens, M.A. B.D., when he was denied, or driven from the pulpit of the Methodist Church, because of his pacifist views. The Walker Theatre meeting was planned because the workers realized that the Trades Congress officers were impotent in the matter of securing from the Government redress of the grievances complained of, and were

*The actual trials, which were held before the Court of King's Bench, began at the end of November 1919 and were concluded in April 1920. This reference would indicate that although this book appeared after the trials, much of it consisted of material written or published earlier.

3

determined that the voice of protest should be heard. The Majestic Theatre meeting was one of a series planned by the Socialist Party to propagate their views. The Western Convention, held in Calgary, March, 1919, was arranged to form some plan of organization that would free Western Canada from the control of a Trades Congress machine which the Western workers claimed defeated their every plan and proposal. The plan of industrial organization was launched at that convention and was accelerated by the active and persistent opposition of international officers to the Winnipeg strike. The strike itself grew spontaneously out of the refusal of the "iron masters" — owners of the contract metal shops — to recognize the unions or the Metal Trades Council, and the refusal of the Builders' Exchange to recognize the Building Trades Council or to pay the men engaged in all branches of the building industry a living wage.

The idea of a conspiracy is preposterous. The contention of the Crown that these activities were part of an attempt to set up a soviet and to bring about a revolution, is a **pretext** by which they hope to **railroad active leaders of the working class to jail**, and an excuse for them to carry on an active propaganda against "Reds," "Revolutionists," "Left Wingers," "Radicals," "Progressives," or whatever they may be called. "Bolshevists" is, of course, the most telling expression from their standpoint.

If they are successful in this endeavor it is quite clear that **the Government will pass legislation, or, more orders-in-council, suppressing every organization, and imprisoning every person** who in any way seeks to better the general condition of the workers.

That **this is no mere suspicion** on our part is proven by the fact that, while the strike was in progress, the **Immigration Act** was re-introduced into the Federal Parliament. It had already been amended and signed by the Governor-General, not more than a couple of days previously. When **re-introduced it was re-amended purposely to destroy the right of trial by jury for all British born citizens**, and also make it possible to deport the strike leaders, without legal trial.* This act was re-introduced into the Ottawa Parliament, and amended within the short space of time of twenty minutes. It was next rushed

---

*The Immigration Act was amended on June 6, 1919, to permit the deportation without trial of persons of British birth accused of sedition. The act had already been amended to permit this to happen to persons who came from other countries, but when it was discovered that most of the strike leaders came from Britain, this new amendment was rushed through the House of Commons and Senate in forty minutes. Years later, Meighen defended this action by saying: "All that was done in 1919 was to add another class to those who were not entitled to jury trial. The class we added were those who came from the Old Country and were anarchists. In a word we added anarchists to prostitutes and beggars." (House of Commons *Debates*, June 2, 1926, vol. 4, page 3996.)

through the Senate, then to the Governor-General for signature. From first to last the time taken for the whole process was less than 45 minutes. There is not a parallel for this stampede legislation in the whole of British history.

Shortly after this amendment was passed the accused were **arrested, rushed to the penitentiary**, and, on the third day, brought before the **Board of Enquiry**, so that they **might have a secret hearing and then be deported**. That this plan was not carried out was due, we believe, wholly to the **storm of protest** raised in all parts of Canada against the outrage.

The fact that they were unable under the re-amended Immigration Act, at that time, to accomplish their designs, halted them for the moment, but it also accentuated their determination to crush the whole progressive working class movement.

This means that a publicity campaign such as that secured by these long drawn out trials, where their side of the case is published in the daily press down to the slightest detail, while we have no such means of setting forth our side of the case, will, they hope, create an atmosphere where not only the conditions of the Immigration Act — which are still intact — may be enforced, but also **such additional legislation** as shall accomplish their designs.

Because of these facts it is necessary that at this time we should present to the entire Labor Movement a complete statement of the various events mentioned in the charges, and the causes leading up to the same, so that it will be able to form an intelligent, complete and accurate opinion of the whole matter, assist us in protecting labor's right to organize, and work out its own emancipation.

We therefore set forth in order the progress of events as follows: —

1. The reason for calling the Walker Theatre meeting and a report of the same.
2. The Majestic Theatre meeting as planned.
3. The formation and aims of the Labor Church.
4. The calling of, and report of, the Calgary Convention.*
5. The calling of, reasons for, and progress of, the General Strike.
6. The Arrests, etc.
7. The prosecutions and progress of the Trial.

---

*The crown in its indictment linked these first four events with the general strike, alleging that the accused had "conspired" and "plotted" at these meetings to call an unlawful general strike and to overthrow the government by revolutionary means. These events are therefore included here by the strikers to give their side of the story, and to show how ludicrous was the charge of a "conspiracy" being "plotted" at open public meetings.

Section I.

THE WALKER THEATRE MEETING
SUNDAY, DECEMBER 22nd, 1918

The Walker Theatre meeting was called by the Winnipeg Trades and Labor Council, in conjunction with the Socialist Party of Canada, for the purpose of passing three resolutions.
These were as follows: —
1. Protest against Orders-in-Council
2. Withdrawal of Troops from Russia.
3. Release of Political Prisoners.*
1. **Orders-in-Council** had been passed and enforced by the Government, and resented strongly by the workers.

Here are a **few samples** of this protest, as printed in the Western Labor News, the official organ of the Trades and Labor Council.

Oct. 4th, 1918, issue, reports raids on homes in North End of city for banned literature.

Oct. 18th issue, Trades Council discusses general strike against Order-in-Council forbidding the right to strike.

The same issue prints in full the Order-in-Council banning many organizations, and foreign papers.

Editorially, the paper severely condemns at length the whole policy of Orders-in-Council.

Oct. 25th issue prints the result of the strike ballot against the "No-strike" order, and shows a vote of 92 per cent in favor of the strike.

Nov. 8th, protest against arrest of Bainbridge, of Toronto, for having banned literature in his possession.

In the same issue there was a protest against seven men at Sault Ste Marie being fined $16,700.00 for belonging to the Social Democratic Party, which had been made illegal by Order-in-Council.

Nov. 22nd the paper contains strong articles condemning the censorship, and further arrests for sedition, and for possessing prohibited literature.

Nov. 29th the Government's Russian policy was condemned and further protests against Orders-in-Council voiced.

Dec. 6th there appears a **Toronto protest**, which says in part: —
Resolved. That we, the delegates of the International Association of Machinists, representing the Province of Ontario, in convention assembled, **do hereby protest against government by "Orders-**

---

*Many of these arbitrary and undemocratic actions of the government were done under authority of the War Measures Act of 1914. As is pointed out in this book, the act was still in force at the time of the strike even though the war had ended November 11, 1918. But even while the war was still being waged, the labour movement felt that these actions were motivated out of class hostility and had nothing to do with the safety of the state.

in-Council" as being prejudicial to the best interest of organized Labor and a subversion of political democracy and civil liberty. Under the provisions of such orders **many political organizations of the workers have been suppressed and scores of their members thrown into prison. Their papers are banned by the censor and their editors subjected to a most vicious form of political persecution. Trial by jury is not permitted and sentences that are an outrage upon human decency are imposed upon them for the possession of literature in which are expressed the greatest thoughts of the liberators of mankind.** And be it further resolved;

That this convention is strongly of the opinion that conditions in this country do not, and never have warranted such an unjustifiable interference with the liberties of the people. **We view with apprehension the introduction of autocratic methods and the increasing tendency of a few men to usurp the prerogatives of the people which are alone vested in their elected representatives.** And whereas, the constitution of the International Association of Machinists declares the necessity of changing the industrial conditions existing at the present time, — these orders are a direct contravention of its principles and purpose, which, if enforced, will prejudice the liberty of our members, and be it still further resolved;

That in view of the present world movement toward freedom and democracy, when the world rocks with internal ferment, when thrones tumble, when autocrats flee the countries they have brought to the verge of annihilation and Labor is asserting its right to rule, — these orders become a danger to social peace. **We therefore demand, that all "Orders-in-Council" under the "War Measures Act" restricting the rights of Labor be immediately rescinded and that all persons imprisoned under its provisions be set at liberty. We affirm our adherence to the constitutional methods of procedure and call upon all labor organizations to give their unstinted support to the purpose of this resolution,** and that copies of same be sent to the Premier, Minister of Justice, Trades and Labor Congress of Canada, also all local unions and the press.

PRESS CENSORSHIP SUPPRESSES TRUTH

The censorship of the press under Orders-in-Council was made especially obnoxious to Labor by virtue of the manifest policy of the Government to dictate arbitrarily to Labor as to what it should or should not print and read.

For instance, the editor of the Western Labor News states he was visited by the Winnipeg representative of Colonel Ernest Chambers, the Dominion censor, who protested against an article reproduced from The Union of Democratic Control, written by E. D. Morel, of London,

England. The editor took the ground that articles printed in Britain
and allowed to enter Canada by the open mails should be entitled
to reproduction in Canadian papers. Furthermore, if they were true
there should be no desire on the part of the Government to suppress
them.

The censor replied that it was not a question of truth or the reverse,
but it was a question as to whether it was in harmony with the policy
of the Government to print such articles.

Upon further protest by the editor, the censor stated with emphasis,
that "The people are cattle" and that the Government intended "to
drive them where it wished," and they did not intend that he, the
editor, should print articles that would lead them in any other direction.

Once again the editor protested against the people being described
as cattle, and the censor replied: "They are d ... d cattle, and you
know they are."

Such an attitude did not strengthen confidence in the Government,
but did strengthen the volume of protest against the whole batch of
Orders-in-Council promulgated by the Union Government.

The foregoing will make it quite clear that the Orders-in-Council,
etc., were rankling in the minds of the workers. It was quite natural,
therefore, that the workers decided to protest, and, on Dec. 13th we
find in the Western Labor News this extract from the report of the
Trades and Labor Council: —

MASS MEETING DECIDED UPON

**Mr. Geo. Armstrong* was given the floor. He recommended
that a mass meeting be held to discuss the various results of
the Orders-in-Council. Members were in Stony Mountain, not
because they were criminals, but because they had run up against
Orders-in-Council.**

Mr. Blumenberg wanted to know when we should celebrate
the downfall of Canadian autocracy.** Liebknecht has pleaded with
the German soldiers not to fight against enemy workers. For this
he was jailed by the German autocracy. But today the Canadian
autocrats out-Herod the German autocrats. **Resolutions are not sufficient, meetings must be held to inform the general public as
to the facts. The daily press refused to let the people have the
facts of the international situation. He advocated that if necessary**

*A member of the Carpenters' Union, founding member of the Socialist Party in
    Winnipeg, later a member of the Manitoba legislature. His wife Helen was leader
    of the Women's Labour League, which played an important role during the course
    of the strike.
**Sam Blumenberg, a popular Socialist orator in Winnipeg, held for deportation
    later, left Canada for the us rather than be deported to Europe.

a general strike be called to force the Allies to withdraw from Siberia.

Bill Hoop said that the war to overthrow the German military autocracy had brought us under a military autocracy and a big fight would have to be staged to regain any semblance of liberty.

Geo. Barlow was in favor of the abolition of Government by Order-in-Council. But votes must do it.

R. Russell* regarded it as useless to hope that the Trades Congress officers at Ottawa would do anything to get the Orders-in-Council repealed. They were in league with the powers that were suppressing the papers and magazines that stood for liberty.

New Orders-in-Council still more oppressive of Labor had been passed during the last three weeks. A mass meeting would draw attention to the facts of the hour.

Delegate Flye said that if Joe Murray was to be freed from the penitentiary there would have to be publicity, followed, if necessary, by drastic action.

Ald. John Queen** said that the military authorities today had refused him permission to hold a meeting on Sunday next to raise money for their new Labor Temple. Only persistent action would bring results.

Delegate Jas. Winning drew attention to the depressing effect the Orders-in-Council had had on the Ruthenians. Their efforts to erect a temple should be encouraged and the Orders-in-Council must be repealed.

Mooney

Mooney's death sentence, he said, was repealed only under the threat of a general strike.***

*Robert Russell, a leading member of the Machinists' Union, a Scot. In many ways the main leader of the general strike, a socialist, and eventual leader of the One Big Union until it merged with the CLC in the 1950s. A school in Winnipeg has been named in his honour.

**Member of the Social Democratic Party, co-founder of the Winnipeg Socialist Sunday School, also a Scot. Elected member of the Manitoba legislature in 1920, served as mayor of Winnipeg seven times in the depression years.

***Thomas Mooney, head of the San Francisco Street Car Employees Union, convicted, many thought falsely, of plotting to bomb a military parade in 1916. Sentenced to death, his sentence was commuted as a result of world-wide protests. He was released in 1937 and died a few years later.

Mass Meeting Ordered

It was ordered that a mass meeting against Orders-in-Council and repression in general be held.

In the issue of [the Western Labor News] Dec. 20th, this advertisement appeared: —

ON SUNDAY, DECEMBER 22nd, AT 2:30 p.m.
WALKER THEATRE
Under auspices of Trades and Labor Council
Orders-in-Council — Allied Intervention in Russia — And to Demand Release of Political Prisoners
CHAIRMAN — ALD. JNO. QUEEN
Speakers:
F. J. DIXON, M.L.A.
W. HOOP   R. B. RUSSELL
GEO. ARMSTRONG   S. BLUMENBERG
REV. W. IVENS
Workers, Rally to the Colors in the Fight for Liberty

The next issue, Dec. 27th, has the following report of the meeting which was held on Sunday, Dec. 22nd, in the Walker Theatre: —

RED LETTER DAY IN HISTORY
OF THE LABOR MOVEMENT

Monster Mass Meeting Cheers the Russian Revolution

When the curtain at the Walker Theatre rolled up at 2:30 Sunday afternoon, December 22nd, Alderman John Queen, Chairman, faced a capacity house. He explained that the **meeting had been called by the Trades and Labor Council and the Socialist Party of Canada as a protest against three things: (1) — Government by Orders-in-Council; (2) — The continued imprisonment of political prisoners; and (3) — The sending of further military forces to Russia and demanding the immediate withdrawal of Allied Forces already there.**

In commenting on the autocracies fastened on the Canadian people during the war, the Chairman impressed upon those assembled that eternal vigilance is the price of freedom and that the Orders-in-Council now on our Statutes will remain there unless we show in no unmistakable terms that the working class will not tolerate them. (Loud applause.) It was said at the time they were passed, that, since Canada was at war, they were necessary — today the armistice has been signed, hence the alleged reason for these measures has vanished. The people generally are beginning to feel them irksome, and in different parts of the country protest meetings similar to this are being held, and the Government is being constantly urged to restore to the people the freedom they used to have. (Cheers).

Comrade "Bill" Hoop started the fireworks by moving the following resolution:

Orders-in-Council Resolution

"Whereas, we, in Canada, have the form of Representative Government; and, whereas, Government by Order-in-Council takes away the prerogative of the people's representatives, and is a distinct violation of the principles of democracy, therefore, we, citizens of Winnipeg, in mass meeting assembled, protest against Government by Orders-in-Council, and demand the repeal of all such orders, and a return to a democratic form of Government."

"The Order-in-Council is a negation of all that we have fought for and obtained for centuries. We do not propose for one moment to sacrifice those liberties — not for one moment. It is true that we have had a world-wide war. It is true that the capitalist class of the world has fastened upon the rising democracies chains which bid fair to stay, and unless we rise to the occasion and break them, the Labor movement throughout the world will forever be in bondage. Today, in spite of the world-wide suffering, we have a glimpse of a world just a little beyond which looks beautiful to the intelligent element belonging to the Labor movement, and the hope and glory is stimulating us — very much to the fear of the capitalist class. Democracy begins with the pay envelope — if it doesn't begin there it doesn't begin anywhere, and the Trade Union movement generally has organized its forces so that if democracy means anything, the capitalist class has to loosen up if they are going to save their own pockets. The Order-in-Council is the sum total and reflex of the doctrine of property — property is the corner-stone of all capitalistic constitution. There can be no salvation for the common people until they know the nature of property and with that intelligence seek to abolish it." Mr. Hoop recalled how King Charles the First lost his head in attempting to use Orders-in-Council against the liberties of the British constitution, and maintained that so long as there is a capitalist class, from time to time there would be repetitions of the attempt to use this form of Government. The speaker ridiculed the present Government in their attempt to take away the "right to strike," and heavily scored them for lack of preparation for the period of reconstruction, and advised the soldier boys in the audience to go back and demand another six months' pay as soon as the first is exhausted.

In seconding this resolution, Mr. George Armstrong pointed out that the S.P. of C. are sometimes erroneously accused of being enemies of authority, while in reality, although they may be enemies of this or that particular authority, this is no proof that they are enemies of authority, but merely proof that authority has passed from that position where it derives its power from the Government of the nation to where it maintains itself by physical force. He commented on the established rights of minorities under the British constitution, which is referred to by the whole world, and drew attention to the fact that when inequalities develop, the rights of the privileged small minorities get first consideration at the expense of the vast majorities — the workers and other minorities are ignored. A striking comparison was drawn between Labor conditions in England after the Black Plague swept the country and present-day conditions, and the speaker caused a ripple of merriment by asking if the Governments here and in Washington had interceded because they feared Labor would set its price too low?

The entrance of Mr. Charitinoff, the Russian editor, whose case is now before the Courts on the charge of having prohibited literature in his possession, was loudly applauded. He, however, made no statement about his sojourn behind the bars.

Rev. W. Ivens* then introduced the following resolution:
Liberation of Political Prisoners
"Whereas, since the outbreak of the recent European war, certain men have been imprisoned for offences purely political; whereas, any justification that there may have been for their imprisonment vanished when the armistice was signed; therefore, be it resolved, that this mass meeting of the citizens of Winnipeg urges the Government to liberate all political prisoners; and be it further resolved, that a copy of this resolution be sent to the Acting Premier and the Minister of Justice."

In moving the above resolution the Rev. W. Ivens said that human nature was inherently restless. Men who were full-blooded always had, and always must, protest. Progress was impossible without protest. Therefore the men who refused to accept the dictation of the powers that be in the various nations were not necessarily criminals. Quite often posterity recognized in such men the saviours of the

---

*A methodist minister, he broke with the church over his pacifism, founded the Labour Church, edited the daily strike bulletin, was elected a member of the Manitoba legislature in 1920 and served many terms.

race. He was not, therefore, asking for the release of criminals, but for the release of crimeless criminals.

The first duty of the state, as of the individual, was self-protection. Then the government had said that their enemies must be punished. Christianity, in opposition, said "Forgive." But we had forgotten the principles of Christianity.

Who are the enemies of the State? he asked. The answer came back — alien enemies. Germans were enemies, and must be interned. President Wilson had drawn a distinction between the German people and the German Government. The people had fought against and overthrown the enemy we were fighting against, namely the autocracy. Therefore, by their own admission, since the German political prisoners we have are of the people who have overthrown despotism, they are our allies today and should be given their liberty.

Speaking of the Austrian alien enemies, he drew attention to the fact that they, too, had dethroned the autocracy we fought, and were by that fact virtually our allies. But, in addition, Austria was composed of Czecho-Slovaks — a nation we were actually assisting in their attack on the Bolsheviki, therefore it was insane to intern longer these people here. Among the Austrians there were also Roumanians. These, too, were our allies. Bohemians were there, too, and we were in sympathy with their aspirations. In the case of the Poles, the facts were the same. Hence, the day for their release was here.

Another class of political prisoners was the citizen enemy. If these were traitors outright, they were shot, not imprisoned. The Order-in-Council made it a crime to belong to certain organizations. Bainbridge was a criminal under this order. But some were fined a few dollars and some thousands, while others were imprisoned for five years, and still others were dismissed for this crime. This proved that these men were, at worst, crimeless criminals and should now be released.

The Government also imprisoned men for circulating literature, and for having it in possession, and for speaking in contravention to the Orders-in-Council. He instanced men who had given magnificent service to their various nations who had served sentences under these various charges. Milton had demanded freedom to THINK, to have convictions, and to EXPRESS those convictions above all other liberties. The Star Chamber that oppressed had gone, but freedom lived on. So, too, would go the Canadian Government, that, in the name of liberty, oppressed men and women with convictions.

Men conscientiously objected to war on religious and socialistic grounds. The question at issue was whether the voice of the nation was the supreme voice for the individual, or whether there was an authority higher than the State. Mr. Ivens took the ground that conscience and the Divine command was the higher authority. Yet men were imprisoned for being true to their highest convictions, not for being criminals. Either the system that made the oppression of men with ideals and convictions possible must go, or liberty must go. This was the time to make the choice, and he would stand with conviction and conscience, no matter what the cost. The political prisoners had made the same choice, therefore he demanded their immediate release.

In seconding this resolution, F. J. Dixon* **stated that he did not believe** that a man who follows the dictates of his conscience is necessarily a criminal, and men who were willing to suffer the tortures of the penitentiary rather than be false to their convictions cannot be bad citizens. The greatest danger to this, or any other country, are those unscrupulous men who stifle the voice of their own conscience while they suck the life-blood of the nation. The men whose liberation we seek were sent to jail because the powers that be thought in some mysterious way they were giving aid and comfort to the enemy. Personally, continued the speaker, I think those responsible for the Ross rifle, defective shells, shoddy clothes, paper boots, and the whole black record of profiteering and graft gave ten thousand times more aid and comfort to the enemy than all the Socialists and conscientious objectors put together, but the malefactors of great wealth are not sent to jail. The Rosses, Allisons, Flavells, and the shareholders in the Crescent Creamery still have a place in the sun. (Loud applause.) Mr. Dixon scored the Union Government for rank discrimination, exempting some men on the ground of conscientious scruples while sending others to jail. The speaker concluded with a strong appeal for concerted effort to free political prisoners, not only for their own sakes, but for the freedom of the general public, also that the nation may not gain the reputation of rewarding its hypocritical knaves with titles and its honest men with shackles.

Withdrawing Allied Troops from Siberia
R. B. Russell moved the following resolution: —
"We, citizens of Winnipeg, in mass meeting assembled, hereby protest against the sending of further military forces to Russia, and demand that the allied troops already there be withdrawn, thus allowing Russia to work out her own political freedom without outside intervention."

*Elected to the Manitoba Legislature in 1915 as a Labour member, first president of the Dominion Labour Party, re-elected to the legislature in 1920. Probably the most popular of the strike leaders, he was a brilliant orator, but had to retire due to ill health. Died of cancer in 1931.

Mr. Russell concurred with the Chairman's assertion that this was the most important resolution confronting the audience. Britain stated that she entered the war on account of the invasion of Belgium, yet four years later we find her invading Russia, the country that sacrificed five million lives in the Allied cause. When the Allied troops first went to Russia, the plea was made that they were to re-establish the Eastern front against Germany, but this plea will no longer be heard as a reason for the retention of Allied troops in Russia, but there is good ground for suspicion that there is a concerted attempt to overthrow the Proletarian Republic of Russia. There is a wide divergence, Mr. Russell asserted, between the press reports of conditions in Russia and the opinions expressed by travellers returning from that country. For example, Mr. Raymond Robbins, one of the last of the Allied representatives to leave Russia, according to an interview published in the Butte Bulletin, asserts that Lenine is the greatest man in the world, and Trotzky a close second; also that the Soviet Government has the support of the majority of the Russian people, and is doing as well as can be expected under the circumstances. Mr. Robbins complains that on his return from Russia, he attempted to interview President Wilson to lay the facts of the Russian situation before him, but was put off on one pretext or another until after Allied troops had landed on Russian soil. Mr. Robbins claims that he has absolute proof that the Bolsheviki are not, nor have ever been, financed by German gold, and it is his intention to publish a book in the near future setting forth the Russian situation as he knows it. The speaker drew a round of applause when he pointed out that even in Canada, whenever the workers took a stand for their rights, they were immediately accused of accepting German gold, whereas the main trouble with the workers is that they don't get gold of any kind. Capital is international, continued Mr. Russell, and it looks very much as though troops were being sent to Russia to protect the investments of capitalists in Allied countries, and prophesied that capitalism must eventually disappear, just as the feudal system had disappeared to give place to capitalism.

In seconding this resolution, Mr. S. Blumenberg said that the Russian question is an international one, affecting the workers of the whole world, as this is absolutely the first instance of a proletarian dictatorship. Nine-tenths of the people accept the newspaper portrait of a Bolshevist as a man who never had a shave nor a haircut in his life, with a knife in his mouth, a torch in one hand and a bomb in the other, and Bolshevism is considered as something similar to "Flu" or "black itch." A certain business man, a member of the Winnipeg Board of Trade, said we are going to see that the newspapers handle Bolshevism without kid gloves — they are doing it, not only without kid gloves, but without brains. (Laughter.) The speaker reminded the audience of the "turnabout face" of the Free Press in regard to Karl Liebknecht.* A short time ago they were painting him as a hero, now, since they can't make people believe he is a criminal, they are trying to paint him as a fanatic. (Prolonged laughter.)

Mr. Blumenberg referred to the resolution recently introduced in the Senate by Senator Johnson, of California, asking if it were true that the Soviet Government sought the help of the American Government to prevent the ratification of the shameful treaty of Brest-Litovsk, and that the American Government had not replied to this offer, and from this he developed the idea that the Allies had gone back on Russia, and not the Bolsheviki on the Allies, as commonly contended.

Mr. Blumenberg explained how some Socialists in Moscow, in 1903, had got control of the convention, and since then they had been known as Majority Socialists or Bolsheviki. An interesting picture was drawn between the six-hour day and the $12 per day wage now being paid to the so-called ignorant Bolsheviki and the condition of the working class elsewhere. The present distrust of the Bolsheviki by the capitalist class, maintained the speaker, is that they fear the workers here will become enlightened enough to follow the example of the brother workers in Russia. Mr. Blumenberg made a dramatic close by calling upon the class-conscious workers of Canada to send greetings to the Russian Soviet Republic and to wish them success.

Chairman Queen then called for three cheers for the Russian Revolution. The meeting ended with deafening cries of "Long live the Russian Soviet Republic! Long live Karl Liebknecht! Long live the working class!" The meeting ordered that, if possible, the message of congratulations be cabled to the Bolsheviki.

Section 2.

THE MEETING IN THE MAJESTIC THEATRE, JANUARY 10th, 1919.

This meeting was called by the Socialist Party of Canada. It was one of a series planned for educational purposes. Russell, Johns, and Armstrong were the speakers.

The addresses were such as would be made by Socialists anywhere for propaganda.

---

*A Socialist deputy in the German Reichstag, refused to support the German war effort and was imprisoned. On his release at the end of the war, he led a new left-wing group of former Social Democrats which engaged in an abortive recolution. In January 1919 he was killed by German Police who were ostensibly conducting him to prison.

The following is the report of the Majestic Theatre meeting held by the Socialist Party of Canada, as reported in the Western Labor News, January 24th, 1919:—

Socialist Party Holds Mass Meeting in Majestic Theatre

On Sunday last, at 2.30 p.m., after the failure of the Walker Theatre meeting to materialize, the Socialist Party of Canada held a meeting in the Majestic Theatre, under its own auspices.* Comrade Breeze occupied the chair.

George Armstrong was the first speaker. He dealt with the nature of wealth in present-day society. He said: —

"During the four years of war, the wealth of Canada had increased from eight and a half billions to nineteen and a half billions, in spite of it being the most destructive period in the world's history. What better scheme had our ruling class for the future to increase the nation's wealth than that just past?

"All the plans for reconstruction brought forward by capitalist or semi-capitalist parties must be based on a property relationship, hence all their suggestions must contain certain material for the protection and stimulus of property.

"With this knowledge, we will, for a few moments, examine the nature of it. In the early history of Canada and the U.S.A., farm lands, forests, etc., was about all the property existent. Why? Their superior qualities consisted in their being more responsive to the efforts of Labor than the poorer, this being the basis of all value contained in them. In plain words, on these resources the wage laborer could produce a surplus over the necessities of life.

"As time passed, much improvement in machinery and method took place, bringing more land, forests, and also mineral deposits into the realm of property. The increase of wealth being enormous, wage slaves became more plentiful, and poverty presented itself in our large cities. The greater the wealth in capitalist society the larger is the percentage of its population in absolute poverty, and it could not be otherwise, as the wealth of this society is but the expression, or estimate, of the surplus value wrung from the hides of the workers; also the worker must be kept in poverty and increased numerically as a guarantee to the security and expansion of the property of this society.

"Now, fellow workers, we ask you to take this facts into consideration when any scheme of reconstruction is presented to you. Your interest as workers is in opposition to all forms of property, we ask you to support only such schemes as will abolish all exploitation

*Planned as a follow-up to the Walker Theatre meeting in December, the meeting changed to the Majestic Theatre when the Trades and Labour Council withdrew its joint sponsorship with the Socialist Party.

of the working class, which means the destruction of all property rights in the wealth of society.''

Comrade Johns* was the next speaker.

He dealt with the reconstruction policy of the Manufacturers' Association. He quoted from their official publication, and analyzed them from the workers point of view. He appealed to the workers to get hold of all the working class literature, for, in the rapid changes of today, bloodshed could be avoided only by an educated working class.

R. B. Russell speaks.

Comrade Russell said that the question of reconstruction was being so much talked about that he was afraid if we were not careful it would be included as part of our standard of living. In fact it was being fed to us from day to day by every paper and magazine; and it was even suggested that a new edition of the Bible be issued to deal with this question of reconstruction. (Laughter.)

He then proceeded to analyze the reconstruction programme of the Winnipeg Labor Party, stating that all he could see in their programme was an attempt to cover every possible freak thought that existed, and thereby increase the membership of their party numerically. He then proceeded to show that the Dominion Labor Party,** or any other party that attempted to reconstruct the capitalist system was doomed to failure. Let us look around and see what is taking place in Winnipeg. Just before the war started, we can remember the army of 15,000 unemployed who marched to the Parliament buildings on Kennedy Street, and, today, after four and a half years of war, wherein the development of machinery had been so great that with thirty million men actively engaged in war, and two-thirds of the remaining population engaged in the production of munitions, one-third of the workers was sufficient to produce all the food, clothing and shelter, to keep the entire world.

This they had done, and this did not take into consideration the foodstuffs that had been sunk by submarines. What chance, he asked, was there for the capitalist system to function when we take these facts into consideration.

*R. J. Johns, a young machinist from England, a fiery orator, member of the Socialist Party, and a leader of the OBU. Blacklisted after the strike, he became a high-school teacher specializing in industrial arts, and later was considered one of the top people in Canada in the field of vocational training.

**Dominion Labour Party, one of several labour parties which had sprung up towards the end of the war. F. J. Dixon, MLA, was president of this party, which espoused the doctrine of the single tax, a popular radical cause in those days in Canada, the US and the UK. Though Dixon and Russell were opposed to each other's brand of radicalism as seen in Russell's attack above, they co-operated together and with other political tendencies during the strike.

In Great Britain it is estimated that ten million men and women were directly engaged in war work, either as fighters or as munition workers, and, today, with less than one million demobilized, the Government's insurance departments are carrying 276,000 on their pay rolls. Think of it, with over nine million still to demobilize.

The speaker then attacked the attempts of the Canadian Reconstruction Association, who had opened offices in Winnipeg to distribute literature to try to bring harmony between capital and labor, and, in their pamphlets, outlined the plans of J. D. Rockefeller, Jr., as idealistic.*

The speaker then referred to the brutal murder of Liebknecht and Rosa Luxembourg, and said the capitalist press openly welcomed such news.

Referring to the attempts to suppress the activities of the workers in the U.S.A., where they were passing laws prohibiting men from wearing red neckties or carrying red flags, the speaker said that although we did not place much significance on the symbol or its expression, yet the fact remained that whenever the capitalist class attempted to suppress in one corner of the globe, such as the U.S.A., we have the reports now coming through that in Australia the effects of the suppression of the symbol in the U.S.A. had created a desire in the land of the Kangaroo for its use, and today the red flag flies over their labor temples.

In closing he appealed to the workers to be up and doing and forget reconstruction bogies. What we wanted was a new system wherein the working class, which is the only useful class, would have control.

Blumenberg Last Speaker

Blumenberg opened with an attack on a Winnipeg "Daily," respecting the mass meeting held in the Walker Theatre, which, said Sam, had refused to disclose his nationality. Laughter followed his statement that such a question was entirely unnecessary since the map of Palestine was written on his face, and on his nose was the mount of Zion.

He spoke of the capitalist boast of winning the war, and maintained that they had not fought, but had made profits out of soldier's dependents. Reconstruction policies next came in for review, and he suggested that it would be well for us to know the "reconstruction gang," and questioned their fitness to reconstruct anything beneficial to the workers.

He then remarked that he would not state what he thought of

---

*These plans were actually the work of Mackenzie King, who had acted as a labour consultant to Rockefeller during a bitter strike in 1914 among the Colorado miners.

the Canadian Government for fear of being landed in jail, but he
proceeded to read an editorial from the Winnipeg Tribune, wherein
it characterized the politicians of Canada as tricksters and pirates.

Dealing with the question of reconstruction, the speaker then stated
that when you reconstruct a building you do not do it on an old
foundation, as, if you did, the plaster would crack and the shingles
fall off, and you would find yourself in the same position you were
in before. They tell you that we are going to have prosperity, but
let me tell you that capitalist prosperity means poverty for the working
class.

He showed that in the United States, in the year 1917 — the
most prosperous year in its history — poverty had increased eight
per cent. In conclusion he called upon the returned soldiers, farmers,
and workers, to unite and overthrow the capitalist system.

At this meeting it was announced that another meeting would take
place the following Sunday, in the same place, to discuss the causes
of the German Revolution. During the week the management of the
theatre were warned that this meeting, if held, would be broken up
by returned soldiers. In order to avoid trouble, the Socialist Party
immediately cancelled the meeting. It was later discovered that one
of the members of the party had, on his own responsibility, announced
the meeting for the following Sunday to take place on Market Square.

When the Sunday arrived some 2,000 returned soldiers arrived on
the Market Square and started a demonstration. This was followed
by the raiding of the Socialist Party headquarters, and developed into
two days of rioting and demonstrations against foreigners, and ended
by the soldiers marching in a body to various industrial establishments,
demanding that Alien employees be dismissed and returned soldiers
be employed in their places.

Very little need be said concerning the Labor Church.

It was organized July, 1918, by the Rev. W. Ivens, who was up
to that time pastor of a Methodist Church in the city.

He had taken a Pacifist position throughout the war, and was compelled
to vacate that particular church on that account. He then started a
church for the workers in the Labor Temple.*

The platform was open. Subjects pertaining to the fundamental problems of the day were discussed. This, naturally, placed emphasis on
both international and economic questions, and brought the church under
suspicion of the Government.

From the first it has been a popular movement with the workers,
and they have now ten branches in Winnipeg, alone. Other cities are

---

*For more on the interesting Labour Church movement, see R. Allen, *The Social
Passion* (Toronto, 1971).

also forming similar organizations.

It stands entirely on its own feet. It has no connection with any other organization. But, being composed of workers, it is keenly alive to their interests.

During the strike it was held in the open air and was attended on Sunday nights by tens of thousands. All its finances were given to the strike funds.

Section 4

THE CALGARY CONVENTION

The Western Convention met in Calgary in March, 1919. It was not a hastily called affair, nor was it the work of a few hot-heads. It was the culmination of a long line of suggestions growing out of deep and long continued discontent of the Western workers. This discontent was largely caused by the fact that the Canadian Convention was always held in the East. Each local had to pay the travelling expenses of its delegates and the vast distances the Western delegates had to travel under this arrangement, deprived them of their proper representation. Many attempts were made to have the convention held at a more central point, but without success.

No better case of this unfairness and the grounds whereon it rested can be found than the conduct of the Trades Congress which met in Quebec in October, 1918.

This Congress defeated all the resolutions sent from the West, with two exceptions. Furthermore, the East succeeded, for the most part, in defeating the candidates for office who were favored by the West, and elected those to whom the West was bitterly opposed.

The result was strong protest which resulted in a series of meetings of the Western delegates while at Congress; the appointment of a **provisional executive for the calling of a Western Convention**, and suggestions as to date and place of meeting for same.

On the return of the Western Delegates, the Winnipeg Trades and Labor Council endorsed the stand of its representatives at the Congress, and the executive of the Council on January 10th, 1919, made the following recommendations re Western Conference:*—

Western Conference

In the matter of a special Western Convention the following action was taken: —

---

*Although the Western Conference represented most of the Western locals of unions affiliated to the Trades and Labor Congress, the top officials of the TLC and the heads of international unions were opposed to it, because they saw in it a breakaway from the main body of the trade-union movement.

The importance of making the coming Inter-Provincial Convention an expression of Labor in the West cannot be over emphasized.

To accomplish this end at least two things are necessary:

1. The necessity for every organization to be represented if possible.

2. A policy to be well thought out and discussed before being adopted by the Council to be sent to the Convention.

We recommend that a committee be appointed to wait upon the unions that have not expressed approval of the Conference, to stimulate their enthusiasm and to get the closest co-operation. A committee of three together with the executive (incoming) to draft a policy to lay before the Council, and the affiliated organizations for approval.

Organizations to be asked to send suggestions along this line to the Council Secretary so that they may receive due consideration.

Respectfully submitted,

E. ROBINSON, Secretary.

Official Call for Calgary Convention

Early in February the following **official "call"** was sent out from V. R. Midgely, of Vancouver: —

Call for Western Conference

A letter from V. R. Midgley was read calling the Western Labor Conference to meet at Calgary on Tuesday, March 13th, at 10 a.m. Del. Russell supported the Conference, especially in view of the present unrest. He moved that a committee be struck to visit every local to get delegates appointed.

Call for Convention

"To all Labor Organizations in the West: Greeting.

"The Western Inter-Provincial Convention will convene in the Labor Temple, Calgary, Alta., on Thursday, March 13th, 1919, at 10 a.m.

"Last November a circular letter was sent out from this office advising the membership throughout the four Western Provinces that arrangements were being made for a Western Conference. The arrangements necessary for a successful Convention have been completed, and every organization should make an effort to be represented by at least one delegate.

Representation

"Representation at the Conference will be based as follows: —
One delegate for one hundred members or less and one additional

delegate for each additional hundred members or major fraction thereof. Central Labor Councils will be entitled to two delegates each.

"The election of delegates to the Western Conference does not entail the payment of any per capita tax.

"Write the delegates' credentials on the letterhead of your organization and send them to this office, room 210 Labor Temple, Vancouver, B.C., or the delegates can present them to the Secretary of the Conference at Calgary."

Del. Logan moved that the council appoint its full quota of delegates at the next meeting. Del. Flye moved in amendment that the delegates be now appointed. The motion carried.

Council Appoints and Instructs Delegates.

The Trades Council, on February 11th, appointed R. J. Johns and R. B. Russell as its two representatives to this Convention.

At a meeting held on February 18th it was suggested that **special meetings should be held to discuss a programme for the Western Convention. It was further suggested that the delegates to the Conference from all unions should meet for discussion as soon as possible.**

On March 7th the delegates met as suggested. Then, on Sunday, March 9th, a special meeting of the Trades Council was called to decide the policy of its delegates at the Convention.

Calls for "Industrial Unionism," "Thirty-Hour Week"; Opposes "Industrial Commissions" and "Liquor Traffic"

The special meeting of the Trades and Labor Council, held òn Sunday evening, March 9th, to discuss matters pertaining to the Western Convention, was a "humdinger." Every seat was filled, and every person was keen. Everything suggests that this Convention will be a land-mark in the history of Canadian Labor.

The following resolutions were adopted: —

Industrial Unionism

The first resolution was on industrial unionism: —

Whereas the capitalist class of this country has in the past used every means at its disposal to defeat the workers in their attempt to ameliorate the conditions under which they live; and

Whereas, to successfully conduct a strike, all crafts in an industry must act together; and

Whereas, the present craft union organization which makes it necessary for each craft to secure sanction from its international tends to defeat this object;

Therefore be it resolved that a referendum vote be taken of all affiliated crafts on the following questions: —

"Are you in favor of scientifically reorganizing the workers of Canada upon the basis of industrial organization instead of craft unionism?"

Carried unanimously.

Industrial Committee

In order to more effectively work out the plan of the sympathetic strike in Western Canada, the matter of the appointment of a Central Industrial Committee was introduced. Following is the resolution adopted: —

We recommend; "the appointment of a Central Industrial Committee to function in any dispute that may take place in the West, with a view to united action, and that representatives be elected according to industries."

Delegates Lovatt, Durwood, Johns, Anderson, Flye, Higley, Hammond, Barlow, and Robinson spoke to this resolution. Carried.

30-Hour Week

The shorter work day again was to the fore. The immediate cure for unemployment is shorter hours even though profits are thereby reduced. The following resolution was passed:

"Whereas the cessation of hostilities has, because of the demobilization of troops and the shutting down of munition factories, caused a state of chaos in the labor market through unemployment; and

"Whereas no provision has been made for such a crisis;

"Therefore, be it resolved, that the Western Convention at Calgary take cognizance of such an emergency and immediately take steps to promulgate a six-hour day, and a five-day week for all labor in this Dominion, so as to assist in absorbing the surplus labor and safeguard against unemployment."

Because of the importance attached by the Crown to the resolutions passed by that Convention, we append **the report of these delegates**, back to the Council, in full.

Delegates Johns and Russell Report Western Convention

Before starting our report as delegates to the Western Conference, it has come to our notice since arriving in the city last night, that the local press have been attempting to raise a propaganda to disrupt the work accomplished at the Western Conference by unanimous voice; and for the information of the delegates attending here tonight, let us say, **that the reports of the Convention in the Calgary** papers were exactly what transpired and are fairly accurate and were sent to all newspapers in Canada by the Associated Press (as they appeared in the Calgary papers) and yet, on arriving here we find the Convention proceedings are all misconstrued. However, a verbatim report was taken and will be published shortly, which will clear away any room for doubt — but to proceed with our report: —

At 10 a.m. on Thursday, March 13th, R. J. Tallon, President of the Railway Shopmen Organization (known as Division No. 4) called the Western Conference to order. In his opening remarks he reminded the delegates that, while the Conference was brought about by the differences in the viewpoints of the workers in the East from those in the West, that the Eastern movement was rapidly waking up — and he trusted the Conference would result in a definite policy being laid down for Labor.

He then called upon David Rees, Vice-President of the Dominion Trades Congress, to take the gavel and open the Convention. Bro. Rees, in his opening remarks, stated that he was pleased to act as temporary chairman, pointing out that the Conference had not been called for the self-aggrandizement of any individual, but in the interests of Labor — he referred to the work the committee had done since the Quebec Convention, to bring about this meeting, and hoped the Conference would at least be as good as the one just finished by the B.C. Federation.

The Credential Committee then reported and recommended the seating of **237 delegates**, made up as follows: B.C., 85; Alberta, 89; Saskatchewan, 17; Manitoba, 45; after which a committee on resolutions was appointed, with J. Kavanagh, of Vancouver, as chairman; and also a committee on ways and means, with Bro. Miller, of Winnipeg, as Chairman, after which the resolutions in the hands of the Secretary were read and handed over to the Resolutions Committee.

On reconvening Thursday afternoon, Bro. Tallon was elected Chairman of the Convention (by unanimous vote) after which the Resolutions Committee reported they were prepared to give their first report.

At this time it was decided to wire to Fernie, B.C., for a stenographer — it being impossible to secure one in Calgary, everyone being so busy they could not undertake the work.

Chairman Kavanagh, of the Resolutions Committee, then stated that the committee desired to offer a resolution as to the general policy of the Conference, so that the delegates would be able to deal intelligently with the matters that were brought before them. **The resolution was as follows: —**

"Realizing that the aims and objects of the Labor movement

should be the improving of the Social and Economic conditions of Society and the Working Class in particular; and

Whereas, the present system of production for profit and the institutions resulting therefrom prevent this being achieved;

Be it therefore resolved, that the aims of Labor as represented by this Convention are the abolition of the present system of production for profit and the substitution therefor of production for use, and that a system of propaganda to this end be carried out.''

A lengthy discussion followed the presentment of this resolution, and on the vote taken **the resolution carried without a dissenting voice, amid prolonged cheers.**

The Resolutions Committee then presented the following resolution, as a substitute for the many resolutions presented on Industrial Organization: —

''Resolved, that this Convention recommend to Organized Labor in this Dominion, the severance of the present affiliation with the International Organizations, and that steps be taken for an Industrial Organization of all workers; and that a circular letter, outlining the proposed plan of organization be sent out to the various organizations; and that a referendum on the question be taken at the same time; the votes east of Port Arthur to be compiled separately from those of the West.''

This resolution caused considerable debate, but in the main it centered around the question of what form of organization it would be, and seemed to draw out ideas as to the details of the form of organization, in order to provide for a further discussion of the details of the organization. **A Policy Committee of representatives of the five provinces was appointed,** with Bro. Johns representing Manitoba. After a lengthy discussion, the resolution was finally passed without a dissenting vote, amid ringing cheers from the entire Convention.

The debate on the above resolution will be found in the Labor News, next issue, provision having been made for same.

During the debate on the above resolution, Vice-President Rees, of the Trades Congress, took the floor — stating he was not going to speak on the resolution, but was rising to a point of privilege, and then proceeded to state that there might be a number of Police Spotters and Secret Service men in their midst; and that one man, William Gosden, alias Smith, alias Brown, well known in Calgary Labor circles, as an ''Enemy'' was in the Balcony of the hall. Every head turned in the direction of Mr. Rees' fingers as he pointed to the figure of a man who sat in the balcony of the hall.

''That man,'' Mr. Rees stated, ''was well known to Labor men as Smith. He went to Fernie, B.C., and tried to make strife there. Some time later he made a visit to Hillcrest. Thinking it would be better for his plans, he changed his name to Brown, and succeeded in getting in on the Miners' Committee, and secured credentials to come to this Convention as a Miners' delegate. On the night he was to have left Hillcrest, he was put under arrest by the police, and the Miners, thinking it was an innocent Labor man that was being put under arrest, stoned the policeman who made the arrest.''

A Vancouver delegate stated Gosden came to Vancouver at the time of the Island strife and tried to create sabotage.

Another delegate suggested that Gosden be hailed into the front of the hall so all and sundry could get a look at him. The suggestion was greeted with shouts of laughter.

Friday morning session brought forth the report of the Policy Committee, as follows: —

1. We recommend the name of the proposed organization to be "The One Big Union."

2. We recommend the Conference elect a committee of five, irrespective of geographical location, for the purpose of carrying out the necessary propaganda to make the referendum a success.

3. We further recommend that delegates from each province meet and elect a committee of five to work in conjunction with the Central Committee in carrying on the necessary propaganda to accomplish the wishes of the Convention.

4. We recommend the drafting and issuing of the referendum be left to the "Central Committee," also receiving and publishing returns of the vote.

5. In the opinion of the committee it will be necessary in establishing an industrial form of organization to work through the existing Trades Councils and District Boards, and no definite plan of organization be submitted until after the referendum has been taken.

6. The committee further recommends that after the return of the vote is received the Central Committee call a Conference of Representatives of Trades Councils and District Boards to perfect the plans of organization; basis of referendum of affiliated membership of 5,000 or less to be one delegate; over 5,000, two delegates; over 10,000, three delegates.

7. We recommend that an appeal be made to the Trades Councils and District Boards for the payment of two cents per member affiliated to finance the educational campaign for the inauguration of "The One Big Union."

The seven resolutions covering policy were taken up separately, and after a lengthy discussion on each, were passed without a negative vote.

At this time a Telegram was received from the Seaman's Union of America, complimenting the Western Conference in sounding the death-knell of Gomperism, which was handed to the Resolutions Committee to deal with.

Free Press, Free Speech, Political Prisoners

The Resolutions Committee then reported on a number of resolutions, the most important of which were demand **Free Speech, lifting of the Ban from Literature,** and **the Release of Political Prisoners and the delegates were demanding that a General Strike vote be taken on the question; and after a lengthy discussion, wherein it was pointed out that the resolution calling for the six-hour day, five days per week, for a general strike to go into effect on June 1st, if same was not granted — and it was decided to couple the whole lot of resolutions together, and if not granted, let us call the general strike at the one time.**

After a further discussion, it was decided to **send a wire to Ottawa, demanding the immediate release of all Political Prisoners, and the repeal of Orders-in-Council, restraining the liberties of the workers — and demanding a reply before the Convention adjourned.**

Endorse Self-Determination

The next two resolutions read, were passed without a dissenting vote, and were as follows:

Whereas, holding the belief in the ultimate supremacy of the Working Class in matters economic and political, and that the light of modern developments have proved that the legitimate aspirations of the Labor movement are repeatedly obstructed by the existing political forms, clearly show the capitalistic nature of the parliamentary machinery, this Convention expresses its open conviction that the system of Industrial Soviet Control by selecting of representatives from industries is more efficient and of greater political value than the present form of Government;

Be it resolved, that this Conference places itself on record as being in full accord and sympathy with the aims and purposes of the Russian Bolshevik and German Spartacan Revolutions, and, be it further resolved, that we demand immediate withdrawal of all Allied troops from Russia; and further, that this Conference is in favor of a general strike on June 1st should the Allies persist in their attempt to withdraw the Soviet administration in Russia or Germany, and that a system of propaganda be carried out and that a referendum vote be taken.

Another recommendation of the committee which was unanimously adopted and without debate read: —

Proletariat Dictatorship

That this Convention declares its full acceptance of the principle of "Proletariat Dictatorship" as being absolute and efficient for the transformation of capitalistic private property to communal wealth, and that fraternal greetings be sent to the Russian Soviet Government, the Spartacans in Germany, and all definite working class movements in Europe and the world, recognizing they have won first place in the history of the class struggle.

Yet another resolution, on which there was no discussion, and which was adopted, read: —

That the interests of all members of the working class being identical, that this body of workers recognize no alien but the capitalist; also that we are opposed to any wholesale immigration of workers from various parts of the world and who would be brought here at the request of the ruling class.

Six-Hour Day Resolution

The resolution that was adopted at the Convention of the British Columbia Federation of Labor, demanding a six-hour day; five days a week, to come into effect on June 1st, this year, was adopted by the Congress with acclamation.

The following resolution was then taken up, which changes the attitude of Labor towards Legislation: —

Whereas, great and drastic changes have taken place in the industrial world; and

Whereas, in the past the policy of the organized workers of this country in sending their Provincial and Dominion Executives to the Legislative Assemblies pleading for the passage of legislation which is rarely passed, and which would be futile if it were, is now obsolete;

Therefore be it resolved, that this Conference of Western workers lay down as its policy the building up of an organization of workers on industrial lines for the purpose of enforcing, by virtue of their industrial strength, such demands as such organizations may at any time consider necessary for their continued maintenance and well-being, and shall not be, as here-to-fore, sending Executive officers to plead before Legislatures for the passing of legal palliatives which do not palliate.

After a lengthy discussion, wherein it was shown that the time had come for Labor to take a definite position — **the resolution was carried unanimously.**

The election of the Central Committee to carry on the propaganda necessary for the establishing of the One Big Union was then taken, and after an interesting election, the following were declared elected:

Pritchard, of Vancouver.

Johns, of Winnipeg.

Knight, of Edmonton.

Midgley, of Vancouver.

Naylor, of Cumberland, B.C.

The meeting then adjourned to allow the provinces to elect five men from each to carry out the propaganda, and the following were elected to represent Manitoba: —

Russell, Winnipeg.

Lovatt, Winnipeg.

Scoble, Winnipeg.

Roberts, Winnipeg.

Baker, Brandon.

After which a number of resolutions, calling for the formation; also Joint Councils of Soldiers and Labor were carried; also resolution condemning Gompers and Draper, for refusing to participate in Labor Conference was passed and numerous others of less importance. The Convention was declared adjourned to allow the Central and Provincial Committees to get together and start their work.

In closing let us say that our reason for only reporting the most important features at this time was in view of the fact that we have made arrangements to have the proceedings of the Convention published verbatim in the B.C. Federationist and the Western Labor News and also in pamphlet form later.

Thanking the Council for the opportunity of being present at the most important Convention ever held in the North American Continent.

R. B. RUSSELL,
R. J. JOHNS.

The above report completely explodes the theory of any "Conspiracy."

It was a gathering of trades unionists, and was dominated by the spirit of working class solidarity.

Resolutions similar in spirit and content have been passed in every part of the empire, but it remains for the Canadian Government alone to use them as part of a seditious conspiracy.

Causes and Development of General Sympathetic Strike.
Was the Strike a Revolution?

The Crown alleges that the strike was an attempted revolution. We must, therefore, now describe the issues involved in the calling of the general sympathetic strike, on May 15th, 1919.

The two issues of the strike were: —

1. The recognition of the principle of collective bargaining.
2. A living wage.

After the general strike was called a third demand was added; namely, the reinstatement of all workers on strike.

The general strike did not take place until May 15th, after the metal workers and the building trades workers had been on strike for two weeks.

An Ordinary Strike at First, on May 1, 1919

It was in the month of February that the Building Trades Council got into negotiations with the Builders' Exchange upon a new schedule, based upon recognition of the Council as representative of the workers in the industry, and embodying a new scale of wages.

The only objection to the former was the recognition of the laborers. So far as the wages were concerned, representatives of the Builders' Exchange admitted the reasonableness of the claims to the men, but gave as the reason for their inability to grant the increase, that the bankers refused to do business upon the new basis.

A counter proposition was submitted by the employers seeking to divide one craft from another, which was refused by the men, and a deadlock ensued, as a result of which the men went on strike on May 1st.

We reproduce from the Western Labor News of May 2nd, the statement re the Building Trades' strike, as it affected, at that time some 1,400 workers: —

Wages only 18 per cent higher than in 1914 — cost of living up 80 per cent — Bosses say demands of men reasonable and necessary to maintain standard of citizenship, but others must take responsibility for increase men demand. — Blanket increase of 20 cents an hour.

All workers, including the Building Trades' Council, went on strike on Thursday morning, May 1st, after holding in the convention hall of the Industrial Bureau, the greatest meeting in the history of the Building Trades Council. The vote was 1,199 for strike to 74 against.

A. E. Godsmark, Secretary of the Building Trades Association states that "the firms have reached the limit of their ability to pay with the proposal they had submitted to the men." The following figures do not bear out his contention. The fact is, that, while building expenses have increased 35 to 40 per cent during the war, the wages of the men have increased on the average of all trades involved, only 18 per cent. An increase of only 18 per cent in wages while the cost of living has increased 80 per cent, proves both the justice of the present demands of the men and their lack of responsibility for the added cost of building construction.

The average increase offered by the master builders is 15 1-3 per cent, while the men are determined on a flat increase of 20 cents per hour, or approximately 32 per cent on present prices. This still leaves them considerably worse off than before the war. This is the reason the bosses themselves admit that the claims of the men are reasonable and justified. But, they say, other persons than the builders must bear the responsibility of increasing the cost of construction. The defence of the worker is that he is worthy of his hire and he must have a living wage.

Here is the schedule of wages now paid, the offer of the bosses, and the demands of the workers:

NAME	Present Rate	Rate Offered
Bricklayers and Masons	.80	.90
Painters and Decorators	.55	.65
Plasterers	.70	.80
Sheet Metal Workers	.58½	.68½
Structural Iron Workers	.75	.85
Asbestos Workers	.60	.70
Steamfitters	.70	.75
Plumbers	.65	.75
Mill Hands — Class A1	.55	.65
Mill Hands — Class A2	.50	.57½
Mill Hands — Class B2	.47½	.55
Mill Hands — Class C3	.40	.45
Stone Cutters	.75	.80
Stone Carvers	.87½	.92½
Planermen	.60	.70
Hoisting Engineers — A	.75	.85
Hoisting Engineers — B	.70	.80
Hoisting Engineers — C		.70
Firemen	.42½	.60
Carpenters	.60	.75

Strikers demanded an increase of 20 cents per hour on present rates of pay.

Master Builders Say Demands Are Reasonable.
The Figures Speak for Themselves

And the master builders openly acknowledge the reasonableness of the demands.

The fight in this case, therefore, is not on because the men are unreasonable, but that the employers say that a further rise in wages will make building prohibitive.

Here is the crux of the whole thing, so far as they are concerned. The master builders say, your demands are reasonable, you cannot live on less than you demand, yet we cannot pay the increase. The reply of the worker was a perfectly natural one. He said, well, if I work I must have a living wage. I cannot live on less than a living wage. His only resource and his only alternatives were work and starve, or strike for a high enough wage to live. And now let us say once more, the bosses themselves agreed that his demands were reasonable.

Demands of Strikers Exceeded When Strike Smashed

It is a fact not generally known, that, when the strike was smashed, and, after the Government had railroaded the workers into jail and penitentiary, the employers actually agreed to pay wages in excess of the schedule demanded by the Building Trades Council. In the case of the plasterers, as an example, the demand was for an increase of 20 cents per hour, while the wages actually agreed upon was an increase of 30 cents per hour.

The Bankers and Financial Magnates Dictate

There has never been any misunderstanding on the part of Labor as to the real merits of the case, or as to the real source of the denial of a living wage to them. There has not been written a single line of vituperation concerning individual employers in the various building trades. There was no need for this. They were not the impossible ones, but **the persons who were responsible for the refusal of a living wage were the men who control the finances of this city; bankers and brokers and the big interests.**

These are the very same men who are directly responsible for the high cost of living. They controlled the markets — the workers did not have a say as to the increase in the cost of living. Their part was to pay the higher price as it was demanded at the store. The storekeeper charged higher prices because the wholesales charged higher. The wholesales raised the prices because they and the bankers, etc., were in absolute control. Full proof of this contention is supplied by the parliamentary committee that investigated the High Cost of Living.

Prices of Living Go Up, Up, Up!

Flour jumped in price over night. Bacon did the same. So did butter and eggs. So did shoes, and clothing and beef, and coal, etc. The only salvation for the workers was to ask more wages, and when this was denied his only way of enforcing a higher wage was through organization.

Then, when he presents his schedule, the boss says his demands are fair and reasonable, but he cannot pay the increase. This has been so with a vengeance for five years. The result is that the financial magnates have heaped up wealth as never before, while the struggle for the workers has steadily become harder and more impossible, till at last they have reached the point where it is impossible to live on the wages offered. Then when they ask for a further raise of pay they are told that the limit has been reached. That is why the crisis has been reached at this time. That is why Labor as a whole is standing behind the men.

Cost of Living as Submitted to Mathers' Industrial Commission.

We take a set of figures presented to the Mathers' Commission while in Winnipeg in May, 1919, on the amount that an average working family must spend to maintain life and decency. The figures are not exaggerations, nor are they the absolutely irreducible minimum, but they are based on an actual statement as taken from the books of the person who presented same.

We were informed that the second column was the amount this family actually spent, and the first column is his deduction therefrom as to where some slight reductions could be made in his monthly budget.

Cost of Living at Winnipeg, Monthly, During the Year 1918, for a Family of Five, Including Three Children of School Age

	Minimum Healthful	Comfort Reasonable
Groceries	$25.00	$27.00
Meats	9.00	9.00
Bread	4.50	4.50
Milk	6.00	6.00
Fruit and vegetables	6.00	6.00
Total Food	**$50.00**	**$52.50**
Clothing for children	$10.00	$10.00
Clothing for husband	5.00	7.50
Clothing for wife	5.00	7.50
Total Clothing	**$20.00**	**$25.00**
Rent	$25.00	$35.00
Fuel	8.00	11.00

Water and Light	1.00	2.50
Total Shelter	**$34.00**	**$48.50**
Help and Laundry	$ 9.00	$ 9.00
Medical	5.00	11.50
Replacements	5.00	5.00
Gifts	2.00	4.00
Total Sundries	**$21.00**	**$29.50**
Recreation	$ 2.00	$6.50
Education	1.00	7.00
Car Fares and Lunches	3.00	9.50
Subscriptions, Telephones, Church, etc.	2.00	9.50
Health Insurance, Lodge Dues	3.00	8.00
Total Extras	**$11.00**	**$40.50**

Recapitulation

Total Food	$50.50	$52.50
Total Clothing	20.00	25.00
Total Shelter	34.00	48.50
Total Sundries	21.00	29.50
Total Extras	11.00	40.50
Grand Total before providing for Life Insurance	**$136.00**	**$196.00**

Let anyone compare this budget with the schedules demanded by the building workers and it will be seen that they are not asking that their wages reach these figures. That is why their demands are said by the Master Builders to be reasonable.

Building Trades Council Makes Statement.

Once more we quote from the Western Labor News, issue of May 16. In that issue appeared an official statement from the Building Workers in part as follows: —

What does the future hold for the workers in the building industry? During the last four years they have been the victims of the great world war. Transformed from a country engaged only in the art of extermination. With practically no building going on these men have been forced to leave the country or compete with the laborer in an open market. The result is he has not been getting that standard of living a citizen of the community is entitled to. He has not been getting a living wage. The building trade worker is less fortunate than the worker in most other industries, due to the fact that his work is purely a seasonal occupation. There seems to be a mistaken idea abroad that the building trade mechanic is one of the most highly paid workers in industry. This is easily understood when all that is taken into consideration is the rate per hour the worker receives while working, no consideration is given to the actual time lost due to climatic conditions and other unforseen circumstances that arise from time to time or the actual wages earned from year to year. A little investigation would show the average time worked by the average mechanic in a normal building season is between seven and eight months. At the present rate of wages this is totally inadequate to maintain an average family of five, self-supporting and in a normal state of health. After going very carefully into this very important matter, the workers decided that in order to maintain their families' self-supporting it would be necessary to make substantial wage demands upon their employers. This has been done. A committee of five representatives of the workers in the industry met in negotiations a like committee from the Builders' Exchange, representing the employers.

Demands Reasonable

After stating our demands and setting forth our reasons why we thought they should be considered, we were met with the bold reply: "We know what you say is true, you are not earning what can be considered a living wage, but half a loaf is better than none, and if you persist in your demand for more wages, it will have the effect of stopping all building, so that there will be no work for anybody." This statement would seem on the surface to be a very logical statement, but we who have given this matter our careful consideration know how absurd it is, and we believe the public should know the truth. We have stated that the average time worked by the mechanic in the industry is between seven and eight months, this would be approximately 32 weeks, taking the average paid worker at 65c per hour, 44-hour week; this would mean that he would earn in the year $915.20, a sum totally inadequate to meet living expenses, as we shall see. Going into the cost of living very minutely, we have arrived at the following conclusions: The average increase in the cost of living over pre-war prices (1913) as at Sept. 1918, is 68 per cent. Since Sept. 1918, up to last month it has increased another 7 per cent, which means that the cost of living since 1913 up to the present day has increased approximately 75 per cent. After making an extensive survey a cost of living budget has been drawn up and which can be verified at any time, showing that for a family of five it took $1,503.21 (Winnipeg prices) to pay for living expenses for one year. This does not include a great many articles that the family should have had, but could not afford to get. This also shows that if it takes $1,503.21 to maintain a family of five and the worker only earns $915.20, he has gone in debt to the extent of $588.01. It becomes necessary, then, in order to wipe out this deficit to get a hold of some other fellow's job, sometimes he is successful, other times he fails; so the struggle for existence continues. We believe that labor used in the construction of buildings is about the cheapest in the labor market today.

Wage Increase Only 18 Per Cent.

The average increase in wages received in this industry since pre-war days is about 18 per cent, and because the trades doing the largest amount of work on the building have received the smallest increase, the net increase in the labor cost of a building has not exceeded 18 per cent. Assuming that the labor cost amounts to one-third of the total cost, 15 per cent increase in wages would amount to about five per cent on the total cost of the building. Should the workers get this increase they have asked, which is about 33 per cent on their present wages, the net increase on the building would amount to about 17½ per cent over pre-war prices, we are prepared to accept responsibility to that extent and no more.

Compare this with, say, the increase in the price of wheat. Wheat sold in the pre-war days at about 96 cents a bushel. Today it is almost three times that amount, or an increase of 200 per cent. If the farmer gets this large increase, there can be no argument against an increase for the building trades in excess of 18 per cent.

To this official statement nothing need be added. It is self-evident that the building trades were compelled to strike to secure an increase.

It must not be forgotten, however, that during the whole time of the war, if any of these trades talked of a strike, it was thrown at them that they were purposely "retarding production" in order to aid the enemy, and reference was made to the "Foreigners" in their unions to back up the preposterous claim of the bosses and the press. When the war was over and they called a strike, it was a "Revolution," fomented by "Foreigners."

Smash Them, One by One!

When the workers refused an offer of the employers of half the increase asked, the employers came back with the threat that if their offer was refused they would refuse to recognize the Building Trades Council and would deal with the unions separately.

This meant, in essence, that they would smash them one at a time. As a matter of fact the council was afterwards ignored by the employers, and, faced with these facts, the building trades workers called upon the whole body of labor to come to their aid in their fight against the master builders, backed by the banking interests.

Metal Trades Workers Also on Strike

In addition to the strike of the building trades, there were other strikes in progress, and, among these were the metal trades workers.

For several years the metal trades workers have attempted to negotiate schedules with the employers, but have always been met by the same obstacle, viz., the obstinate refusal of the three big contractors: The Dominion Bridge, the Manitoba Bridge, and the Vulcan Iron Works, to recognize, in any way whatever, the men's organization.

In 1918 the Metal Trades Council was formed, which included all the employees in the metal contract shops in the city, and on the presentation of proposed schedules, based on recognition of this Council, the men were again met with a refusal.

The matter was brought to a head by a strike being called. The men received an advance in wages, but did not attain the recognition of the union.

Again, in 1919, the same proposition was submitted, but met with absolute refusal. After consultation with the Trades and Labor Council Executive, and after, upon their advice, submitting to the employers a much modified proposal which met with no better reception than the previous one, the men struck work on May 2nd.

Of the dispute in the metal trades, the Western Labor News, of June 27th, says: —

When we turn from the Building Trades Council dispute to the case of the other large factor in the strike, the denial of recognition of the unions and council of the metal trades workers, we have the same factors as before, and one new factor.

Here the demands are for increased wages, shorter hours and for the recognition of the right of labor to form its own effective organizations.

Their Wage Demands

That their wage demands are reasonable is demonstrated by the fact that they are asking that they be paid a wage similar to that paid on the railways for similar work under the McAdoo award.*

Their argument in this regard is that a wage fixed and agreed upon by a commission in the U.S. and Canada for the metal trade work of the railway shops is a reasonable thing to ask. That the claim is well based is proven by the fact that it is now being paid

*This refers to a decision made in the US awarding railroad workers generous increases over a two-year period. The award was made by William G. McAdoo, director-general of the US railroad administration.

in Winnipeg by the railways to the men who do similar work.

Their Demand for Reduced Hours

Their demand for a reduction of hours from ten to nine is in absolute agreement with the decisions reached by all the Allied Governments at the Paris Peace table. These Governments have signed the treaty that includes the eight-hour day. In addition, there are thousands of schedules in other trades based on the eight-hour day. It is the standard for the railroads over the whole continent.

There is a demand in Britain for a six-hour day for miners, etc. And that demand found a response at the Western Conference in Calgary a short time ago. But the demands of the men did not include a six-hour day. They simply asked to be placed on a level with the millions of workers in other plants.

The employers refused point blank to even discuss an eight-hour day. They offered a nine-hour day to their respective shops, but would not in any way open up negotiations on the eight-hour basis.

Recognition of Unions

Their further demand is the recognition of their unions and its affiliation with the Trades and Labor Council.

Once more they are standing on the agreement reached at the Paris Peace Conference. The same principle is recognized by Britain and France, and the U.S.A. and the Canadian Governments. Nor is their recognition a mere matter of form, for when these Governments wish to confer with labor they approach in Canada the Dominion Trades Congress; in the U.S.A. the American Federation of Labor and in Britain the Parliamentary Committee of the Trades Congress. Yet Mr. Deacon, speaking before the Mathers Commission, and his compatriots, Barrett and Warren, at various times and places, take the stand that labor has no right to organize, and they refuse to recognize any union they form.

The most they have been willing to do is to meet a committee of their men. This, provided they have no connection with the Trades Union Movement. Barrett and Deacon and Warren may meet and plan together, but this right is denied their employees. They can form their associations with the Winnipeg Board of Trade, with the Canadian Manufacturers' Association, etc., but Labor has no such right. And if it forms such unions, the members are dismissed at the first opportunity.

In the Robertson agreement, 1918, made with the Vancouver Shipyards, the Minister of Labor recognized, and initiated just such a council as the Winnipeg workers demanded.

Furthermore, the Minister of Labor — Senator Robertson — May,

1919, recognized the Building Trades Council at Ottawa, based on principles identical with those for which the workers of Winnipeg were demanding recognition.

Peace Table Terms Support Strikers

Lest some should feel that we do not state fairly the position when we say that certain things have been recognized by the Paris Peace Conference, we quote their **nine demands** which received the signatures of all the Governments concerned. Sir Robert Borden signed the agreement for Canada.

"The Commission on International Labor Legislation issued the full text of their report. It is proposed that the following nine clauses be inserted in the Peace Treaty as embodying the ideals of organized Labor throughout the world: —

"1.   In right and in fact the labor of a human being should not be treated as merchandise or an article of commerce.

"2.   Employers and workers should be allowed the right **of association for all lawful purposes.**

"3.   No child should be permitted to be employed in industry or commerce before the age of 14 years, in order that every child may be ensured reasonable opportunities for mental and physical education. Between the years of 14 and 18 young persons of either sex may only be employed on work which is not harmful to their physical development, and on condition that the continuation of their technical or general education is ensured.

"4.   **Every worker has a right to a wage adequate to maintain a reasonable standard of life**, having regard to the civilization of his time and country.

"5.   Equal pay should be given women and to men for work of equal value in quantity and quality.

"6.   A weekly rest, including Sunday or its equivalent, for all workers.

"7.   **Limitations of the hours of work in industry on the basis of eight hours a day or 48 hours a week**, subject to an exception for countries in which climatic conditions, the imperfect development of industrial organization or other special circumstances, render the industrial efficiency of the workers substantially different. The International Labor Conference will recommend a basis approximately equivalent to the above for adoption in such countries.

"8.   In all matters concerning their status as workers foreign workmen lawfully admitted to any country, and their families, should be ensured the same treatment as the nationals of that country.

"9.   All States should institute a system of inspection in which women should take part, in order to ensure the enforcement of the laws and regulations for the protection of the workers.''

Reasonableness of Demands Brought Labor Solidly Behind Building and Metal Workers

Had the demands of the workers concerned been unreasonable they could not have secured the united support of the whole Labor movement they have at this time. That the tens of thousands of workers have rallied to the help of those who at first went on strike is proof that they believe their cause was just.

There is no royal way of calling a general strike. Each union must decide the issue for itself, and each union must cast a secret ballot. This gives to every worker the right to express his convictions without fear or favor. Furthermore a union may refuse to take a vote. This course has been followed by the Typographical Union in this city up to this time. Let us say it again, therefore, NO UNION CAN BE COMPELLED TO STRIKE. This must be done upon its own volition after the facts are presented.

Section 5
HOW THE GENERAL STRIKE WAS CALLED

The steps taken to call the general strike are well known. First, the unions concerned in disputes with their respective employers were already on strike. One after the other they ceased work at the hour their agreements ceased. Then they presented the matter to the **Trades and Labor Council**.

This body is composed of elected representatives from every union in the city that decides to affiliate. Some unions, such, for instance, as the Railway Engineers and Conductors, and some of the Telegraphers, etc., have not asked for affiliation, and have no connection whatever with the Trades and Labor Council. Other bodies ask for affiliation and are not received for reasons adduced. Sometimes it is impossible to secure a charter for a union from the Internationals and so the unions are not received into affiliation.

But such as compose the council elect their delegates on the basis of proportional membership. These delegates vote only on issues that affect the whole council. The council on its part, has NO CONTROL WHATEVER over the affiliated unions. All it can do is to make a recommendation upon the known facts, and this recommendation is carried back to the various unions concerned by the delegates of that union.

The reports of the Metal and Building Trades Councils were given to the Trades and Labor Council on May 6th.

There the matter was thoroughly discussed. It was shown that every means had been tried to come to an amicable arrangement, but everything had failed and they came before the council to ask for the support of the organized movement of which they were a part.

The council endorsed the demands of the men on strike and agreed to call for a strike vote of the affiliated membership, as to whether support was to be given or not, the report to be given at a special meeting of the council on May 13th, and a majority vote was to decide the issue.

The local union delegates reported to their organizations, the ballots were taken and the membership recorded their opinion.

This is How it Works

The men chosen by the unions to the council are elected by open nomination and secret ballot. In the council the vote is taken after full discussion upon the floor of the council, and the majority must be convinced before a vote can carry.

There are some who seem to think that Labor can be stampeded. But if these persons had attended a few meetings of the council and realized how often their leaders were recalled from office, or their recommendations turned down, they would realize how wholly democratic the Trades Council is.

No wild-eyed agitators lashed the membership to fury, no fiery speeches were required and none were given. It was the most spontaneous response ever given to a request for assistance.

When the general strike was recommended, there was NOT ONE DISSENTING VOICE ON THE FLOOR OF THE COUNCIL. The delegates were instructed to report back to their unions and have a vote taken by a certain date.

For the most part this was done by that date, and the vote sent forward to the Secretary of the Council. Let it be clearly understood that the only persons to make the report back to the respective unions were the elected delegates. These are from the rank and file of the unions themselves and are elected for one year. There is never a meeting of the Council when old members do not drop out and new members come in. These delegates present the matter under discussion to their own local union, and their vote is taken by ballot.

In spite of this procedure there are those who urge that Labor is dominated by agitators, etc., etc. Such a charge is wholly beside the truth.

The report given on May 13th was only a partial one, some of the organizations not having had an opportunity to call meetings, but it showed the overwhelming feeling of revulsion against the attitude of the employers and of sympathy with the men.

Partial Vote for the General Strike

Just how Labor regarded the crisis is revealed by the vote. We quote once more from the Western Labor News, May 16th. This is the partial vote that had at the time of going to press reached the Secretary of the Council. Returns since that time have possibly been even more favorable for the strike. We present the figures so that all may know whether Labor is in the general strike unwillingly, and whether it looks as if the workers were out unwillingly.

Partial vote, as reported Wednesday morning, previous to calling of strike. Several thousand votes came in after this list was compiled.

	For	Against
Boilermakers, 126	124	26
Boilermakers, 529	82	0
Boilermakers, 566	152	0
Boilermakers, 451	101	8
Carmen, 550	656	26
Carmen, 6	133	10
Carmen, 371	706	68
Blacksmiths, 147	113	8
Blacksmiths, 61	121	6
Railway Clerks, 613	91	14
Railway Clerks, Unity	126	15
Municipal Employees, Winnipeg	173	86
Municipal Employees, Assiniboia	28	3
Municipal Employees, St. Boniface	14	0
Firemen, City	149	6
Firemen, St. Boniface	14	0
Police, City	149	11
Waterworkers	44	9
Electrical Workers	22	8
Bakers and Confectioners	272	2
Retail Clerks (partial vote)	450	10
Lithographers	28	2
Printing Pressmen	50	21
Bookbinders	37	24
Sleeping Car Porters	67	2
Caretakers	133	5
Upholsterers (partial vote)	11	8
Stationary Engineers, 498	182	4
Brewery Workers	152	22
Flour Mill Workers	58	34
Machinists, 122	269	75

Machinists, 189	80	0
Machinists, 457	138	1
Machinists, 484	292	7
Machinists, 863	106	15
Mill Hands, 172	283	5
Carpenters, 343	371	4
Postal Workers	250	19
Pipe Fitters, 479	181	10
Plumbers, 254	60	0
Sheet Metal Workers, 420	56	2
Cooks and Waiters (partial vote)...........	278	0
Garment Workers	143	27
Motion Picture Operators	26	0
Moulders	59	1
Patternmakers (partial vote)	4	0
Tailors	155	13
Teamsters	611	3
C.B. of R.E. (Transcona Stores)	17	1
C.B. of R.E. (Transcona)	112	4
C.B. of R.E., 67	78	3
Jewelry Workers.........................	70	6
Plasterers, 34	72	0
Other votes	31	1
Other votes	62	6
Other votes	118	1
Other votes	21	1
Other votes	56	2
	8,667	645

An Unparalleled Response

These figures show a clear determination on the part of the workers as a whole to do their part. But they do not tell the whole story. There are some thousands of men and women, as before stated, who are not in any way affiliated with the Trades Council. These could not be reached in any way by the Council against their wish. But many of these struck work at the same time as the affiliated workers; this, in many cases without even the knowledge of the Council. Others came out when the matter was presented to them and their assistance requested. The decision was entirely in their hands.

The membership affiliated with the Trades and Labor Council at this time was about 12,000, whilst figures tabulated during the strike showed that approximately 24,000 men and women were on strike.

Claim Police Under Orders of Strikers

The Police voted 149 to 11 for strike.

Before the strike began, violence and mob rule were hinted at quite openly in quarters opposed to Labor. Letters appeared in the daily press stating that disorders would occur in the event of a general strike being called.

Desiring to remove all foundation for the expressed fears of lawlessness and rioting, the strike committee, as its first official act, requested the Police to remain on duty.

This the Police agreed to do, but gave the committee distinctly to understand that they would do one thing or the other. If they stayed on the job they would carry out their duties and would "break the heads" of the strikers if they were so ordered by the chief if disorders occurred.

The committee replied that it was in order to prevent disorder that they requested the Police not to act on their strike ballot, but to remain on duty so that the city would not be placed under Martial Law.

Would Not Support Revolution

For the benefit of those who fear the strike had some ulterior purpose, such as the overthrowing of the present system, the establishing of a Soviet form of Government, and the calling of a revolution, let us say calmly and with conviction that the workers of Winnipeg would respond to no such call. Even supposing a few hot-heads made such an appeal, the mass of the workers would defeat it by their votes as overwhelmingly as they supported the strike.

No, the workers are dissatisfied, but they are not revolutionists. They want the control of industry in their own hands as soon as possible so that they can get the full product of their toil and eliminate production for profit. But they will wait until this is accomplished by constitutional processes. Some of the leaders who are most maligned and suspected at this juncture are members of the Labor Party, whose platform is that of gradual change from the present system to that of a more equitable one. Were they revolutionists they would form some revolutionary society of their own or link up with some already in existence wherever they were found.

It was this fact that the workers were prepared to carry on the process of education so that reform could be achieved by peaceful means, that was behind the general strike, for the amelioration of their position. Their demands were for the recognition of the right to organize, and the establishment of a living wage and there were no other demands.

Strike Supported by Returned Soldiers

If there is one body of men more than another that has declared its opposition to revolution and Bolshevism, it is the returned soldier. Yet he was with the strikers in May and June.*

In a united mass meeting called to line them up with forces opposing the strike they turned down the prepared resolution and passed a resolution strongly supporting the strikers in their demands.

In face of these facts it is impossible to misunderstand the situation. The returned soldier delegates were never absent from the Strike Committee; they knew everything that transpired; they had an equal voice with the other delegates from all other striking bodies in the decisions rendered; they were supported by over a score of returned soldier delegates from other bodies. So that the element that is staunchest for law and order was there at the centre of things in full force.

There are some who think that only a small percentage of the soldiers were with Labor at that time. This is not correct. The majority of returned men were with Labor; some persons place the figure as high as eighty-five per cent.

Strike Called May 15th, 1919 — A Memorable Morning

The arrests that smashed the general strike, together with the unprecedented solidarity manifested during the progress of the strike, have made Thursday, May 15th, 1919, a date that will live long in the history of Winnipeg.

The workers in every occupation, with but few exceptions, walked out on strike to help their fellows, and the whole city was tied up in a general strike.

Within a short time the telegraphers and the newspaper men were also on strike and the city was practically cut off from the world.

The first issue of the Strike Bulletin, published with the greatest difficulty, on Saturday night, May 17th, said: —

"About 95 unions are out 100 per cent strong. The phones are closed, the waterworks are out," etc., etc.

General Strike Committee Organized

When the Trades and Labor Council called the strike it decided to ask each union to appoint two delegates to a Strike Committee. Later this was increased to three delegates.

The Council elected, by ballot, five of its members, in addition

---

*The support of the returned soldiers for the strike was a key factor in maintaining the morale of the strikers. In spite of strenuous efforts of the Citizens' Committee to turn the veterans against the strikers, the returned men never wavered in their support.

to the Executive officers, to be the nucleus of the Strike Committee until the unions should have time to elect delegates. This is the origin of "The Red Five."

From this Strike Committee a Central Strike Committee of fifteen was later struck off to expedite business. This committee had no power of its own, but considered matters of vital importance and reported periodically back to the main committee.

The General Strike Committee decided all matters of policy and appointed all subsidiary committees, such as press, relief, organization, food committees, etc.

Strike Bulletin Issued Daily

When the daily press was closed it was discovered that the demand for a daily strike paper had to be met, so a Press Committee was appointed.

This committee discovered that the Pressmen's Union had, by resolution, decided to do no printing whatever during the period of the strike; and had specifically mentioned in their resolution that they would not print even for the Labor Paper. To overcome this difficulty the union was asked to supply men who would volunteer to print a daily strike bulletin without pay. This request was granted.

The Strike Committee controlled the policy, size, finances, circulation, and appointed the editor of the Daily Strike Bulletin. It also appointed a **Censor Committee**, after complaint had been made by the G.W.V.A., that a notice detrimental to their organization of a meeting to be held, had been published, and the Secretary of the G.W.V.A.* was made a member of that committee.

THE STRIKE AND ITS PROGRESS

As the hour fixed for the strike approached, the feeling on all sides was one of tense expectancy. The daily press, true to form, had freely circulated alarmist reports, had consistently worked up an agitation on behalf of the interests which own and control it. The workers on the other hand had only their weekly paper to offset these efforts of the vested interests. On the whole, however, the morning of May 15th, 1919, was marked by a firm determination on both sides to bring the fight to a successful issue, and the bitterness that marked the later stages was happily not manifest. For some days previous there had been feverish preparations on the part of all local organizations to gather in all the unorganized workers and to those heroes of many fights, old and young, in the ranks of labor, the desire on all sides to join forces with the recognized labor organizations augured well for victory,

*Great War Veterans Association.

but even the most ardent and optimistic had but faintly gauged the unanimity of feeling on the part of the workers.

In less than two hours the whole productive industry of a whole city was tied up, as men and women, boys and girls came trooping out of shop and store and factory, not a wheel was turning in the big plants, not a street car was visible, and on the face of every worker was the cheerful optimistic smile of confidence in the justice of their cause, and the firm determination to assert the workers' right to organize in any manner, for any lawful purpose, which would better their conditions and assure to all a living wage.

Not only was the productive industry tied up, but the workers in almost all branches of the distributive system were out, in sympathy with their fellows, and this provided problems that required executive ability to handle satisfactorily.

The General Strike Committee had already requested the policemen to stay on duty in the interests of "Law and Order," and to this request the loyal men had readily agreed, even going so far as to offer to remain on duty for twenty-four hours a day and forfeit their holidays, but for some reason or reasons unknown the offer was not accepted by the city authorities.

The waterworks employees of the city had also been requested to stay at work and maintain a supply of water at 30 lbs. pressure for domestic use. It may also be pointed out in this connection that the firemen's organization, which had gone out with the civic employees, also offered to the civic authorities a full and complete life-saving crew for service in case of fire where human life was in danger. This offer, like that of the police, was also rejected without any reason being given. The only inference to be drawn is that the civic authorities and the Citizens' Committee (who had virtually assumed control of the civic government) had decided to line up with the reactionary interests and to fight the workers to a finish.

At the outset it was realized that the question of the bread and milk supply was the one most likely to call for all the ability and ingenuity of the workers to handle, as not only were the bakers out, but all the teamsters of all the bread and milk firms. Realizing the urgency of this matter, the Strike Committee at once appointed a sub-committee to wait upon the City Council and discuss with them the best methods to adopt in order that the city might be fed, and especially that the necessary supplies might be obtainable for women, children, and invalids.

The City Council expressed their appreciation fully and officially of this offer of co-operation of the Strike Committee, and at once appointed Aldermen Fisher, Sparling, Hamlin, and Queen as a sub-committee of the City Council to devise ways and means and put them

— Foote Collection, Manitoba Archives
Headquarters of the Citizens' Committee of 1,000, in the Winnipeg
Board of Trade building on Main Street just south of Portage Avenue.

PERMITTED BY

AUTHORITY OF

STRIKE COMMITTEE

— Public Archives

The card printed at the instigation of the manager of the Crescent Creamery, and used on milk wagons to indicate to strikers that the Strike Committee sanctioned this activity.

into effect, in co-operation with the sub-committee of the strikers. At this joint meeting of the sub-committee from the City Council and Strike Committee there also appeared two leading members of the Citizens' Committee, in the persons of Messrs. A. J. Andrews, K. C.,* and W. J. Botterell (albeit, they stated that they were there as private citizens, and not as members of the Committee of 1000) who stated that they were anxious that the milk deliveries should be resumed for the children's sake, and expressed their satisfaction that arrangements had been made to that end. It was at this meeting that the cards were first discussed, and at the instigation of the manager of the Crescent Creamery Co., Mr. J. M. Carruthers, it was decided to have a card printed in order that the general public and the strikers would know that these employees were not scabbing, but discharging a very necessary duty at the request and with the sanction of their fellow-workers.**

It was thought advisable at the outset by this Joint Committee to operate through the medium of food depots, but on investigation this plan was deemed unwieldy, and in all probability would result in the unequal distribution of the commodities, leaving a loophole whereby those in affluence could secure more than a fair share of the necessaries, and those less fortunately placed financially would be at a disadvantage.

It was eventually decided to ask the bakers, teamsters, etc. directly concerned, to resume their labors, which they were willing to do, provided they had something to show their fellow-workers and the general public that they were not scabbing — which sentiment was fully concurred in by the sub-committee of the City Council and by the managers of the particular firms concerned; in fact two of the aforesaid managers, distinctly instructed their employees not to take out their delivery rigs without first securing the cards agreed upon by the Joint Committee of representation from the Strike Committee and City Council, which cards were to be obtainable at the Labor Temple. These cards, about 12 x 16 inches in size, bore the inscription: **"Permitted by Authority of the Strike Committee."** Employers of labor, from the firms involved, voluntarily went to the Labor Temple to secure these cards, knowing

*A. J. Andrews, KC. Winnipeg lawyer who headed up the Citizens' Committee of 1,000, became special deputy minister of Justice with wide powers to act against the strikers, and chief Crown counsel in the trials that followed. The Toronto Star, in a report from its staff correspondent in Winnipeg on June 27, 1919, stated that Andrews devised practically every move made against the strikers: the dismissal of the police force, the organization of special police, the ultimatum to civic employees, the amendments to the Immigration Act, the arrest of the strike leaders, their immediate transportation to a penitentiary twenty miles from the city; also, that he had a hand in deciding the activities of the RNWMP.

**This was the origin of the most controversial action of the Strike Committee: the issuance of authorization cards to keep milk deliveries going. It was suggested by management.

what was printed thereon, and **themselves** placed these cards upon their own property.

Notwithstanding the campaign of lies, misrepresentation and calumny of the vested interests, through their Citizens' Committee and the kept press, the vast machinery of supply and distribution of these two essential commodities, milk and bread, was not dislocated for more than one day and for anyone to have suffered inconvenience, not to say hardship, was proof of their own shortsightedness and bad management.

If proof were needed that there was absolutely no desire on the part of the workers to cause hardship, it is abundantly supplied by their action in requesting the elevator operators and stationary engineers to resume their work at all the City Hospitals and in the fact that volunteers were sent to some of the hospitals in response to a request to take down the storm windows and put on the screens, which involved several days' work, and which was done gladly and without remuneration of any kind by striking carpenters.

Both sides realized that the large number of returned soldiers in the city would affect the result of the struggle, and both laid claim to their support. The executives of the three returned soldiers' organizations then in existence in the city were largely reactionary in their stand and tried to line up the rank and file behind the Citizens' Committee of 1000. To that end they called a mass meeting of returned men in the Convention Hall of the Industrial Bureau, and submitted a carefully prepared resolution to hand over the rank and file to the forces of reaction. This meeting was called for the evening of May 15th (the first day of the strike). However they failed in their object, as the following clipping from the Strike Bulletin, of May 17th, will show:

VETERANS DECLARE SYMPATHY WITH PURPOSES OF STRIKE.
Rank and File Turn Down Recommendations of Executives

Any hope that the employers may have entertained that the returned soldiers would in any way oppose labor in the present strike must have been dissipated by the mass meeting of veterans held in the Convention Hall of the Board of Trade Building last Thursday night. The meeting was called by the executives of the Great War Veterans, the Army and Navy Veterans Association, and the Imperial Veterans of Canada. After a stormy meeting the following resolution was passed unanimously:

"That this meeting declares its full sympathy with the purposes of the present strike to meet the general condition of the people, and pledges itself to use every legitimate means to preserve law and order; and that after the strike is settled labor and the returned soldiers get together and discuss the deportation of the enemy alien.''

A much longer resolution submitted by the executives was defeated. It read:

"Whereas, a state of social and industrial unrest has existed in the City of Winnipeg for a considerable time, which has this day resulted in the outbreak of a strike of large dimensions.

"And Whereas, by far the largest number of returned soldier-citizens are drawn from the ranks of labor, with whose legitimate demands they are in complete sympathy; but at the same time it is apparent that an insidious campaign has been inaugurated amongst certain sections of labor and of the returned citizens for the purpose of spreading propaganda of the most virulent and disloyal type with the avowed object of causing unrest and instigating a revolution.

"And, Whereas, we stood shoulder to shoulder on the battlefields of Europe; where thousands of our comrades laid down their lives, to uphold and maintain the ideals of true democracy, British justice and fair play, all of which are now threatened by revolutionary doctrines and propaganda mentioned as well as by the undesirables, enemy aliens and others, permitted to remain at large in our midst and in many cases to debase the labor unions and obtain the employment to which we are justly entitled.

"Now, therefore, be it Resolved, by this mass meeting of three thousand returned soldier-citizens of Winnipeg that we do:

"(1) Endorse the policy of strict neutrality in this present strike adopted by our various associations.

"(2) Stand shoulder to shoulder now, as we did in the past, to uphold the same principles for which we fought, the preservation of law and order, and the public peace and safety, for the remedying of our grievances by constitutional methods and for the suppression of all agitators and revolutionary propagandists, no matter what their nationality.

"(3) Place ourselves at the disposal of the civic, provincial and military authorities in order to carry out these purposes to the best advantage and to combat any attempt to introduce into Canada the doctrines of the so-called Russian Socialist Federated Soviet Republic.

"(4) Once again inform the Dominion Government in clear and unmistakable terms that unless it immediately shakes off its apathy, disposes of undesirable enemy aliens and other agitators, eliminates the profiteers and monopolists, takes steps to reduce the high cost of living and shows a disposition to conduct the affairs of the country with business foresight and acumen, it cannot be considered other than an inducement to disturbance and a menace to the public peace and safety it purports to maintain.

"(5) Call upon our Dominion governing bodies to impress upon the Government the necessity for immediate action, failing such that they demand that the Dominion Government shall resign.

"(6)   And be it further resolved that this meeting request all loyal British members of labor unions to support returned soldiers' organizations in maintaining law and order now and at all times."

The discussion which took place before the shorter resolution was passed was lengthy and heated at times, but the result showed that the great mass of veterans realized that they had a common interest with labor.

Comrade R. A. Rigg had the honor of drafting and moving the resolution, with the exception of the last issue, which was added at the suggestion of Comrade Mansfield, following a very able speech which did much to clear the way for action.

This declaration of the veterans in sympathy with the purpose of the strike is a big contribution toward victory for the workers. Its importance, in view of the whole issue is decidedly far-reaching.

By this time it was realized that the campaign carried on in the newspapers was calculated to unnecessarily alarm the people of the city, in that they were deliberately attempting to incite the populace to riot and disorder by attributing dishonorable and revolutionary motives to the Strike Committee, especially the Central Committee (who were constantly and incorrectly referred to as the "Red Five") so much so that reports were made to the General Committee that inhabitants of the wealthy residential districts were refusing, through fear, to sleep in their own homes and were preparing to sleep in barracks and churches. Reports were circulated in American and Eastern Canadian newspapers that the City of Winnipeg was in the throes of a revolution, that the streets of the city were running with the blood of its citizens and that whole residential districts were being burned down.

By noon on Friday, May 16th, the Stereotypers and the Webb Pressmen had taken their vote and had joined the ranks of the strikers, and as a result, the daily press was automatically closed up for five days.

Mayor Gray, when addressing a meeting of returned soldiers in Victoria Park, some time later, referring to this matter, expressed the opinion that: "It was a good thing the press was closed down during the early days of the strike." That this did much to clarify the situation there can be no doubt, and had it been possible to keep them closed up for the duration of the strike there would have been no disorder, there would never have developed that bitterness which became so marked a feature as the strike progressed.

The press, when it resumed publication, howled about this "outrage" — the Citizens' Committee of 1000 howled in unison — but the general public were fairly well content.

But the closing of their chief channel of misinformation and misrepresentation was not at all to the liking of the reactionary Citizens' Committee. If the press was lost to them their cause was lost, for how could they convince the innocents that this was a revolution and not a strike? How convince them that theirs was the only pure and disinterested view and that they had a monopoly of loyalty and patriotism? How convince them that their lies were truths and that they were the real saviours of democracy, if the columns of the prostituted yellow press could not blaze it forth to the world?

In this closing down of the daily press, the workers of Winnipeg learned a lesson that time can never erase from their memories — the lesson that the popular idea of the freedom of the press is a myth and a delusion — the lesson that the press is the willing servant of the big interests.

However, "Needs must, when the devil drives," and this so-called Citizens' Committee, robbed of the usual means of spitting forth its venom, rose to the occasion and published a sheet styled "The Winnipeg Citizen" — a paper which puts to shame forever the most yellow of any of the yellow Northcliffe effusions — which out Bottomlied the one and only Horatio.

Get, for instance, extracts from "The Winnipeg Citizen":

THE WINNIPEG REVOLUTIONARY STRIKE

For nearly a month, all eyes in Canada have been turned upon Winnipeg. For nearly a month the citizens of Winnipeg have been fighting whole-heartedly and with a very generous measure of success, against a determined attempt to establish Bolshevism and the rule of the Soviet here and then to expand it all over this Dominion.

In their fight, the citizens of Winnipeg have contended against great odds. When through the machinations of a number of confessed Bolshevists in the Winnipeg Labor Temple, between twenty and thirty thousand were tricked and betrayed into striking, the issue went right to the heart of the great body of middle class citizens whom the strike leaders sought to deprive of the very necessaries of life, of food and water, and of light, police protection and fire protection.

It aroused them to organization and to action, and it sounded a note of warning throughout Canada as to what might be expected all over the Dominion if this effort to fasten Bolshevism upon Winnipeg were not decisively defeated. From the moment that the general tie-up took place over a dispute between some metal workers and their employers, the general strike was recognized as an attempt at revolution — and the citizens proceeded to combat it as such.

The revolution in Winnipeg was the outcome of a Bolshevist movement started at Calgary last March and directed by the I. W. W. Organization in the United States. That convention elected a "Red Five" Executive for Canada. One of these is Victor Midgley, of Vancouver, a notorious agitator whose expulsion from Vancouver was demanded by returned soldiers last August when he and others led a one-day general strike in that city in memoriam to a military slacker and defaulter who was shot while resisting arrest.*

The second is W. A. Pritchard, of Vancouver, who participated in the same unpatriotic escapade. The third is Joseph Knight, of Edmonton, one of the most notorious of Western agitators of the mining districts and a man who demands the release from internment of men who were actively working in Canada for the German Government during the war.

The fourth is Joseph Naylor, a Bolshevist by his own frank admission, who is out to overturn the present system of Government. And the fifth is R. J. Johns, one of the worst Red agitators in Canada, a Winnipeg man who in 1917 at a public meeting of the Trades and Labor Council urged a general strike against conscription and national registration.

Johns is one of the prime organizers of the Winnipeg strike and he also went to Toronto and was largely instrumental in bringing about the abortive general strike there. Another local leader is Mrs. Helen Armstrong who, according to her own word, has spent some years of her life in an insane asylum. Her husband, George Armstrong, another notorious "Red," is one of the local leaders, who drew down upon himself the wrath of returned men both over the conscription issue and latterly when returned soldiers went on a rampage against a Bolshevist meeting which sent greetings to the Soviet Government of Russia, and the Spartacans in Germany.

F. J. Dixon, a soap-box orator who is a member of the Legislature, had to flee for his life and was battered by returned soldiers when he addressed a meeting in the Market Square in 1917, counselling everybody to burn their registration cards and to resist conscription. He is another of the leaders of the local revolt. Still another is John Queen, a Socialist alderman, who participated in the same meetings and was one of the objects of the patriotic soldiers' ire.

Andrew Scoble and R. B. Russell, two more of the prime agitators in this defiance of constituted authority, were active participants in the Red convention at Calgary which passed resolutions for the release of German agents, others for the establishment of Soviet Government

---

*Albert (Ginger) Goodwin, an organizer for the Mine, Mill and Smelter Workers Union, was shot and killed by a police officer who was looking for him as a draft dodger in July 1918. On August 2, 1918, a twenty-four-hour general strike took place in Vancouver to protest this murder.

and proletarian dictatorship, and still further resolutions favoring minority dictatorship of labor by manipulated votes such as that which brought about the general strike here.

A further leader is R. E. Bray, who poses as a returned fighter, but who never saw the firing lines, and who told Premier Norris in cold-blood on June 2, that he was a Bolshevist and out for the establishment of Soviet Government in Winnipeg. The historical survey of facts and the editorial expressions thereon, published below, clearly present the viewpoint of the great middle class of Winnipeg, the innocent victims of the revolution.

In the columns of this sheet are to be found the best samples of journalistic prevarication that human (or inhuman) ingenuity could conceive — not only were its columns full of deliberate lies both about the cause and the conduct of the strike — but they also contained what should be anathema to old Ananias himself — half truths and distortions of the truth.

Whoever were responsible for its printing and publication were and are to this day so heartily ashamed of their creation, that they have never dared in one issue, or in the pamphlet published since the strike and distributed all over this continent by the hundred thousand, to publish one single name. They had, however, the saving grace of humor in paying an indirect compliment to every sensible person who should come in contact with it, to print in large type on the front page: **"This paper is free, please do not pay for it."** This was the medium through which they vented their spleen, this the outlet for their hysteria — in it they raised their cry of revolution, Soviet and Bolshevism — they were totally ignorant of what these expressions meant and as is usual in such cases, they howled the louder and spilled the more ink, on the assumption of the professional politician: "That if you throw enough dirt, some of it will stick."

This was the medium through which they incited the Provincial Treasurer to resort to intimidation of the proprietors of moving picture houses, by sending representatives from his department with threats of cancellation of licenses unless they removed these cards from their theatres — indirectly through this medium they had the mounted police assume authority to tear them from the delivery rigs and resort to various other little practices that were convincing of their desire to maintain "Law and Order" so long as it was their own particular kind of law and order that was being maintained. All this despite the fact that the cards had been tacitly accepted by the official representatives of the City Council on the Joint Committee.

Through the columns of this sheet they howled about the inhumanity and brutality of the Strike Committee in shutting off the supply of milk to women and children — yet the very interests which were and are behind the Citizens' Committee were responsible for the shutting off of the entire milk supply of the city for three days in 1918 because the City Council had appointed a Commission to examine the books of the Milk Trust, to find and report the profits that were being made, prior to allowing the Trust to raise the price of milk.

Partly owing to this campaign of the Citizens' Committee and partly owing to the increasing duties of the Central Committee of seven, it was decided to increase the membership to fifteen. The committee had no inherent power to act, but acted only in an advisory capacity; all their actions had to be ratified by the General Committee, consisting of three delegates from every striking organization, and which numbered approximately 300. There were daily interviews with the City Council, at which the Citizens' Committee was fully represented, and on these occasions Mr. A. J. Andrews was one of the leading spokesmen, as well as Mr. Isaac Pitblado, Mr. A. T. Sweatman, and Mr. Crossin, the first three of whom are now figuring as counsel for the crown in the prosecution of the eight strike leaders.

THE MAYOR AND THE IRONMASTERS

As an indication of the feeling existing between the two factions up to this time and as indicating the attitude of the Citizens' Committee of 1000 towards the demands of the strikers, the following partial report of a meeting of the City Council, taken from the "Strike Bulletin" is given:

CITIZENS' COMMITTEE PREVENTING SETTLEMENT
Metal Trades Employers Not Own Bosses

Mayor Gray, at Council meeting Thursday noon reported that Messrs. Barrett, Lyall, and Warren, representing the Metal Trades employers, had met him yesterday. He had shown them the letter from the Strike Committee, containing the terms of settlement. They said they were requested by the Citizens' Committee of 1000 not to open negotiations and were acceding to that request.

Ald. Heaps*: "Then the Citizens' Committee is standing in the way of a settlement."

Mayor Gray: "I wrote this in front of those three gentlemen and told them it was my report to Council."

Fireworks Banned

The Council resolved to ban the use of fireworks during the strike.

*A. A. Heaps, a member of the Winnipeg city council, member of the Upholsterers Union, arrested as a strike leader, acquitted. Was elected to the House of Commons from Winnipeg North in 1925, where he served until 1940.

— Brown Brothers, Public Archives
Mayor Gray at the door of City Hall.

Papers Not to be Distributed From Fire Halls

Ald. Heaps moved, seconded by Ald. Queen, that the distribution of papers from Fire Halls be stopped. It was so ordered. This motion arose from a notice in "The Citizen" telling people to call at the Fire Halls for that paper.

Running Trades Appear Again

Wm. Best, on behalf of the Running Trades once more urged the Council to take some action toward a settlement. Their men, he said, were excited, and many of them were anxious to "go over the top." They looked to duly constituted government to see justice done no matter how it hurts or whom it hurts. They stood solid and united for the right of workers to the right of self-determination in the selection of their representatives to deal with their employers. If the Committee of 1000 was standing in the way, he would tell them that the workers standing behind the strikers were as numerous as the leaves of a forest.

Learning to Shoot

Messrs. Andrews, Pitblado, and Sweatman, for the 1000, all declared that before any settlement could be made, the sympathetic strike must be called off.

W. T. Cox, admittedly of the middle class, said he did not care how long he worked. He was prepared to eat grass. He was learning to drill and shoot at Minto Barracks. The best thing they could tell Robertson and Meighen was: "Go back to Ottawa." (Applause from members of the Citizens' Committee.)

Ald. Simpson: "It is your duty, Mr. Mayor to call representatives of the employers, the strikers, the Citizens' Committee, the Dominion and Provincial Governments together and try to effect a settlement."

Ald. Fowler: "I don't agree. I'm out to do all I can to put this sympathetic strike out of business."

Council adjourned till 10.30 tomorrow.

MEIGHEN AND ROBERTSON ARRIVE FROM OTTAWA

After the strike had been in progress for nearly one week, there appeared in Winnipeg the Hon. Arthur Meighen, Minister of the Interior (and at that time acting Minister of Justice, in the absence of Hon. J. C. Doherty) and Senator Robertson, Minister of Labor. It had been rumored on the street that certain leading lights of the Citizens' Committee of 1000 had gone East to meet these two representatives of constituted authority and it has subsequently been fully proven and admitted by Senator Robertson that two members of that Committee did meet the train at Fort William, and that one of these two was the man who was subsequently made the Deputy Minister of Justice to handle the Winnipeg trials. A few miles outside the city a further delegation of two from the same Committee of 1000 met the train, and of the four, three of them, A. J. Andrews, K.C.; Isaac Pitblado, K.C., and W. A. T. Sweatman, are the leading lawyers for the Crown in the prosecution of the men on charges of Seditious Conspiracy.

Under the circumstances there is little wonder that the average man feels convinced that there was a "Conspiracy," not on the part of any of Labor's spokesmen, but on the part of the Committee of 1000. The minds of these two ministers already poisoned by the highly colored reports from the West, were well prepared for the reception of the plausible stories poured into their ears by the spokesmen of reaction, and without taking the trouble to find out the truth or otherwise of the tales that were told them (and this much was admitted in his own office by Senator Robertson) they proceeded to denounce the so-called leaders as undesirable agitators who were anxious to overthrow constituted authority and bring about a revolution.

With the usual shortsightedness of the professional politician they could not (or would not) see what was apparent to a child, that had the Strike Committee any sinister motive, there would have been no consultation or co-operation with Civic, Provincial or Federal Governments. But the facts are that at the very time these gentlemen were pouring out their hearts to the Committee of 1000 and through them to the world, the Central Strike Committee was in attendance on the City Council, and as soon as the Strike Committee learned of the presence of these gentlemen, they sent a delegate to wait upon them, and invited Senator Robertson, as Minister of Labor, to come and give whatever information and counsel he had to the representatives of the strikers as a whole. This he declined to do, although it is the specific work for which he draws his salary, but he preferred to stand on his dignity and sent a reply to the Strike Committee that: "It would not be consistent with the dignity of a Minister of the Crown to attend the Strike Committee meeting, but he would be ready any time the following morning to receive a deputation and hear the strikers' side of the story." At the same time intimating that he thought the sympathetic strike was unlawful and must be called off.

MAYOR GRAY'S ROUND TABLE CONFERENCE

About the same time (May 23rd) Mayor Gray had called a special Round Table Conference to go into the causes of the strike and to seek, if possible, a solution.

Following is a brief resume of the proceedings. From it the readers will gather many pointers that need no elaboration, but which throw a good deal of light on many phases of the situation and the attitude of both sides.

This is taken from the "Strike Bulletin" of May 26th:

MIDNIGHT SESSION ABORTIVE
(Fine Debate But No Decision)

Mayor Gray, on Friday night, called together a Committee to consider the strike and, if possible, recommend some solution. The Committee consisted of His Worship, in the chair, Aldermen Fisher and Simpson, Messrs. Winning and Russell, of the Strike Committee; Messrs. Andrews and Sweatman, who said they were acting as individuals; Messrs. Carroll and English, of the Running Trades, and D. J. Scott.

No Big Five

Mr. Anderson, chairman of the Central Strike Committee explained that there were 300 men on the Strike Committee, which had elected 15 of their number to a Central Committee. The members of this Central Committee would attend all conferences or negotiations to give the lie to the statement that five men were running this strike. This Committee is composed of Messrs. Anderson, Pickup, Allen, Veitch, Russell, Flye, Robinson, Smith, Miller, Lovatt, Shaw, McBride, Winning, Greer, and Scoble.

Russell Reviews Strike

R. B. Russell reviewed the history of the strike and the efforts of the Strike Committee to get a settlement. Much capital was being made out of the Iron Masters' statement that they had submitted a plan of collective bargaining to the Mathers' Commission on May 10th. Their insincerity was shown by the fact that on May 13th, in the presence of the Mayor, they had refused to deal with the Metal Trades Council. This Council had written every Metal Trades Employer and never received one reply.

More Chicanery

Members of the Strike Committee had been told that the Ironmasters were prepared to recognize collective bargaining under the auspices of the Industrial Commission Bill. The Strike Committee did not object to this course — but it now appeared that the employers were not free to act on their own behalf, but were controlled by the Committee of 1000.

Collective Bargaining

A lengthy discussion occurred on different forms of collective

— CBC Winnipeg, Public Archives
The only known photograph of members of the Citizens' Committee,
this is a banquet held sometime after the strike. The committee included
members of the Builders' Exchange, bankers and grain dealers,
insurance-company executives, auto dealers, metal-shop owners, and
heads of other employers' associations who financed the committee
— a *Who's Who* of Winnipeg business.

bargaining. Alderman Fisher said: **"The man who opposes collective bargaining is 20 years behind the times."** A. J. Andrews said very few were opposed to it.

J. Winning: "Will the T. Eaton Co. recognize it in any form?"

A. J. Andrews Explodes

A. J. Andrews said this strike had gone beyond the original issue. So far as he was concerned there would be no negotiations until the postal employees, firemen, water-works employees and telephone operators were back at work. It would be splendid diplomacy for the Strike Committee to yield that point. Afterwards the principle of collective bargaining would be recognized.

R. B. Russell: "What assurance can you give us?"

A. J. Andrews: "We can't give you any."

R. B. Russell explained that governments had violated agreements in order to uphold a principle. Italy had broken her agreement with Germany to support the cause of the Allies. This was right. The firemen had acted from the same motive. — But this was held to be wrong.

Insurrection Ridiculous Claim

The labor movement was not attempting to overthrow the State. This strike had not the slightest semblance of an attack on the State. Everything had been done in a constitutional manner. The onus for the trouble was on the employers.

Winning Proposes Possible Settlement

J. Winning: "We are fighting under constitutional trade union rules. The duty of the Trades Council is to render assistance to any part of the movement that is in jeopardy. We have conferred with the City Council, the Provincial Government and Senator Robertson; that shows we recognize constituted authority. We cannot request postal employees, firemen, etc., to go back to work. If they did that where would our economic power be? We have a solution to offer. **Give us a guarantee that collective bargaining will be recognized and we will all be back at work in 48 hours."**

A. J. Andrews: "We say you've done a wrong. You now have a chance to retire gracefully. **If you do not do this, we will line up against you the Dominion, Provincial, and Civic Governments."**

Remove the Cause

R. B. Russell: — "We would remove the cause of this trouble, that is the lack of collective bargaining."

J. Winning: "Our action is quite constitutional. The American Federation of Labor, a very conservative body, has a clause in its constitution which says that no local Council shall enter into any agreement which forbids a sympathetic strike."

A. J. Andrews: "If your attitude is that the causes must be removed, we shall have to wait for the millennium."

J. Winning: "This discussion is on the wrong track."

A. J. Andrews: "I'm not here to go into causes, but to advise a certain line of action."

R. B. Russell: "We are prepared to go further and remove the cause of sympathetic strikes."

A. J. Andrews: "This matter is within the rights of the Provincial Government. **Legislation should be passed guaranteeing** the right of collective bargaining, accompanied by a Dominion Law, making it a crime for unions to violate agreements."

R. B. Russell: "How would this do?" presenting resolution passed by Strike Committee.

Strikers Favor Legislation

"That we go on record as being in favor of legislation, making it compulsory on employers to recognize the right of their employees to collective bargaining, through the representatives of their organizations, as expressed in craft unions, industrial unions, trades councils, and trades federations."

Passed by Strike Committee, May 21st, 1919.

Ald. Simpson: "Is it possible to get a guarantee of legislation?"

A. J. Andrews: "I will not make a bargain that I am forced to make by present conditions."

Ald. Simpson: "Let us have a guarantee of legislation backed by the Provincial Government, the Mayor, and the Committee of 1000."

A. J. Andrews: **"I will not negotiate until the men on the public utilities are back. I will not bargain."**

R. B. Russell: "Senator Robertson has promised recognition."

A. J. Andrews: "It is not a Dominion matter."

T. B. Carroll: "Mr. Andrews' position is a threat. It resolves itself into a question of who should yield first. The employers must yield some. I can't see that the men are responsible. In the Running Trades we would go a long way before striking, but we can strike. Our employers frequently yield points. Why can't the Ironmen do the same?"

A. J. Andrews: "This is not a case between employers and employees."

T. B. Carroll: "What about the statement made at the Industrial

Bureau that the policemen and firemen would be put in a position where they would never strike again. Do you intend to prevent that by giving them ideal working conditions and wages?''

A. J. Andrews: ''The sympathetic strike is wrong.''

Ald. Simpson: ''We propose to remove the cause by legislation.''

Ald. Fisher suggested that a smaller committee might act more quickly, but this suggestion was not acted upon. The committee rose at 12 p.m.

EDWARD McGRATH AND THE PROVINCIAL GOVERNMENT

At the very time Messrs. Meighen and Robertson were shouting from the housetops that this was not a strike, but an attempt at revolution, the Strike Committee, determined to leave no stone unturned in their efforts to effect a settlement, and to explore to the limit any avenue that was likely to lead to that end, were in constant communication with the Provincial Government. Mr. Ed. McGrath, formerly closely identified with the Winnipeg Trades and Labor Council, but at this time an employee of the Provincial Government as Secretary of the Bureau of Labor, submitted to the Central Strike Committee what was apparently a bona-fide offer from the Provincial Government to the effect that if the workers would reconsider their opposition to the Industrial Disputes Act, and would appoint two delegates to sit as representatives of Labor on the Board to administer the Act, the Government would withdraw from the Board two members that it had already appointed thereto and would accept the appointees of the Strike Committee, in order that the whole strike situation might be brought before the Board as a means of obtaining settlement.

The Central Committee reported this offer to the General Strike Committee, which body, though opposed to the principle of the Act, finally consented to the appointment of two of its members to the Board. This was done so that it could not be said by the Government that Labor itself stood in the way of a settlement.

Not until these two representatives presented themselves to the Provincial Government was it discovered that this proposition of Mr. McGrath was at best a vision, for the Government disclaimed all knowledge of the offer, and refused to consider it.

The Strike Committee had acted in perfectly good faith and this decision of the Provincial Government came as a shock, especially in view of the fact that the majority of the committee had swallowed in the first place their natural objection to having anything to do with politicians as settlers of labor disputes; but the fact that they did so, will ever stand to their credit as an indication of the lengths they were prepared to go in order to effect a satisfactory settlement without compromising on principle.

SENATOR ROBERTSON, THE POSTAL EMPLOYEES AND THE ULTIMATUM

In the meantime the doings of the representatives of the Dominion Government, Messrs. Meighen and Robertson, had been dark and mysterious. Nobody (in the ranks of labor) knew what they were doing and what steps, if any, they were taking to function in their official capacity, but this was presumably well known to the employers and the Citizens' Committee of 1000.

However, on the Sunday afternoon, May 25th, Senator Robertson called a meeting of the postal employees in the post office, at which a few were present, but the majority left him severely alone, and attended a meeting of their own organization at the same hour in the Labor Temple to take a vote as to whether or not they should accept the "ultimatum" that had been issued, and go back to work, or whether they should play their part like men and **"Stick."** Needless to say it was overwhelmingly in favor of playing the man's part and they **"Stuck."** This ultimatum was issued to every striking postal employee, calling upon them to return to work at 10 a.m. Monday, May 26th, 1919, to sign an agreement never again to take part in a sympathetic strike, to sever their connection with the Winnipeg Trades and Labor Council, failing which they would be discharged from the Government's service, lose their right to pension, and forfeit the right to employment by the Dominion Government.

Under such terms and with so much at stake it would almost have been pardonable if these men had capitulated, but the bond of sympathy was so strong, the justice of the strikers' demand so obvious that only something like sixteen returned to work, and it was reported that four of these quit again, refusing to work under such conditions.

POSTMASTER McINTYRE'S TELEGRAM

Despite this, there was dispatched East and West a telegram bearing the signature of the postmaster (the authenticity of which he denied under oath at the preliminary trials) stating: "Am happy to say that the majority of the employees are returning to work with the exception of a few irreconcilables, and these under **'Bolsheviki'** influence."

A SINISTER CONSPIRACY

Striking evidence of "conspiracy" on the part of the trinity of governing bodies (apparently under pressure from "Big Business") to undermine the morale of the strikers and cause disruption and disintegration of the solid mass of labor, and to smash labor organizations, was provided when the Provincial Government proceeded to follow in the footsteps of the Federal Authorities, and issued a similar "Ultimatum" to the striking telephone girls,* followed immediately by one from the Civic Government to the Civic employees in the various departments, and from the corporations and big private employers.

But a new psychology had developed, something entirely beyond the comprehension of our rulers and statesmen, whose vision was so narrow that they could conceive of no other solution of labor unrest than the application of coercive measures to bring the workers into submission.

Following the lead of their fellow-workers in the postal service the telephone girls voted to stay out and take the consequences, and they in turn were supported by the Civic employees.

DESERTERS AND REINFORCEMENTS

As was to be expected, there were a few deserters. A fight with all the forces of constituted authority and the vested interests lined up in opposition to 25,000 wage slaves, could not be carried on without desertions, but the reinforcements were coming up in the ratio of 100 to 1. Daily, almost hourly, the Strike Committee was receiving offers of help from cities, towns, and villages.

THE STRIKERS STEADFASTNESS AND SOLIDARITY

As indicative of the solidarity of the workers and the grim determination exhibited by the strikers, below are given a few clippings from the "Strike Bulletin" of May 27th, 1919. The first:

A MARVELLOUS STRIKE

We are, we believe, speaking the literal truth when we state that never in any country at any time was a strike of such magnitude as the Winnipeg strike carried on in such a wonderful spirit. There has not been one single case of disorder. Not a cent's worth of property has been damaged. Not a single policeman has been called to take a hand. The record of the police court is lower by far than normal; lower than at any time in months.

What is the secret of it all? Or, is it just an accident?

We are credibly informed that the people living in Fort Rouge were literally terrorized over the thought of revolution. They are reported to have slept in the churches. They swarmed into temporary militia regiments and slept in barracks. And all this when there was not a breath of disorder among the strikers.

Why the terror on the part of the wealthy and the tranquility on

*The Manitoba Telephone System was already owned by the province, so that the telephone girls were considered to be public-service employees.

the part of the strikers?

There are those who say that the whole reason is that there were reports abroad that the strikers were intending to start a revolution. That they had set up a Soviet in the Trades Hall. That the foreigners were ready to overrun the whole city. Are these reasons adequate? Who started the revolution story? Who believed it? And why?

To answer these questions is to enter the realm of both fact and psychology. The rich, who have become rich on war profits, know that this is the price of blood. The gold that has touched their palm has left its stain both there and in their conscience, and they cry: "Out damned spot," but it will not out. They live trembling at the thought of the future. They are afraid of retribution. They live in fear today and dread tomorrow. They feel deep down that there is a day of reckoning. So they fly to the churches — to the altars.

The workers, on the other hand have no need of fears. They have served well and faithfully. They have at last found it impossible to live and so say we must get more. Not the whole do they ask, but a larger share. They know their cause is just. This knowledge gives them confidence.

Wonderful Confidence of Strikers

Are we downhearted? No. This is the tone of the thirty-five thousand workers on strike in this city today. Every kind of attempt has been made to get the workers back on the job, from Government ultimatums to petty bribes on the part of individual employers. But in spite of all the thousands stick and every local stands as solid as adamant. There is no give. Every striker says it is a fight to the finish and we will finish it.

Never was there such a spirit of brotherhood. Offers are tumbling in for homes for girls who are in need of room rent. We have a spare room. Send us up a couple. Tell the committee we can help them out if they are stuck. Tell the girls that they are welcome at our place to such as we have. Such are the magnificent offers that the strike is bringing from every source.

It is not that the homes of the workers are big, or that they have abundance. But the girls and the thousands of men struck for sympathy on a principle, and that principle is today being justified as never before. The spirit is marvellous. It is worth a strike to see this marvellous spirit of comradeship and unselfishness. This is the spirit that will bring such a victory as labor never dreamed of before.

And the second being a short resume of the proceedings of the Labor Church meeting in the Victoria Park on Sunday evening, May 25th, 1919:

VAST ASSEMBLY IN VICTORIA PARK
Addressed by Ivens, Pickup, and Dixon

"No!" Five thousand times "No!" was the answer of the strikers to the ultimatum of the Citizens' Committee given in Victoria Park.

Rev. Wm. Ivens — the terrible — called out: "The Citizens' Committee say you must call off the sympathetic strikes. What is your answer?" Five thousand men and women answered "No!" These speak for 35,000 more. So the strike is still on.

Lawrence Pickup outlined the position of the postmen, explaining that promises made to them a year ago were still unfulfilled. The only hope of the postmen was in the organized labor movement. In spite of the threats of Senator Robertson the postal employees had voted to stay out. (Loud applause.)

F. J. Dixon, in opening, said he felt like the old darky who wanted to join a fashionable city church, and the minister, knowing it was hardly the thing to do and not wanting to hurt his feelings, told him to go home and pray over it. In a few days the darky came back.

"Well, what do you think of it by this time," said the preacher.

"Well, sah," replied the colored man, "Ah prayed, an' de good Lawd, he says to me, 'Rastus, Ah wouldn't bodder mah haid about dat no mo'. Ah've been trying to get into dat chu'ch mahse'f fo' de las' twenty yeahs, and Ah done had no luck.' "

There were churches in Winnipeg being used as recruiting stations for the purpose of drilling men to subdue strikers. The strikers had demonstrated that they were the friends of law, order, and peace. The Lord was certainly not in the churches that were being used for such a purpose.

Jesus was a carpenter's son, not a lawyer, financier, or iron master — it was easy to guess which side he would be on in this struggle.

He was on the side of the poor. It was the high priests, the scribes, and the Pharisees — the same class of men as comprised the Committee of 1000 — who had crucified Christ.

The Persecuted Are Blessed

The fact that the men who had been elected by the strikers to guide the destiny of the strike were being reviled by the opposition was a certificate of good character. The more vile and despicable the attack made upon these men the greater should be their glorification.

Spread the Strike

The best answer they could make to the various ultimatums was

— Foote Collection, Manitoba Archives
A meeting in Victoria Park during the strike. The park was located in a solid Anglo-Saxon working-class residential district, two blocks away from the city hall. Note the houses and factory in the background.

— Foote Collection, Manitoba Archives
Victoria Park. Throughout the strike, the Strike Committee confined
its public activities to meetings held in parks across the city.

to spread the strike. If the strikers started going back to work on any pretext the strike would be lost. The only way to win was to stay out and stick together.

Big Collection for Girls

A collection of nearly $500 was taken up to feed the girl strikers who might need it.

Against the restraint and moderation manifest in the foregoing articles, (and they are in keeping with the general character and tone of the strikers' speech and press at this time) may be set the following choice selection from the Winnipeg Telegram of May 26th, 1919, entitled:

THE CAUSES AND THE CURE

"There are in Winnipeg, unfortunately, a handful of English and Scotch agitators who are openly and even proudly Red Socialists and Anarchists. They are held in contempt by their own fellow-countrymen, are despised and loathed ... That is the complete list of our trouble makers, our revolution masters, our Soviet makers — if we except a more than half-mad preacher who was kicked out of his church for preaching treason ... It was comparatively easy for the traitors and hostile foreigners to lead the loyal element astray." ... It explains all the above by saying: "We all have a pain today — and a severe one."

"The way to solve the problem is to clean up Winnipeg of both human rubbish and quacks." This so "that our nerves will not soon again become so frazzled."

ONE ACHIEVEMENT OF THE STRIKE

From the inception of the strike, meetings had been held daily in many city parks and open spaces attended by thousands of strikers and sympathisers (and incidentally, as we have found out since, by that particular species of the animal kingdom, anathema to every honest-minded man and woman, the **"Spy"** and **"Agents Provocateurs"**) and after the strike had been in progress two weeks, the crowds at these meetings had increased in size and demands were made for speakers, which it was found increasingly difficult to supply.

RELIEF FOR THE GIRLS

By this time also, it was evident that something must be done to assist the large number of girls who had come out with their fellow-workers.

This large body of girl and women workers from the departmental stores, laundries, garment factories, candy kitchens, hotels, and restaurants never had more than a week's margin between the pay-envelope and starvation.

THE WOMEN'S LABOR LEAGUE

The Women's Labor League had secured free of charge for ten days the use of the large dining room and kitchen, with partial equipment of one of our city hotels on Main Street, the "Strathcona," and here the girls were fed free of cost, not luxuriously, but with enough, and in addition were given a cash grant to meet room rent. The men were also invited and made welcome and when they had the money were expected to pay, but if they, too, were without funds then they were fed free on production of a ticket issued for that purpose by the Relief Committee. This activity on the part of the Women's Labor League did not meet with the approval of the financial interests of the city and eventually the proprietor of the hotel asked the strikers to vacate.

Not to be outdone, the women, good fighters that they were, went on the hunt for other premises, where the vested interests could not wield the big stick, and found them at the Oxford Hotel, where a bigger and a better dining room, and fully equipped modern kitchen were put at their disposal. Here were served from 1,200 to 1,500 free meals daily, the expense being provided in part by the Relief Committee, in part by donations, and in large measure by collections taken up at the various meetings of the strikers held throughout the city.

THE LABOR CHURCH

In connection with this, the Labor Church, whose membership is composed almost entirely of workers who were out on strike, contributed approximately $4,500.00 during the six weeks of the strike.

A word concerning the interest and activities of the Labor Church may be very appropriate at this juncture.

The second Sunday the strike had been in progress the service was held in Victoria Park, with an attendance of well over 5,000, and there was a collection of approximately $500.00; the third Sunday there was an attendance of over 10,000 and a collection was taken of $1,504.10.

This was one of the most inspiring episodes of the whole of the never-to-be-forgotten six weeks.

PROFESSOR ALLISON AND THE STRIKERS

As a typical instance of the temperate and reasonable manner in which the vital issues at stake were kept to the fore on the part of the strikers as against the deliberate attempts to sidetrack them on the part of the Committee of 1000, here are appended three short articles from the "Strike Bulletin." They are self-explanatory and shed much

— Foote Collection, Manitoba Archives

"The sympathetic strike was just as religious a movement as a church revival," claimed Rev. A. E. Smith. This is probably a prayer meeting during the strike, such as those addressed by Smith, Woodsworth and Canon Scott of Quebec, to raise funds for needy strikers' families. These "social gospel" meetings took their fullest form after June 30, when Rev. William Ivens began to hold Labor Church meetings at the Labor Temple.

light on the situation:

GOVERNMENT SHOULD RESIGN
Professor Allison Compliments Strikers on Order. — Says They Stand For Constitutional Authority

"The best thing the Union Government could do would be to resign," declared professor W. T. Allison on Tuesday evening at a large meeting in the Selkirk School grounds.

There would not have been this great unrest, he said, if we had a good Government at Ottawa. All Governments since Confederation had been largely directed by the railways, manufacturers, and banks. The Union Government had a great opportunity, but it had fallen down. He hoped to see a Labor Party in Canada similar to that in Britain.

The Professor said it looked as if the whole weight of authority was against the strikers. What will you do? he enquired. "Stick, Stick, Stick!" shouted the crowd.

He regretted the summary action of the City Council and suggested the questions at issue were of sufficient magnitude to warrant a referendum vote of all the citizens of Winnipeg being taken.

He also suggested the formation of a representative committee of 100 citizens — distinct from the self-constituted 1000 — to try to effect a settlement.

Professor Allison complimented the strikers on the perfect order which prevailed and said he was satisfied that all wanted to settle this matter by constitutional means. "Keep smiling," were his parting words.

Strike Bulletin of May 27th, 1919:

WHAT IS A LIVING WAGE?

What is a living wage? This is one of the demands of the strikers. What does it mean? Judge Mathers, while here as Chairman of the Industrial Commission, said that it meant more than a bare existence; it meant, he said, enough to supply all reasonable needs and to put by a little for a rainy day.

In the light of this definition let us examine a few cases from this city. The writer has before him the sworn affidavit of a number of employees. Here are a few. We take them from cafes run by men who are members of the Restaurant Keepers' Association.

Let us take six of these, the C. V. Cafe, the Carleton, the Venice, the Kensington, the Olympia, and the Club Cafe. In these places the hours are:

The long day, 7:30 a.m. to 2 p.m. Then return 5:30 p.m. to 1:30 a.m., or a fourteen and a half-hour day.

The short hours are:

11:30 a.m. to 8:30 p.m., or a nine-hour day.

Meals are supplied while on duty.

THE WAGES ARE 15.00 PER MONTH. No, not per week, but per month. Three days off per month. In several instances only one day off per month.

Out of the above $15.00 per month the girls pay for laundry $1.00 per week, and fifty cents per week to the bus boy. Or six dollars per month.

THESE GIRLS THEN HAVE NINE DOLLARS A MONTH to pay room rent, clothes, recreation, outdoor meals, etc.

It is a sin that cries to heaven.

Men Get Shameful Pay

Here is the record of two men employed in a building owned by a prominent citizen. We forbear the name at this time.

Mr. A. works from 8:30 p.m. to 7:45 a.m. Cleans several floors. Seven lavatories. Brass and glass work. Runs elevator from 5:30 a.m. to 7:45 a.m. One day each week he has to look after furnaces. Wages $50.00 per month. Lives out of building.

Mr. B., fireman in this same building, works from 6 p.m. to 5:30 a.m. Besides his furnaces he runs the elevator from 6 p.m. to 10:30 p.m. In spare time he is required to do general cleaning. Wages $55.00 per month. In both cases the men work 74 hours per week in all.

When we are asked what is a living wage, we point to the above wages for men and girls, and say NOT THAT. But a decent living wage.

Still we are told the workers are avaricious and ought not to grumble. Surely the time to strike has come. It is time the citizens of Winnipeg rose in their might and said, it is enough.

"THE ALIEN CRY"

The workers were content to rest their case with the judgment of the people, but this was not acceptable to the "Big Interests." Red herrings of various degrees of rottenness had been repeatedly dragged across the path, such as cries of "Soviet, Bolshevist, Revolution and Permit Cards," and last, in an effort to arouse the ire of the patriotic element, they started a flag waving campaign, and especially to rally the support of the returned soldiers, they raised the cry of "Alien."

THE ALIEN QUESTION

"Yah! yah! aliens! aliens!" shrieks the self-constituted Committee of 1000 through its megaphonic press. The Strike Committee challenges a comparison of its personnel with that of the 1000.

The bosses love the alien when they can use him to break strikes. In fact in many cases he was brought here for that purpose. For example in the Nova Scotia miners' strike (1913) the bosses circularized southern Europe, offering the princely wages of 11 cents to 15 cents per hour for mine and steel plant workers.

During the war bosses wanted to pay alien labor $1.10 per day and put the difference between that and the prevailing wages into their own pockets. Labor successfully protested against that dastardly project. It had to in self-protection. If the bosses could get aliens for $1.10 they would pay no more to anyone. Remember the bosses brought the aliens here. Remember also that thousands of aliens have asked for passports and have been refused.

The bosses have no quarrel with the rich alien, no quarrel with the unorganized alien. The only aliens they complain about are those who have had sense enough to join the ranks of organized labor and therefore cannot be used to scale down wages.

"But alien is one — of class, not race — he has drawn the line
    for himself;
His roots drink life from inhuman soil, from garbage of pomp
    and pelf;
His heart beats not with the common beat, he has changed his
    life-stream's hue;
He deems his flesh to be finer flesh, he boasts that his blood
    is blue:
Politician, aristocrat, tory — whatever his age or name,
To the people's rights and liberties, a traitor ever the same.
The natural crowd is a mob to him, their prayer a vulgar rhyme:
The freeman's speech is sedition, and the patriot's deed a crime.
Whatever the race, the law, the land — whatever the time, or
    throne,
The tory is always a traitor to every class but his own."

At the time the Committee of 1000 were agitating the public mind against the "alien" with demands for his deportation, "Milady" was touring the alien district in limousine and taxi, begging, pleading, imploring and bribing the "female of the alien species" to come to her aid and replace the female workers who were on strike.

Employers, large and small, sent deputations to beg of the alien to come back to work.

But the alien declined the tempting offers made them and they stuck tight as a postage stamp. For the workers of Winnipeg, the barriers of color, race and creed had been torn down and are now beyond hope of being rebuilt. **"Which is as it should be."**

In the "Strike Bulletin," No. 12, of May 30th, 1919, there appeared on the front page the following reiteration of the strikers' demands, and a statement of what they did not want:

WHAT WE WANT

The Demands of the Strikers are: —
1. The Right of Collective Bargaining.
2. A Living Wage.
3. Reinstatement of all Strikers.

WHAT WE DO NOT WANT

1. Revolution.
2. Dictatorship.
3. Disorder.

THE TORONTO STAR AND THE STRIKERS

As evidence of one of two things, either that there still live some editors of the daily press who will not prostitute their ability for money, or that the "big strike" had not completed its circle, we reprint an excerpt from the "Toronto Star," on May 23rd, 1919:

TORONTO STAR BACKS STRIKERS

IT IS BECOMING MORE AND MORE CLEAR THAT THE ISSUE IS NOT BOLSHEVISM OR ANY ATTEMPT TO URSURP THE GOVERNMENT OF CANADA, BUT A DISPUTE BETWEEN EMPLOYERS AND EMPLOYED ON THE QUESTIONS OF WAGES, HOURS, RECOGNITION OF UNIONS, AND COLLECTIVE BARGAINING. A strike covering a wide range of industries of course causes great public inconvenience. But what is the remedy? IF IT IS LAWFUL FOR ONE SET OF WORKERS TO STRIKE, SHALL IT BE MADE UNLAWFUL FOR TWO OR A DOZEN TO STRIKE? The difference, of course, is that when a strike is general or of very wide range, the matter becomes one of national importance, and the Dominion Government may be warranted and even in duty bound to take strong measures to effect a settlement.

THOSE EMPLOYERS WHO HOLD OUT AGAINST COLLECTIVE BARGAINING — that is, negotiating with unions which have members working in various establishments — ARE CLEARLY WRONG AND THEIR POSITION CANNOT BE MAINTAINED. Collective bargaining is the inevitable result of the modern concentration of industry, and to oppose it is just as extreme as to propose the abolition of organized capital. The organization of labor and the organization of capital are the hard facts of the situation, and must be recognized.

The Star is not a labor paper, but a leading Toronto daily. Yet it supports us on the issues for which we are on strike.

Not a Bolshevist Uprising

Speaking of the wonderful conduct of the strike it says:

The stand taken by the organized body of returned soldiers in Winnipeg is one that has had, probably, a highly corrective influence on affairs.

The ex-soldier citizens have given their full sympathy and support to the strikers in their demands for the betterment of their conditions, on the definite understanding that there is to be no disorder or lawlessness in connection with the strike.

When one considers that Winnipeg has been tied up for a whole week, that over thirty thousand men have been on strike and feeling running high, it is a credit to that city, its people, and all concerned in the whole affair that such excellent order has been preserved. To some extent this desirable result may probably be attributed to the stand taken by the G.W.V.A. and returned soldiers generally. They sympathize with the demands of the workers; they approve of the strike and desire it to succeed, but they want no resort to riot and violence. The labor leaders are doubtless anxious to retain this important support and sympathy.

So far they have retained it, and we have difficulty in reconciling this fact with the statement that Winnipeg is in the hands of Bolshevists and the foreign element.

THE CANADIAN PROBLEMS CLUB

As a further indication of the willingness of the Strike Committee (as representing all the workers) to investigate every possible opportunity that presented itself to effect a satisfactory settlement of the strike, when a delegation from the "Canadian Problems Club" (an organization composed for the most part of professional men) waited upon the Central Committee with a request that they be supplied with certain information, and an enquiry as to the acceptance by the Strike Committee of their organization as mediators, Messrs. Winning and Russell were instructed to wait upon the Canadian Problems Club and give them all the information required. This they did, to the entire satisfaction of that body. They also intimated the willingness of the Strike Committee to avail themselves gladly of the service of any individual or organization that might be able to effect a settlement.

In contradistinction to this friendly and conciliatory attitude of the Strike Committee, must be recorded the actions of the so-called Citizens' Committee of 1000, which refused any information and declined altogether the offer of the club.

THE POLICE ULTIMATUM

This is a copy of the "Ultimatum" to the police and civic employees,

— A. K. Gee, Public Archives

Portage Avenue, looking east near Eaton's department store. This photograph came from a group taken relatively early in the strike, perhaps around the end of May. It could be of the first appearance in public of RNWMP detachments, who are still wearing army uniforms here. Streetcars had stopped running, but cars and trucks supplied by well-to-do citizens and large companies were providing ''jitney'' transport for office workers and shopgirls. Mrs. George Armstrong was arrested several times during the strike outside Eaton's for urging shopgirls to join the strike.

respectively, together with a resolution passed by the Winnipeg Policemen's Union, held in the Police Court room on May 30th, 1919:

To Board of Commissioners of Police
of the City of Winnipeg:

1. I hereby acknowledge that the supreme governing power of the police force is vested in the Police Commissioners alone, and I hereby agree to observe the orders, rules and regulations of said Police Commissioners at all times.

2. I further agree that I will not join or remain a member of any union or association which is directly or indirectly in affiliation with any other organization to whose orders, directions or recommendations such union or association or its members are obliged or agree to observe or conform, or act in concert with; that I will be governed by and observe and comply with all rules and regulations in force from time to time for the management of the force in which I may be employed, whether prescribed by the Police Commissioners or the Chief Constable; that I will not take part in or support or favor what is known as a sympathetic strike; and that upon a breach of any of the above conditions occurring I shall be liable to instant dismissal from the force.

3. I hereby acknowledge that I have received a copy of the rules and regulations governing the department and agree to obey same.

Dated at the City of Winnipeg, this   day of May, 1919.

Name ....
Rank ....

In answer to this the following resolution was passed by a mass meeting of the members of the Winnipeg Policemen's Union held in the Police Court room 30th May, 1919:

Having had no time to consider the ultimatum presented by the Police Commissioners, and feeling that it is a violation of our agreement by the Police Commissioners, just recently signed, we wish to affirm our position, that we stand behind constituted authority and are willing to do all in our power to preserve law and order as loyal British subjects.

Everybody loves the police — except the 1000. The soldiers gave them three cheers.

The police have won almost universal endorsation by the way they have conducted themselves during this strike and almost everyone, outside of the coterie of 1000, feels that the Police Commission has grossly insulted these real men by putting up such an agreement to them at this critical time. All Law-abiding citizens want the civil police kept on the streets. Any attempt, directly or indirectly, to force them off the streets will be greatly resented.

The above was called "The Slave Pact," and the "Western Labor News" comments upon it as follows:

BRITONS NEVER SHALL BE SLAVES

The City Council upon order of the Board of Trade Soviet, has drawn up the following pledge for its employees:

"I hereby agree that if I am appointed to any position in the city's service, I will not join or remain a member of any union or association which is directly or indirectly in affiliation with any other organization to whose orders, directions or recommendations such union or association or its members are obliged or agree to observe or confirm, or act in concert with; that I will be governed by and observe and comply with all rules and regulations in force from time to time for the management of the department in which I may be employed, whether prescribed by the City Council or by the head of such department; that I will at all times be loyal and faithful to the city; that I will not take part in or support or favor what is known as a sympathetic strike; and that upon a breach of any of the above conditions occurring, I shall be liable to instant dismissal from the city's service."

It is this same City Council that asks the Provincial Government to make collective bargaining compulsory.

It is safe to say that no person who understands the nature of liberty and collective bargaining could have drawn up such an abject pledge of subservience.

ONLY A SLAVE COULD SIGN IT. A FREE MAN, A WHITE MAN — NEVER!

In this connection is the following brief report of an incident which occurred during the City Council meeting in the afternoon of Friday, May 30th, 1919, taken from the "Strike Bulletin" of May 31st, 1919:

POLICE GIVEN 24 HOURS' EXTENSION
Canadian Problems Club Suggests Modification of Civic Pledge

At the request of G. K. Wark, Vice-President B.L.F. and E., and A. McAndrew, Assistant General Chairman of the C.P.R. System I.B.M.W., the Police Commission has given the police another 24 hours in which to consider the agreement submitted to them. This was announced by Alderman Sparling to the City Council Friday afternoon.

Remove Root of Antagonism

A delegation from the Canadian Problems Club, consisting of R. A. Rigg, F. M. Black, R. F. McWilliams,* and Professor Chester

*Became lieutenant-governor of Manitoba in the thirties.

Martin, waited on the Council urging a modification of the pledge which the city was asking its employees to sign.

R. A. Rigg pointed out that as the Civic Employees Unions were affiliated with The Trades Congress of Canada the action of the Council was a direct challenge to that body. He pointed out very clearly that the Trades Council had no power to compel any union affiliated with it to strike. Affiliation was purely voluntary and unions acted on their own initiative, free from any outside dictation. He asked the council to modify the stringency of its resolutions.

Alderman Fowler: "No chance."

R. A. Rigg: "I'm sorry to hear that." His concern throughout had been that this quarrel might be settled in the best interests of all. In order to avoid future trouble the root of antagonism should be removed.

R. F. McWilliams suggested that the trouble should be so disposed of that there would be no possibility of recurrence. In its resolutions the Council in endeavoring to ban sympathetic strikes had overshot the mark and by interfering with a man's fundamental right to associate with others for mutual benefit had taken a stand which might create difficulties with the whole labor movement.

Alderman Fowler said they were dealing with facts, not theories. He didn't see how they could change.

Alderman McLean said the question would never be settled. The Council must hedge the civic employees in as the peace conference was hedging in the Germans.

SOLDIER STRIKERS TAKE ACTION

On the evening of May 30th, 1919, a meeting of returned men in sympathy with the objects of the workers in their struggle, was called at the request of Ex-Sergeant A. E. Moore — at that time an employee of the Provincial Government, in charge of the Alien Investigation Board — and now President of the Provincial Command of the Great War Veterans' Association — in order that the advisability of interviewing the Provincial Government could be discussed.

The meeting assembled at a few minutes after eight and did not adjourn until after eleven o'clock.

After going into the matter thoroughly, it was unanimously decided that it would serve a most useful purpose if a delegation of returned men waited upon the Provincial Premier and his Cabinet and asked them to settle the dispute by the enactment of special legislation, making collective bargaining compulsory upon every employer of labor in the province.

The result of these deliberations is briefly stated in the following account taken from the "Strike Bulletin" of May 31st, 1919:

— Manitoba Archives

Liberal Premier T. C. Norris and his minister of Education, R. S. Thornton. Their party had come into office in Manitoba in 1915 on an election promise of "purity in politics," defeating a notoriously corrupt government. They instituted a whole set of reforms, though these were very WASP in tone and often worked against ethnic interests: compulsory school attendance, higher education standards, an independent civil service, woman suffrage, temperance laws, mothers' allowances for widows and deserted wives, improved workmen's compensation, factory inspection and "fair wage" arbitration.

In 1919 they were preparing to set up a Joint Council of Industry along British lines. However, labour-union leaders demanded less paternalism and more bargaining rights to be exercised by the workers themselves. The Norris reforms dared not go so far, and gradually support for them diminished as opposition hardened on both the right and the left.

SOLDIERS' ULTIMATUM TO NORRIS

Demand Police Ultimatum be Withdrawn — Newspaper Bolshevik Campaign Must End — Campaign of Vilification of Labor Leaders be Ended — Will Stay on Job Till Collective Bargaining and Living Wage Granted — Will Meet Government at 11 a.m. Saturday for Reply — Will Not Stand for Threats of Martial Law.

Two thousand returned soldiers waited on Premier Norris on Friday morning and demanded an immediate settlement of the strike on the basis of collective Bargaining being made compulsory by legislation. They will return for an answer at 11 a.m. tomorrow, Saturday.

Soldiers' Resolution

The Honourable T. C. Norris,
  Premier,
    Province of Manitoba.

"Owing to the serious condition of affairs in this city, we feel it incumbent on us as returned soldiers to draw to your notice the desirability of an immediate settlement, which we believe can be done, through either the Provincial or Dominion Governments taking immediate action, and making this disputed question of collective bargaining as it now exists on the railways, effective by statutory action."

Back of Police

The soldiers also pointed out very emphatically that the Police Commission regulation insisting that the police sever connections with organized labor was a bad mistake. They thought the Committee of 1000 had used its influence to get the regular police off the streets in order to replace them with the military. They thought it was grossly unfair to put the police up against such a proposition at this time and said the order must be repealed to avoid trouble.

The veterans made their presentations very strong. They especially insisted on the police commission order being modified. (This demand was cheered with tremendous enthusiasm.)

The delegation was under the chairmanship of A. E. Moore and the several speakers did some plain talking. They wanted to know if the Premier would call them "Bolsheviks" or "Aliens?" Mr. Norris assured them that he would not. The soldiers bitterly and emphatically resented the press attacks upon strike leaders, and were especially incensed at the term: "English and Scotch anarchists" as applied to those men. They made it absolutely clear that this campaign must be stopped, and stopped at once.

They insisted that the Premier use his utmost influence with the press to prevent a recurrence of this abuse. Mr. Norris promised so to do and later informed the reporters in his office of the stand taken by the soldiers.

On Saturday, May 31st, in pursuance of the intimation to the Provincial Government the previous day, the returned men lined up on Market Square and marched to the Legislative Building, Kennedy Street, and the following brief report of events there is taken from the "Strike Bulletin" of June 2nd, 1919:

SOLDIERS BACK STRIKERS TO LIMIT

Ten Thousand Wearing Buttons March to Parliament Building — Tell Norris to Call Off Committee of One Thousand — Urge Special Session to Legislate re Collective Bargaining — Denounce Treatment of Telephone Girls — Going Back to Interview Government Monday Morning — Visit City Hall and Demand Withdrawal of Ultimatum to Civic Employees — Insist That Police Remain on Duty — City Council Leaves it Stand Over Till Tuesday Morning — Give Policemen Ovation — Carry Flag to Labor Temple — Say Sympathetic Strike Cannot be Called Off Till Collective Bargaining Established — Resent Press Campaign of Vilification — Say It Must Stop — Give Three Cheers for Labor News.

At 11 a.m. on Saturday ten thousand returned soldiers followed the flag down Kennedy Street to the Parliament Buildings, to get from Premier Norris an answer to the demands they had presented on Friday.

The legislative chamber was packed and thousands stood outside in the drizzling rain awaiting the result.

Greatly Disappointed

After the Premier had expressed himself, the spokesmen for the returned soldiers expressed bitter disappointment at the attitude the Government had assumed. Instead of demanding that the sympathetic strike be called off they said the Premier should call off the Committee of 1000.

Resent Abuse of Flag by 1000

Some commotion was created at the outset by the fact that an individual in the press gallery was wearing a flag in his button hole. The returned men thought this indicated that he belonged to the Committee of 1000 and demanded the removal of that emblem. One man finally jumped into the press gallery and removed it. Comrade

Bray later explained that the soldiers respected the flag and they did not intend to see it prostituted by the Committee of 1000. He was informed that the man who had worn the flag had a son who had been over there. The soldiers did not wish to hurt anyone's feelings, but they could not stand for any abuse of the flag by the Committee of 1000.

Will Defend Law and Order

Comrade Moore explained that the soldiers had fought for law and order and were always prepared to defend it. They wanted a settlement of this strike and did not think the press campaign of vilification was helpful to that end. Then came cries of "Take the reporters out" and "Give them one more chance."

Comrade Moore said they were there for an answer to their previous demands for legislation compelling collective bargaining. Premier Borden had said this was a provincial matter so they wanted to know when the Government would deal with it.

Comrade Moore then presented a resolution on behalf of the delegation which stated that the announced extension of the ultimatum to the police was entirely unsatisfactory. That ultimatum must be withdrawn. The resolution also asked for an answer from the Government to the request for legislation re collective bargaining.

Let Police Stay on Beats

Comrade Moore was especially emphatic and received tumultuous applause when he demanded that the police remain on duty and be not asked to sell their birthright during the present crisis.

Police Have Proven Loyal

Comrade Bray said the returned men knew what loyalty meant. They had demonstrated their loyalty at the front in order that governments might continue to exist. The police had likewise demonstrated their loyalty; in fact, many of them were returned men. The Premier now had a chance to demonstrate his loyalty by backing the police.

The returned men were out for law and order. The police had done all they could to preserve law and order. They deserved consideration. It was an insult to the police to ask them to sell their birthright, especially at this time.

Sick of Dilly-Dallying

Comrade Bray contended that this was a time for action — not talk. There had been too much dilly-dallying in this matter. The returned men were anxious for a settlement giving all a square deal.

Press Campaign Deeply Resented

The attitude of the press was not helping to effect a settlement. The returned men would be gentlemen and not descend to scurrilous personalities as the press had done. They would like the Premier to think what the boys had done in France, to consider the sacrifices they had made. As for them, they would continue to be soldiers and gentlemen.

Flag Incident Explained

Comrade Bray referred to the unfortunate incident at the opening of the meeting. The man wearing the flag had a son who had been over there. It was inadvisable to wear flags at this time because the men who had fought to defend it were determined that no skulkers hide behind it. They despised the action of the Committee of 1000 in trying to hide behind the flag (cries of "Crime! Crime!") and use it against men who were fighting for justice and a living wage.

The boys, said comrade Bray, want you to represent the people and not that bunch of financial barons in the Manufacturers' Association. In addition to our other demands we want you to withdraw your ultimatum to the telephone girls.

Norris Severely Heckled

Premier Norris said he was wearing a flag, not because he represented any faction, but because he thought the flag represented all classes. (A voice: "It is being prostituted by a faction. It is the same flag as yours." Another voice: "Get on with the strike.") Mr. Norris asserted that his sympathies were with labor. He had conveyed to the reporters the message of the returned men that they resented the press campaign of misrepresentation. He had told the City Council what the soldiers thought about the ultimatum to the police. He understood that representatives of the Railway Brotherhoods were even now trying to get employees together with a view to settlement.

Sends Soldiers to City Hall

Mr. Norris said the police affair was beyond his control. The soldiers should put it up to the City Council. (Cheers and shouts of, "we will!").

The Government has met the wishes of the returned men in many things. He was sure they would not be unreasonable. It was impossible to promise legislation about collective bargaining immediately. The Government would have to find out its power. At the request of the representatives of the Railroad Brotherhoods he had written

Messrs. Barrett, Lyall, and Warren suggesting that they meet their employees through the mediation of those representatives.

Government Opposed to Sympathetic Strikes

He announced that the sympathetic strike must be called off before the Government could act; (loud booing and shouts of: "call off the Committee of 1000").

Mr. Norris continued: If the strike was called off the Government would use all its energies to settle dispute; (a voice: "soft soap!"). The Government had taken the stand that there must be no sympathetic strikes on public utilities and food services. They had attempted to avoid such a condition as this by the Industrial Conditions Bill. If the soldiers would use their influence to call off the strike and get the Trades and Labor Council to nominate two men to the Industrial Council, the Government would see that sittings were held at once and proceedings pushed. (Cries of No! No!! No!!!)

We are in sympathy with labor repeated the Premier.

Question: "How about the postal employees?"

Mr. Norris: "That's a Federal matter."

Question: "How about the telephones?"

Mr. Norris: "There is no ultimatum in that connection."

Question: "How about the firemen?"

Mr. Norris: "They are under the Civic jurisdiction."

"I have stated my case. I have told you what we're going to do." (Shouts of: "Nothing!" and "Resign! Resign!")

Answer Unsatisfactory

Comrade Moore deprecated personalities and said that the Premier's answer was very unsatisfactory. They wanted something done. If the Government insisted that the sympathetic strike must be called off, the strike would last another six months. They wanted the strike settled on the basis of the right of collective bargaining and a decent living wage. Everyone who opposed these things was prolonging the strike. He was going away disappointed. (Cries of: "We all are!")

If the sympathetic strike was called off, the committee of 1000 would say they had won.

"Call off the Committee of 1000," continued Comrade Moore amid deafening applause.

Premier Should Reconsider Decision

Comrade Batsford got the floor and asked the Premier to reconsider his decision. As returned soldiers, who had upheld constituted authority, they had appealed to constituted authority in a constituted way.

The Peace Conference had endorsed collective bargaining and they were asking Premier Norris to call a special session of the legislature and promise to introduce a bill dealing with the matter.

What Government Can Do

Comrade Bray said no man was satisfied with the interview. The Premier had told them what he could not do. He would tell the Premier what he could do. He could put pressure on the Telephone Commission to call off their ultimatum and stop the war on the telephone girls. He could bring pressure to bear upon the City Council to cancel its ultimatum. One Alderman (McLean) had said the city must hedge in its employees as the Peace Conference was hedging in the Germans. "Is that democracy?" he asked. The building rocked with shouts of "No! a thousand times No!"

Spineless Ninnies at Ottawa

Comrade Bray said the Norris Government had helped to elect that bunch of spineless emasculated ninnies at Ottawa and they might now get busy and put some ginger into them or help to get them out of the way. Furthermore, he said, the Government itself should stop paying "scab" wages and become a model employer.

One Thousand Want Martial Law

Comrade Speers, in concluding, asserted that they were sorry nothing had been accomplished. The soldiers wanted this strike settled satisfactorily. They had fought for democracy and had returned to find an autocratic Committee of 1000 trying to run the city.

The city was wrong in putting their ultimatum to the police at this time. He believed the Committee of 1000 wanted to get the police off the streets and put men with bayonets on them. The returned men would not stand for this. The Committee of 1000 must be destroyed. (Deafening applause).

March to City Hall

After the meeting with Mr. Norris the soldiers marched to the City Hall and swarmed into the chamber. The Council was in session, but at once adjourned and Mayor Gray attempted to address the vast crowd, mostly returned men, from the City Hall steps. The meeting was decidedly stormy.

Re-Affirms Council's Position

The Mayor insisted that there must be no more sympathetic strikes on public utilities. He was prepared to stand or fall by that decision. (Shouts of: "Resign! Resign! For you will fall!") He was finally booed into the City Hall.

No Police Ultimatum

There was no ultimatum to the police, asserted Mayor Gray. "Oh! Oh!" shouted the crowd. The representatives of the Running Trades were now meeting with the police and trying to make a settlement.

The crowd made it very plain that it wanted no interference with the police.

Council's Silly Position

Several returned men addressed the meeting, going over much the same ground as covered in the legislative chamber. There was no mincing matters. It was straight talk from strong and determined men.

It was pointed out that the Council had put itself in a ridiculous position in passing a resolution in favor of collective bargaining and then reducing its own employees to the level of slaves.

Comrade Munro announced that he had visited the post office and had seen there a sign "Mail for Business Men Only." He wanted to know who were the citizens.

Aldermen Queen and Heaps addressed the gathering and were heartily applauded.

Police Ultimatum Suspended

It was announced later that the ultimatum to the police had been suspended until next Tuesday.

Soldiers Will March Again

The returned men will wait on Premier Norris Monday morning at the same hour. They say they will go daily until their demands are granted. They will also march on the Committee of 1000 and the City Hall is likely to see them again unless the slave pact is withdrawn from all the employees. They say openly that this is not the thing they fought for and they will not stand for it anywhere in the city.

Never before has Winnipeg seen such a morning. The soldiers and the workers are united into a solid fighting front.

Apropos of the general attitude of the returned men, the following article, reprinted from the "Strike Bulletin" of June 2nd, 1919, gives very concisely some of the reasons for the strong feeling expressed by the ex-soldier:

THE SOLDIER AND THE STRIKE

The severest jolt the financial magnates of Winnipeg ever got was administered by the returned soldiers early in the strike, when the mass meeting representing all the returned soldier bodies reversed the decision of the combined executives and threw in their lot with the strikers.

Since that time these employers have chafed with chagrin and disappointment. They had spent so much time and printers' ink and so many beautiful words on the returned soldier. They have met him as he left the ship and the train with select news items. They met him with brass bands and tinkling cymbals and honied phrases. They pointed out to him the traitorous acts of LABOR while they, the soldier, fought. Labor was their enemy — the masters were their friends.

And now: Presto — Donner and Blitzen — their campaign was a "dud." Their "black besses" failed to explode. Something is wrong.

The Soldier Fought and Fought

The soldier can't be white-livered. No one can call him yellow. His feet are not cold. When he went over the top he silenced all suspicions and overcame all opposition.

What Then is the Matter?

What is the matter? Well he damned the politicians while he tried to "carry on" with a Ross rifle. Jambing rifles while men fall all around don't make contented soldiers. He cursed as he choked in trying to swallow the Ironsides soldiers' meats. He inwardly fumed to see his $1.10 a day melt against the sudden "rise in prices." He ground his teeth while he read his wife's letters telling him how she tried so hard to make ends meet on her small and ever-smaller "allowance." It did not take him long to think of the Hun in Canada — the Hun behind his back. He does not love him today.

Then upon his return he finds a pension awaiting him that is a positive insult. It is so niggardly as to shame the very devil. He thinks hard as he sees the difference between his pension and that of Colonel Sir Punk. He wants to know why, and why and why?

Just as soon as he is discharged and looks for a job he faces life once more as it really is. If he is partially disabled, and has a pigmy pension, he finds Sir Augustus Nanton writing a letter like the following:

This is an extract from a letter received by a returned soldier who won a D.C.M., and lost a leg, from Sir Augustus Nanton.* Lady Nanton was Auxiliary President of the battalion to which the man belonged.

*A Winnipeg investment dealer, one of the most influential of the business elite.

Sir Augustus writes:

"In your case, I have no doubt that, in addition to your salary, you are receiving some partial disability allowance from the Government, which, I sincerely trust, together with your salary, brings in to you an income which will enable you to live.

"Yours truly,
"(Signed) A. M. NANTON."

The letter needs no comment. One such letter is sufficient to do its work with any soldier.

Then he turns around and finds a Lieutenant-Governor paying another returned man $13.00 a week. Others get 31 cents an hour. The railways offer 32½ cents an hour. And at wages such as these he cannot find employment.

Where women are concerned things are no better. Restaurant girls get as low as $15.00 per month. Women who work cleaning offices at night get $15.00 per month. And all along the line it is unemployment and low wages.

Low Wages and High Prices

The low wages would not matter if prices were also low. But prices are controlled by trusts, and combines, and banks, and milling interests, and grain exchanges, and pork packers, and all the long line of profiteers and parasites.

They own cars and mansions and declare their dividends on an ever-increasing scale. They boast of their growing wealth, while he pays a tax on matches, and on tobacco, and on tea, and sugar, and shoes, etc., until a dollar buys only half as much as formerly. He has quit fighting — but he still thinks, and he says, at last, well, I guess we shall have to fight once more.

So he lines up the friends and foes, and his thinking has led him to see his present enemies in the men who buy full page advertisements in the daily press for tariffs, and tirades against labor. He sees his friends in the men against whom these things are aimed.

He Acts Only When He Knows

He does not act in a hurry. He has been taught to wait. So he waits until he gets the facts. Then he acts.

He has decided that the profiteer is the real Bolshevist, and he has signed up against the profiteer. That is why he is in the ranks of the strikers.

He has read the daily press with growing hostility during the last ten days. He has heard himself described as an alien, led by anarchists; so at last he marches to the Parliament Buildings and asks the Premier the question: "Do you call us aliens and Bolsheviks?" The Premier has but one answer. That is — No!

Then says the soldier: ''You must cut this stuff out of your campaign against us strikers; and you must cut it out of your press!''

He Protests Against Injustice

He also sees the real nature of the contemptible campaign of vilification of labor leaders, and he tells the Premier you must cut this out too. We have had all we intend to take of it.

He takes the same stand re the policemen. As a soldier, he has as a class passed the stage of fear, and so the soldier body told the Premier in plain language, that he must see that that ultimatum was withdrawn. Then he gave three cheers for the police.

The absolute unscrupulousness of the employing class is seen clearly by the soldier. He knows what machine guns mean in a mob, and he has found out that he — the returned soldier, with the other strikers — is the mob, so once again he issues a warning, and said once again quite plainly, if you call out the soldiers, you will find that two can play at that game.

Just how much lies behind that lone voice is impossible to tell. But, as the returned soldier demands a living wage and the right to collective bargaining, and says he will ''carry on'' until he gets it, his cry that he can play with guns bears a fearful import.

He Must Get Justice

He smarts under his disadvantages. He has no hall where he can meet en masse. While there are 10,000 returned soldiers, the city hall holds less than a thousand. It seems that he cannot have the Industrial Bureau because the Committee of 1000 has leased it for the period of the strike.

What road hogs they are. They have a monopoly of everything. They own the earth; they dictate over the whole of the soldier's existence. He has obeyed, and has been ordered about as long as he can stand it, he says; ''I fought for Justice and Liberty and now I want a little bit of it.'' This is why the returned soldier has lined up behind the strikers.

It is for him another fight for Justice, and he has said we shall ''Carry on,'' until the fight for a living wage and the right to organize is won.

SOME CHURCHES AND THE STRIKE

From the time the returned men demonstrated on which side their sympathies lay, the Citizens' Committee of 1000 and the interests opposed to the strikers were active in an attempt to secure other support, and some of the leading city churches were used for that purpose.

At Westminster Church a special meeting was called ostensibly to discuss the issues at stake, but it was solely for the purpose of securing recruits for the special strike militia, that was being organized for the purpose of suppressing demonstrations, and for other services during the continuation of the strike, this despite the protest of the Pastor, Rev. Dr. Christie. These special service men recruited from the large offices in the city, and from some of the large department stores, were in many cases confined to barracks where they were instructed in the use of fire-arms.

In addition to this special force, many of the large firms had a ''special force'' of their own. It was an every-day occurrence to see, on the premises of some of these firms, a strong force of men, including many of the despised aliens, being instructed in squad drill and the use of the rifle, under the charge and direction of army and ex-army officers.

It is also a fact that in almost every school playground in the city, as well as in the grounds of the City of St. Boniface, squads were being drilled and instructed in musketry three or four nights of every week.

It was also stated that the O.C. of one of Winnipeg's famous battalions, even as early as ten days before the strike, called a meeting of the old members of his battalion and appealed to them to join up for special service during the troublous times ahead, and in the course of his address to the men, exhorted them somewhat after the manner of ex-Emperor Wilhelm, and told any man there, who would have any scruples about bloodshed, or who would not be prepared to shoot and shoot to kill, to retire from the gathering.

Added to this story (manifestations of reactionary sentiment on the part of the workers' opponents) is the proof of the unscrupulous manner in which the same interests were willing to deceive and mislead, not only the public, but the sympathizing strikers at points outside of Winnipeg.

The following cutting from the ''Strike Bulletin'' of June 3rd, 1919, is self-explanatory, and needs no further comment:

BEWARE OF FAKE TELEGRAMS
Villainous Attempt to Get Railway Workers Back to Work Monday Morning

The following forged telegram, signed Robinson, shows the depth of degradation to which the opponents of labor will descend to defeat the strikers.

The railways had issued their ultimatums to the workers to return to work Monday or they would lose their jobs. This was seized upon as an opportune moment to invent a spurious telegram for the railway workers. It reads plausibly, and is signed Robinson.

But one thing gave the game away — that was the instruction to use the mails. The railway workers did not believe that the strikers would use scab post office workers even to help the strike, so they despatched personal messengers to Winnipeg.

This brought to light the damnable strategy of our enemies. Here is the telegram:

G. N. W. WIRE

"Winnipeg, Man., May 31.

"J. W. Walsh, Sioux Lookout, —

"At meeting last night it was decided to instruct all shop railway foremen, except Transcona and Winnipeg, to resume work at once, and each member must contribute $1 per day towards maintenance all local members in Winnipeg.

"We are badly in need of funds, collect all possible at once and mail by registered letter to Treasurer Trades and Labor Council, Winnipeg. See all further amounts come by assessment forwarded weekly, and return to work not later than Monday morning.

"Robinson, 1040."

MORE FIENDISH TACTICS
Bosses Make "Plants" on Strikers.

The strikers may thank their stars these days that the plans of the other side come to them almost in their entirety. It helps them to avoid pitfalls.

The latest dastardly plot is that there are to be "plants" framed up for the leaders. If a bomb can be planted in one of their pockets and then have them immediately arrested and the thing found on them this will fix them. Complaints of too much Ivens in the past. This is not sufficient to get Ivens, so he is to be made the target for a scheme that will destroy his character, etc.

We shall not here give names, or times, or places, but we warn all strikers to be careful that these inhuman fiends do not get any of you.

THE THIRD SOLDIER DELEGATION

From the same issue of the same paper, we append an account of the third delegation of soldier strikers to the Provincial Government. The sight of these thousands of ex-service men marching with military precision and maintaining such order as could not be excelled under the strictest military discipline, was having a very favorable impression on the minds of all who saw them and they were beginning to realize

how they had been misled by the Citizens' Committee of 1000, through
the columns of the yellow press, and it was a common expression
that "our boys" would not line up so strongly, if there was any cause
to fear revolution. The following is from the "Strike Bulletin" of
June 4th, 1919:

SOLDIERS INSIST ON ACTION

**Provincial Government Again Visited — Delegation Growing in
Numbers — Returned Soldiers Only Allowed in Chamber —
Demand Government Legislate, Resign, or Take Referendum
— Say Majority Favor Collective Bargaining — 1000 a Bunch
of Boodlers — Dixon Loudly Cheered.**

Eaton's store and the Free Press were loudly booed by the returned
men who marched to the Parliament buildings yesterday to seek
from the Government an answer to their demands presented last
Friday and Saturday. A tremendous crowd had gathered on Government ground long before the boys arrived, but none other than returned
men were allowed in the legislative chamber. A few buttonless men
who managed to get in by way of the window were gently but firmly
ejected.

Returned Soldiers Only

The committee in charge of the delegation — distinguished by
white badges — cleared the house of all but returned men. The
chamber was filled to its utmost capacity and thousands were unable
to obtain entrance.

Flag Cheered

When the standard bearer entered a rousing cheer was given for
the flag. Messrs. Norris, Brown and Johnson received the delegation.
Comrade Bray, in opening, asked for perfect order and a fair deal
to every speaker. He then read a resolution which had been previously
passed at a meeting of returned men, stating:

Legislate or Resign

"That, whereas Senator Robertson and Premier Borden have said
that the Dominion Government has no authority to pass legislation
guaranteeing the right of collective bargaining, and whereas they
have declared that the Provincial Governments are the authority having
that power;

"Therefore, be it resolved that we herewith demand such legislation
at once.

"Also that we demand the withdrawal by the Provincial Government of its ultimatum to its employees;

"And, further, that in the event of the Government not complying with our demands we call upon the Government to resign."

This resolution was endorsed with loud applause by the soldiers. Comrade Bray further intimated that the delegation wanted an answer to the demands they had presented on Friday and Saturday.

Norris Again Negative

The Premier congratulated the soldiers on the peaceable and gentlemanly presentation of the resolution. Evidently the soldiers wanted the Government to take drastic action, but the Government must proceed along constitutional lines. He had appealed to the press for fairness and moderation. He had presented civic matters to the City Council as requested.

As to convening the Legislature in special session there was a certain constitutional procedure to be followed. The Government tried to represent all the people and the people's representatives would have to be consulted. He was not sure that the Government had authority to call a special session and therefore it was impossible to announce that he would do so.

Personally he was in favor of collective bargaining and opposed to sympathetic strikes — especially on public utilities.

Conciliation Committee Working

The Premier reminded the delegation that a Conciliation Committee of the Running Trades was in session. He hoped that committee would work out a solution. If collective bargaining could be established by mutual agreement that would be better than legislation. Further, the Premier said, he did not think it would be satisfactory to declare sympathetic strikes unlawful, because men would strike against injustice.

However, he was prepared to submit to the decision of the majority, expressed by constitutional means. His colleagues were prepared to do everything possible along the lines suggested.

Soldiers Deeply Disappointed

Comrade Bray commented very forcibly on the Premier's remarks. He declared that the soldiers were deeply disappointed at the attitude of the Government. The delegation felt that it represented all returned soldiers and that they had the backing of a majority of the people of Manitoba. He had seen in The Telegram (hisses) a report that Premier Norris had promised the City Council that his Government would give the matter of passing legislation, making collective bargaining compulsory, serious consideration. Premier Borden and Senator Robertson had said this was within provincial jurisdiction. If they were wrong to whom could the soldiers appeal?

Helped Elect Norris

Comrade Bray pointed out that thousands of men who had since been overseas voted for the Norris Government in 1914 and 1915. It was they and their class that elected the Government and not the 1000 boodlers at the Industrial Bureau.

Cheers for Dixon

There was only one man in the Legislature, declared Comrade Bray, who had grit enough to come out on the side of the workers at this time and, in spite of the admonitions of the Premier, this man was still being reviled by the daily press. That man had been on the side of labor all the time. His name was Dixon. (Loud and prolonged cheers.)

Government Must Choose

You speak of the hardships to women and children, continued the speaker. What about the profiteers? What about Flavelle? — (Boo's) — What about the 1000 that raised the rent? Did they think of the women and children when they profiteered while we were "over there"? It was for the Government to choose whether it would tacitly side with that shameless bunch of profiteers or, at this late date, come over to the side of the workers. If the Government could not supply the need of the hour it should resign. The strikers certainly had a majority of the people on their side.

Running Trades Called Tories

As for the Running Trades effecting a settlement. They were the old Tories of the labor movement, but the Strike Committee, in accepting their offer of mediation, had shown its willingness to try all avenues that might lead to a settlement.

The Strike Committee had tried, and would try, every means to achieve an honorable settlement, but they would never compromise on a principle. This sympathetic strike would never be called off till effective recognition had been given the principle of collective bargaining. (Loud cheers.)

Stop War on Telephone Girls

Comrade Bray said the soldiers had been informed that Superintendent Williams had notified six telephone girls that the Citizens' Committee would not allow the Government to reinstate them. What usurped authority did that Soviet bunch at the bureau enjoy?

He also stated that he had reliable information that there was a plot on foot to place bombs upon the persons of some of the strike leaders and then arrest them.

He was credibly informed that a squadron of the Fort Garry Horse was kept at attention last Saturday from the time the returned men gathered to parade until they dispersed.

He wanted to know if it was true that the military authorities had placed machine guns in strategic positions in the Parliament Buildings?

Premier Norris said he had no knowledge of any such action.

Comrade Bray, in concluding, challenged the Government to take a referendum vote on the principle of collective bargaining.

Fifty-Fifty

Comrade Bathie protested that he had been misunderstood. He was for the returned men all the time and any man who would not back the workers was no man. When he said fifty-fifty — he meant a square deal for every speaker. He contended that an element other than returned men had tried to get into the parade on Saturday. (Shouts of, "No! No!").

"How about Mrs. Armstrong?" "She is with Labor."

He has suggested going to the Industrial Bureau and letting only returned soldiers in.

A voice — "It was too late."

Comrade Bathie — "Is this a returned soldiers' meeting or a labor meeting?"

Chorus — "Fifty-Fifty."

Who Would Be Hurt

Comrade Farnell pointed out that Mrs. Armstrong had not spoken on Saturday. The committee in charge had restricted the speaking to returned men.

Comrade Bathie's suggestion about the Industrial Bureau had been made too late to be acted upon. He thought the Premier would like to pass the Legislation asked for, but that in some way the Committee of 1000 had tied his hands. But he hoped the Premier would have backbone enough to call a special session and legalize collective bargaining. Such action would benefit the great majority and hurt nobody except the Committee of 1000.

Oration on the Flag

Comrade Munro had been taught that red in the flag represented bravery; white, purity; and blue, justice. He asked the Premier to be brave and act for the welfare of the majority on behalf of purity and justice. Act, said he, according to the colors of the flag.

Return in the Morning

Comrade Bray thanked the Premier for the interview and announced that the delegation would return in the morning to ascertain if, after further consideration, the Premier would either call a special session or resign.

March to St. Boniface and Industrial Bureau

Appealing for a continuance of the perfect order which had prevailed, Comrade Bray announced that on leaving the Parliament the soldiers would parade to St. Boniface to insist that the City Council there withdraw its ultimatum to its employees, and from there parade to the Industrial Bureau.

On the way to St. Boniface the march was past the Industrial Bureau. There, the big sign, reading: "Headquarters of Citizens' Committee of 1000," caught their eye, and it was soon in their hands.

The Committee of 1000 were nowhere to be found, and, on the advice of the police, the crowd started for St. Boniface.

Their march was headed this time by the Union Jack and the "Committee" sign mounted on two tall poles. It was evident that the headquarters had suddenly been transferred from 1,000 men to some 10,000.

Mayor of St. Boniface

The boys say that they found the Mayor of St. Boniface white. He agreed to call off all scabs from civic employ and man the plants wholly with volunteers. He had called a meeting of the Council and the policemen's ultimatum would be discussed thereat, and he would be prepared to give them an answer at 11 a.m. tomorrow.

City Hall Again

From St. Boniface the soldiers returned to the Winnipeg City Hall. But their quarry had again escaped. Mayor Gray and the Council had been run to earth on Saturday and they had no desire to meet the soldiers again.

The boys laughingly said: "We'll call again in the sweet by and by."

On to Victoria Park

Leaving the City Hall the flag once more swayed across Main Street. Some of Eaton's rigs were unloading at a warehouse, and the drivers had an uncomfortable fifteen minutes. Finally someone called out: "A guilty conscience needs no condemnation. Leave them to themselves," and then on surged the marching army.

Just behind the same warehouse a Cocoa-Cola wagon was unloading. The soldiers wanted to know whether it was loaded with machine guns or "pop" guns, and they made a speedy examination.

When it was found to be "pop" the crowd booed the drivers and gave them generally a hot time.

Then the move was made to Victoria Park.

They speedily filled this to overflowing. Various speakers dealt with the strike situation, and all were once again urged to maintain order under all conditions.

The crowd here was composed of soldiers and civilians, and both were on the platform as speakers.

Nothing but the best of good humor was manifest. They had made their jaunt. They were tired and hungry. But, for a few minutes before they went home to eat, they had to have a good time.

Determination, optimism, and solidarity are there as never before. It is only a matter of days when their tremendous power will compel a satisfactory solution.

Tomorrow morning at 10.30 the Market Square will again be the place for the gathering of the class.

DOINGS IN THE HOUSE OF COMMONS

On June 3rd, whilst the returned soldier strikers were having their third interview with Premier Norris and the Provincial Cabinet, Mr. Ernest Lapointe, M.P., was saying in the House of Commons at Ottawa:

"The hand of the Government should not be hampered, and that full liberty of action should be given it in order to effect a speedy settlement of the industrial troubles. Still he regarded the situation as largely the result of negligence, maladministration and blunders on the part of the Government. Troubles were spreading in places where formerly there was peace. Governmental action had been impotent and inadequate."

Which statements are in somewhat startling contrast to the words of Dr. M. R. Blake, representing North Winnipeg in the same House of Commons, who, speaking on June 2nd, is reported in the Manitoba Free Press as follows:

Ottawa, June 2. — Dr. M. R. Blake, of Winnipeg north, moved the adjournment of the Commons this afternoon to discuss the strikes in Winnipeg and other Canadian cities. He was seconded by W. F. Nickle, of Kingston.

Dr. Blake stated that the great majority of labor men in Winnipeg had not voted in favor of a strike. This was evidenced by the fact that only 8,600 cast the votes for a strike, although about 35,000 were now out. The heart of labor was all right, he said, but many of the labor leaders were wrong. He agreed with the Minister of

— Manitoba Archives
On their way from a meeting with Premier Norris at the legislative
building to St. Boniface city hall on June 3, a large group of pro-strike
veterans passed the offices of the Winnipeg Board of Trade, which
were serving as headquarters for the Citizens' Committee. The text
describes the incident shown in these two photographs in which the
Citizens' Committee sign was removed.

Labor that the situation in Winnipeg partook more of the nature of a revolution than a strike.

As a result of this report, a mass meeting of his constituents was held in St. John's Park, on the evening of June 4th, attended by over six thousand, to protest against this attitude of Dr. Blake, and stating that he had not represented the views of his constituents.

In further contrast to these statements of Dr. Blake was the speech of Major G. W. Andrews, D.S.O., M.P., speaking on June 2nd, in the House, in relation to the Winnipeg Strike as taken from the Hansard report:

MAJOR G. W. ANDREWS, D.S.O., M.P., DEFENDS WINNIPEG STRIKERS IN PARLIAMENT

Strikers Are As Loyal Citizens As Canada Ever Had — Collective Bargaining Necessary — Demands Backed by League of Nations — Sympathetic Strike Natural and Logical — Repudiates Bolshevism — Time For Change of Government.

Winnipeg Member's Testimony

Major G. W. Andrews, D.S.O., M.P., (Centre Winnipeg) in House of Commons, June 2, 1919. (Hansard report).

When the election was on, a year and a half ago, it was my privilege to address an audience of Winnipeg workingmen on the subject of winning the war. The issue at that time was quite clear cut. I told them I was a candidate for the Union Government and as such stood for the conscription of men. I pointed out that this meant the particular men I was talking to. I also told them that I stood for the conscription of money, which meant their money, and for the conscription of the last dollar and the last man in Canada, if need be, to win the war. That was pretty straight talking. When I got through one of the men got up and said: "Well, we understand exactly what you mean now." I told them I would not think of going over the top with men who were not prepared to go all the way. When the 17th December came they knew exactly what it meant for the men who were going to the war. When the election was over, in spite of the fact that my opponent was the secretary of the labor union, it was found that they had voted for me in the proportion of three to one.

These are the men who, today, are on strike. There is certainly something wrong somewhere. **In addition to those men, as good and as loyal citizens as Canada ever had, there are many of my own comrades who stood in the trenches in France; they are on strike. I say, standing in my place here, that eighty per cent of the returned men of Winnipeg are in sympathy with**

the strikers and the object of this strike.

On the first of May the men of the Metal Trades went on strike, partly because the masters refused an eight-hour day and a larger hour wage, but chiefly because of the employers' refusal to recognize their union. The building trade employees presented their schedule to the masters who frankly admitted its fairness and reasonableness, but declared their inability to meet the demand. Here we have the two vital causes of the strike **(1) a living wage, and (2) the right to organize. This is the cause of the strike in my opinion after the most careful consideration and after using every means in my power to find out the facts.** When the ironmasters let it become known that they were going to make it a trial of endurance, the Trades and Labor Council called for a sympathetic strike of all organized labor in the city. A vote was taken, and all unions, including public utilities, came out.

The single workman is helpless against the great corporation; the individual union or craft is equally so. Collective bargaining is the logical outcome of organization, and it is now too late in the day for any corporation to refuse it — that principle is embodied as one of the provisions of the charter of labor formed by the League of Nations.

The sympathetic strike is the natural and logical sequence of organization. What more natural than that men who have interests in common should stand together in an emergency? A particular union or craft in striking may be striking for a principle that is absolutely vital to every man in the industry and just as the employers can down one single man so they can down a single union unless all stand together. This is co-operation; it is brotherhood, and it is absolutely the same principle of sticking together that was employed in France.

There is another point I want to touch upon for a moment or two. **Twice this afternoon I have heard the term "Bolsheviks" applied to the strike leaders in Winnipeg. Gentlemen, if you apply the term to those men you apply it to me, because they are my friends**. There is a man called Jas. Winning, a good, level-headed Scotchman, who has spent practically all his life working for his fellowmen. The only erratic thing he has done in this agitation has been closing down the press and participating in the strike. As to the press, I had the misfortune to hear an Honourable Gentleman, one of the oldest members in the chamber, state his opinion that the press was corrupt, and he was not called a "Bolshevik" for saying that. **If ever a strike by workingmen in newspaper offices was justified it was in this case if the newspapers were not playing the game**. There is another man called Russell in Winnipeg. Russell is a Socialist and not a man who advocates force. I know these men, and for them force would be absolutely the last resource. Russell wants a change. So does Robinson, so does Simpson, and so does Rigg. They want a change because they are not satisfied with present conditions. **How many Honourable Gentlemen in this House are satisfied? I venture to say many of them would welcome a change of Government.**

Mr. Andrews: "I feel a little that way myself, but I would like to see some further action by the Union Government first."

Some Honourable Members: "Hear! Hear!"

PARADE AND COUNTER PARADE

Wednesday, June 5th, was perhaps one of the most interesting days of the whole strike. It was in the morning of this day the soldier strikers paraded with such effect through the wealthy residential districts of South Winnipeg, some four thousand strong. It was to the "boys" a reminder of some of the happier days of service, when "marching at ease" they would sing some of the old favorites or whistle to their heart's content. This was the day when the first counter parade was held at the instigation of the Citizens' Committee of 1000, and those they represented, a parade of any returned man, who has sunk to the level of a scab.

In the afternoon of this day, three crippled veterans limped into the Labor Temple, and told the Strike Committee of the plot by which they had been lead to lend themselves to such mean purposes, and this is their story:

"About 3.30 a.m. about 25 of the best cars in Winnipeg came out to Tuxedo Military Hospital and asked how many of the boys would like to join in the soldiers' labor parade, and, of course, lots of us went, but instead of being taken to Victoria Park, which we knew was used as the assembly place for the real parade, we were taken to near the corner of Broadway, in the rear of the Hudson's Bay Co., and though we thought there must be some mistake, it was not until we heard some of the speeches that we realized how we had been mislead, but it will never happen again."

Some of these same crippled veterans were placed in special positions at the City Hall to excite the sympathy of onlookers and help the cause for which this scab parade was called. It is a fact that almost all large plants in the city paid their scab employees for all time lost in attending these parades, and some went so far as to threaten their employees with dismissal, if they refused to attend. Notwithstanding these despicable tactics the forces of reaction could not muster a sufficiently strong parade to suit their purpose, and so the ranks were numerically improved by calling up the lawyers, insurance and real estate

— Manitoba Archives

June 4, 1919. Citizens' Committee volunteers, including university students, line up on Broadway near the old buildings of the University of Manitoba. This was probably a prelude to one of the "Loyalist" (anti-strike) soldiers' parades to the Manitoba legislature and Winnipeg city hall "to assist duly elected authority in re-establishment of law and order." As one of the organizers recalled later, "We formed an army . . . we formed infantry units . . . we had some men on horses . . . The parades of the other side quit. We scared the hell out of them."

— Manitoba Archives

The "Loyalist" veterans in a counter-parade, June 4. Middle-class officers were outraged that the Great War Veterans' Association had taken a pro-strike position. Attempting to play upon prejudice against foreign-born workers (the "alien enemy"), against the alleged unconstitutionality of the Strike Committee, and appealing to soldiers' grievances against war profiteers and inflation, these officers brought large numbers of veterans to support the city, provincial and federal governments during the strike.

War hysteria helped them identify "Bolshevists" as allies of "the Hun," and strikers as tools of a "Red" or "alien" plot to set up a Soviet in Winnipeg. Many of these men served as Citizens' Committee volunteers or as special police in the next few weeks.

clerks. If readers of this pamphlet could see the moving picture film of the two parades they would have no doubts as to which was composed of real veterans.

This counter parade attended upon the Premier and upon Mayor Gray and tendered resolutions, couched in honeyed phrases, of their devotion to "Law and Order" and Constituted Authority" and various members who were spokesmen for it boasted of the dire consequences that would follow if they were permitted to visit the Labor Temple. After listening to the lip service these men rendered the Governments, Civic, Provincial and Federal, Mayor Gray expressed his satisfaction by saying: "It is like a drink of new wine to hear such expressions of loyalty." But it is a singular fact that at the close of this much talked of "Loyalist" — law and order demonstration, the police were called upon to arrest a man for carrying a gun (the first arrest during the strike) and despite the fact that to comply with his request would be a grave violation of the Law, Mayor Gray ran bare-headed through the street after the policeman in charge of the prisoner and demanded his release.

THE G. W. V. A. MEETING
End of Neutrality

On this same date for the first time during the course of the strike no fewer than four gunmen were arrested, two of them strangers to the city, but as different people in authority vouched for them, including Mayor Gray, they were released and no charge was laid against them.

In the afternoon of this day James Duncan, of Seattle, addressed an enthusiastic audience of over 10,000 in Victoria Park; the following account of the G. W. V. A. meeting of Wednesday, June 4th, taken from the "Strike Bulletin," speaks for itself:

GREAT WAR VETERANS ENDORSE STRIKE

Neutrality Ended — Mass Meeting, 2,000 Strong, Overrides Chairman — Emphatic Resolution Passed — Monster Parade Visits Crescentwood — Spectator Arrested For Pulling Gun — Counter Demonstration Organized — Some Soldiers Deluded Into It — Soldier Strike Supporters Meet in Victoria Park at Ten This Morning.

Some two thousand members jammed the Great War Veterans Association meeting in Manitoba Hall, Tuesday evening. It was soon evident that the great majority of those present were strongly in favor of the strike and its objects. Some returned men who were working at Eaton's and had only joined the Association that afternoon were refused the privilege of the floor. An officer present said this treatment was an insult to those men. He was asked to apologize, but refused and left the meeting.

Resolution Instructing Executive to Support Strikers

"Whereas great changes have taken place in the strike situation in Winnipeg;

"And, whereas the time has come for the G. W. V. A. to declare its position as to which side is right in the present struggle;

"Therefore, be it resolved that this mass meeting of the G. W. V. A. go on record giving their entire support to the present strikers and that our Executive Board be instructed to give all necessary assistance to the workers now on strike in order to bring an early settlement."

Chairman Over-Ruled

Vice-Pres. J. O. Newton, who was in the chair, expostulated that this resolution was out of order, as the policy of the Association was one of neutrality.

The meeting, however, over-ruled his decision by more than a two-thirds majority and the resolution was sustained.

The following excerpts from the same source are worthy of reproduction at this time, as throwing considerable light upon actual happenings:

THE NAMELESS ONES

Where is the anonymous Citizens' (?) Committee? Who are they? Who is their chairman? Who elected them? Where are their headquarters? How many of them are there? Who gave them power over the City Council and the Parliaments? Who? Why? When? Where? What? It is all a mystery to the citizens as a whole.

They are rich men, of course. They can spend money on full page advertisements. They can publish the names of the labor delegates to the Calgary Convention. But their own names are never allowed to appear in public. Who are they? Why their timidity? Who is their chairman? Who? Who? Who?

Ah, said the owl: Who? Who? Who-oo? They work in the dark. They burrow underground. They hire others to plant their dark designs. They enroll a militia to fight their fight. They order the dailies to throw their mud bombs. The editors who take the pay for their advertisements are the same men who malign and vilify and mislead and misrepresent, but who gives them their orders? The labor leaders are known, but who are these who fear the light and work in the night?

We venture to say that they are as much ashamed of their identity being known as they are of their cause being known. They pay others to say that the principles of the strike are not those of collective

— Manitoba Archives

June 4. Premier Norris addressing members of the anti-strike Loyalist
Veterans' Association. At first he had feared they were pro-strike demonstrators, but soon learned differently. Norris declared that all sympathy
strikes must cease before his government would confirm the right of
collective bargaining, and thanked the rightist veterans' group for its
stand on "law and order." Later, one labour leader alleged that Norris
would have passed compulsory collective bargaining laws as late as
mid-June 1919 except for the hard-line stand of Meighen and Borden.

bargaining and a living wage. They hire lawyers to erect a straw man over the definition of collective bargaining. They purchase a press to prove that Bolshevism is the deep design of the workers. They concoct schemes about alien uprisings. They invent and design and lie "ad nauseum." But who are they?

Worry not as to who they are. Sufficient to know that there are the celebrities of the Manufacturers' Association, the Greater Winnipeg Board of Trade, the Canadian Manufacturers' Association, the Real Estate Men's Association, etc. They are the men who believe in a living wage and the right to organize for themselves, but deny it to others. They cannot in decency give their names. So we must not ask the impossible.

After the arrests had proved the presence of hired thugs and gunmen (the usual policy of capitalism all over the world) the appeal of the Strike Committee to all strikers and their sympathisers to preserve law and order and beware of agitators was reiterated and the following appeared on the front page of the "Strike Bulletin," on the morning of June 5th:

STRIKERS, HOLD YOUR HORSES!
This is the hour when you can win
STEADY, BOYS, STEADY
KEEP QUIET
DO NOTHING
KEEP OUT OF TROUBLE
DON'T CARRY WEAPONS
Leave this to your Enemies
Continue to prove that you are the friends of law and order

The following account of what was perhaps the best and most inspiring of the many parades of the returned men, also appeared in the same issue. This parade was acknowledged to be the finest and best disciplined parade ever seen in the City of Winnipeg:

TEN THOUSAND MARCH FOR JUSTICE

Returned Soldiers Demonstrate Strength
Ten Thousand March For Strikers — Perfect Order Maintained — Clash Narrowly Averted — Labor Temple Not Visited by the One Thousand — Counter Demonstration a Side Issue — Provokes Some Trouble — Tribune Lies Exposed — Meet Again Today at 10 a.m.

Incensed by the despicable tactics of the Committee of 1000 and the gross misrepresentation by the kept press in reporting Wednesday's parade, the returned boys turned out yesterday morning, ten thousand strong, to demonstrate that they were supporting the strike in dead earnest. No sane man can now doubt where they stand. Yesterday's parade made the workers of Winnipeg thrill with pride and confidence and struck terror into the hearts of the one thousand autocrats. It was an inspiring sight to see the boys stepping blithely along behind the old flag to the skirl of the pipes and the roll of the drum. They marched south on Main, Portage and Kennedy, swung back along Broadway to Main, north to Selkirk, and back to Victoria Park.

Something Nearly Happened

When the boys reached the Royal Alexandra on the return march word was passed through the ranks that the One Thousand had carried out their threat and marched to the Labor Temple. The parade immediately became electric. In a trice every man had his handkerchief tied round his right arm. Teeth were set and steps quickened. The report, however, proved to be a false alarm; as our boys swung from Main Street down James Street to the Labor Temple, the crowd deserted the counter demonstration, which was at the City Hall, and left them to their own devices.

This parade not only proved beyond a shadow of a doubt that the returned men are backing the strikers to the limit, but it was also a demonstration of the strength of labor. The soldiers kept the crowd clear of the parade, but on each side of them marched at least twenty thousand strikers and their sympathizers. Cheer after cheer from the bystanders proved that the real public is with the strikers.

Banners a Feature

Wednesday some of the soldier strikers got into the wrong parade by mistake. But this was remedied yesterday. A dozen banners proclaimed the objective of the soldiers. "Britons Never Shall Be Slaves." "Down With the Profiteers." "Deport ALL Undesirables." "We Stand For 35,000 Against 1,000" and "We Fought the Hun Over There. We Fight the Hun Everywhere," were some of the inscriptions.

On Guard

When the boys assembled in Victoria Park they were asked to stay there until it was seen if those who had threatened to raid the Labor Temple would attempt to carry out that threat. When it became evident that there was nothing doing they gradually dispersed to meet again in the morning.

THE EVENTFUL SIXTH OF JUNE, 1919

June 6th, 1919, is a day that will ever live in the annals not only

of Winnipeg and Canada, but of the whole British Empire, for it was
on this day that the infamous **"Forty-minute"** legislation was enacted
at Ottawa. While these Winnipeg dailies were carrying full page
advertisements, paid for by the Citizens' Committee of 1000, of which
the following, taken from the "Free Press," of June 3rd, is a sample:

THE UNDESIRABLE CITIZEN IN OUR MIDST

How much longer is the alien to run amuck, to insult our flag,
take it by force from Canadian-born citizens in our streets, continue
his threatening attitude to Law and Order, is the question thousands
are daily demanding our Citizens' Committee of One Thousand to
answer.

During the past four years when aged fathers and mothers, when
wives and sisters were bullied and insulted by this element, they
consoled each other by saying: "Just wait till the boys come home."

Must Deal With the Alien Now

There are some 27,000 registered alien enemies in Winnipeg district. The same "Reds" who are prominent leaders in this strike,
led them during the war to hamper and block in every conceivable
way, recruiting our reinforcements and supplies from going forward
to the front.

The demand pouring in on our Citizens' Committee from thousands
of loyal citizens that the alien question has reached the limit of
endurance and must be dealt with now is receiving your Committee's
grave consideration.

CITIZENS' COMMITTEE OF ONE THOUSAND.

And whilst the kept press of the Dominion were bending all their
energies in the same direction, presumably at the instigation of the
same interests, the Senate at Ottawa defeated Senator Bradbury's amendment to the Immigration Act, expressly forbidding immigration from
enemy countries, an amendment which, he said, was "called for by
the blood of 55,000 Canadian dead," by a vote of 26 to 19, an achievement which should prove to the most sceptical the shallowness of capitalistic pretentions.

WHO SAID CONSPIRACY

The doings of this day afford conclusive proof of one of the most
dastardly "conspiracies," not on the part of the workers or any of
their organizations, but on the part of organized capital and the Government it controls. It was about this time that the Government of Canada
was seeking a loan of $100,000,000 from the financial magnates of
Wall Street, and it was rumored in Winnipeg, and it was the report
in Ottawa, that one or more representatives of these same interests

were insisting that drastic action be taken by the Government to put down the "Revolution" in Western Canada, before the loan would be made. The Immigration Act, which had already been amended during that session of the House, was further amended to enable the Government to deport **British Born** subjects. This was done and the bill read the third time in both houses and given the Governor-General's assent in **less than 40 minutes.**

GENERAL KETCHEN AND THE LOYALISTS

Whilst this was being done at Ottawa, the so-called "Loyalist Returned Soldier Association," (the outcome of "scab parade" referred to earlier in these pages), was holding a meeting in the Amphitheatre and listening to violent speeches of an inflammatory nature from various speakers. It was at this gathering that Mayor Gray stated that he could not countenance any violence, "but he would advise those present to march around the Labor Temple, seven times seven, as the Israelites of old did around Jericho, and perhaps the walls would fall down."

The principal speaker at this gathering and the guest of honor was Brig.-Gen. H. D. S. Ketchen, O.C., M.D. 10, and that he was in on the conspiracy to rob British-born men and women of their citizenship is proved by his words as reported in the following article taken from the "Free Press Evening Bulletin," of June 6th, 1919:

TO DEAL WITH UNDESIRABLES, SAYS KETCHEN

Military Head Cheered to Echo by Loyalist Veterans at Mass Meeting — Further Response to Mayor's Appeal for Constables.

Brig.-Gen. H. D. B. Ketchen told a mass meeting of the Returned Soldiers' Loyalist Association* in the Auditorium Rink this morning that all undesirables, alien and otherwise, would be fully dealt with. This assurance, coming from the officer commanding Military District 10, encouraged the veterans to a wild demonstration of enthusiasm. Following a second appeal by Mayor C. F. Gray, hundreds of the returned men remained after the meeting to be sworn in as special constables. The Mayor's proclamation, banning parades, was received by the loyal veterans in good spirit and without a single voice in opposition. With hand raised in salute, General Ketchen stood on the platform while the immense gathering of returned soldiers roared out three cheers and a "tiger." Mayor Gray also was greeted with deafening applause and cheering when he appeared.

*This was an organization created by a lawyer, Captain F. G. Thompson, to rival the Great War Veterans Association which remained steadfast in supporting the strike. Thompson failed, however, to enlist much support for this group.

Gen. Ketchen Speaks

Brig.-Gen. Ketchen first said to the men — "I want to congratulate you, the loyal veterans, on the stand you have taken, showing that you are absolutely behind law and order and for the constituted rights of this country. I know there is one point on which you would like assurance from me. Is the undesirable element, alien and otherwise, to be dealt with? I am not permitted by the Government or anybody to make this announcement to you. However, I want to tell you, as one of yourselves, that I can give you my assurance that at this present moment steps are being taken in that direction.

"Every one of those fellows, alien or otherwise, who have shown themselves to be undesirable, will be dealt with fully."

Here clamorous cheering forced the general to pause. He was unable to speak for about two minutes.

Continuing, he said — "I think that when the time comes for this information to be given to you officially, you will realize that I have told you only a part of it. Right now it is our duty to support civic authority, and I would ask you to do your best in backing up the Mayor in whatever he puts before you.

"If the time comes when the Mayor is unable to handle the situation he knows what he can do. And if that situation arises I know that every right thinking returned soldier in Winnipeg is going to support me."

Mayor Cheered Loudly

Mayor Gray, on rising to speak, was cheered with wild enthusiasm. He said — "Yesterday I had the privilege of addressing you. When I got back to the City Hall one of my own aldermen said to me, 'I was at that meeting, Gray, and you did nothing but incite riot.' "

"Name him! Name him!" the crowd shrieked.

"Alderman Robinson!" the Mayor shouted in reply.

"Shame! Shame!" the crowd returned, many continuing to jeer until the Mayor raised his hand to speak further.

"I am in a very difficult position," he continued. "When that trouble occurred in front of the City Hall yesterday people came to me and said, 'Read the Riot Act! Call out the military!' But not a bit of it. We do not need that action yet." (Prolonged applause.)

Acts Constitutionally

"I am going to appeal to you, as I did yesterday, to stand behind me and help me all you can smashing this thing constitutionally. If I cannot handle the situation with two thousand men I want to feel that it is only an advance guard and that I can call on every one of you. When this thing is over the British flag will still be

— Manitoba Archives

June 4. Mayor Gray at City Hall addressing anti-strike veterans. The professionally made signs were supplied by sympathetic businessmen. Already "Loyalist" leaders, anti-union aldermen and a police commissioner member of the Citizens' Committee were planning to fire the regular police and replace them with special police drawn from the veterans. Some specials were sworn in on June 5; more volunteers were formed from the Loyalist group the next day for a "home defence force" against the alleged alien menace.

on the City Hall, and not the red flag!"

Someone called from the audience, "What about Duncan, of Seattle?"

"He is out of town," the Mayor replied. "We can trust to the general to deal with men of Duncan's type. He is not going to lie down until he finishes the job."

Capt. Charles Wheeler delivered another characteristic anti-Bolshevist speech and appealed to the men to remain behind after the adjournment of the meeting, to be sworn in as special constables.

C.V. Combe appealed for volunteers to ensure distribution of the Manitoba Veteran, the official organ of the G.W.V.A., the second issue of which is just off the press. He declared that posters would be placed around the city today saying, "Neutrality means Bolshevism, says the G.W.V.A."

Start Referendum

A good start was made Thursday by Secretary Laidlaw, of Winnipeg Great War Veterans, in sending out circulars for a referendum vote of the 10,000 members on the action of the Executive in repudiating the proceedings at Tuesday night's fiasco meeting and in lining up the Association unequivocally on the side of constituted authority as against the forces of Bolshevism. There is no doubt in the minds of the officials as to what the result of the vote will be. They are absolutely confident that the overwhelming majority of the returned soldiers will vindicate the Executive's action.

The strong stand taken by the Executive, it is of interest to note, was enthusiastically confirmed yesterday by the Returned Soldiers' Loyalist Association, which has been formed for the purpose of prominently displaying the attitude of the great mass of veterans in the city while the strike is on.

MAYOR GRAY BANS PARADES

It was on this day also that Mayor Gray issued his proclamation banning parades, a procedure which is unconstitutional. But the big parade planned for this day, headed by the Pipers' Band, with the Transcona Brass Band, and a Drum and Fife Band, were requested by the police not to continue the parade, as they had instructions to stop it, and it would likely cause disorder, and as this was the one thing desired by the reactionary interests it was decided to comply with the request, and the parade was marched back to Victoria Park, where cheers were called for the police, and drew a hearty response from all present.

A committee was then dispatched to interview the Mayor and ask his reasons for banning the parades, and his answer was that it was on instructions from the Attorney-General for the Dominion, Mr. Arthur Meighen. He was then invited to speak to the returned men in the park the following day, which he consented to do.

ARRIVAL OF DOMINION DELEGATES

By this time the strike had spread to towns and cities, East and West, and in view of the general situation it was deemed advisable to have delegates from all outside points to sit on the Strike Committee in order to better keep in touch with the workers who were so practically demonstrating their sympathy with the workers in Winnipeg in their fight for the recognition of collective bargaining and the right to a living wage.

The following two messages received by the Strike Committee and reprinted from the "Strike Bulletin," of June 7th, will give the reader some idea of the widespread interest that was being taken in the Winnipeg situation:

VANCOUVER GOING STRONG

A wire from Vancouver stated that the whole waterfront was tied up, the strike was progressing, and a complete tie-up was expected within 48 hours.

Minneapolis Offers Aid

The Minneapolis Trades and Labor Assembly voted unanimously Wednesday evening to send fraternal greetings to the men and women of Canada who are so courageously winning a victory, not only for themselves, but for the workers all over the world. Your solidarity will be an inspiration to American organized labor in these days of turmoil. Be assured that we are with you to the end. In whatever way we can assist you command us.

Yours fraternally,
**Minneapolis Trades and
Labor Assembly,**
L. SINTON, Secretary.

MAYOR GRAY BEFORE SOLDIERS' PARLIAMENT

On Saturday, June 7th, Mayor Gray addressed the Soldiers' Parliament in Victoria Park and made many significant statements and admissions. He stated that General Ketchen had been pressed continually by a certain section of the community to call out the military, but he had refused each time. In answer to requests for permission to parade, he said:

"No, gentlemen, you are for law and order. I know it. I wish all the people could see you, it would remove a lot of misunderstanding. This is the most orderly meeting I have addressed for

some time. I honor and respect you."

One comrade present asked: "What did you do for the babies when the Crescent Creamery put on milkless days?" And the Mayor answered, while scratching his head: "How would you like to be me."

STRIKE COMMITTEE

At this time the chief business of the General Strike Committee was the receiving and dispatching of wires and communications from outside points, though there were almost daily conferences between the Central Committee and different bodies in the city anxious to effect a satisfactory settlement.

Added to these duties was the provision of speakers for the daily meetings in Victoria Park, St. John's Park, St. James' Park, Norwood Ball Park and the many other places where the strikers gathered to hear the progress that was being made.

WOODSWORTH ARRIVES

On Sunday, June 8th, there arrived in Winnipeg Mr. J. S. Woodsworth, formerly Methodist Minister, later in charge of Social Research work for the three Prairie Governments, and still later, a longshoreman on the water front in Vancouver, and the crowds that assembled to hear him at the Labor Church service in Victoria Park in the evening, was a testimony to the high esteem in which he is held in the city, that was the scene of his activities in his ministerial capacity.

It was at this gathering the workers of Winnipeg were introduced to a man of sterling worth, and of whom they cherish the most pleasant thoughts in the person of the Rev. Canon Scott (Lieutenant-Colonel) who has been referred to as the "Idol of the first contingent." Canon Scott came all the way from Quebec, when he heard that some of his old boys of the 27th Battalion were engaged in another "war," and of his excellent services we shall speak later.

The following is from the "Strike Bulletin," of June 9th, 1919:

WOODSWORTH ADDRESSES 10,000 AT LABOR CHURCH

Dixon, Robinson, Rev. Canon Scott, and J.S. Woodsworth Speakers — Offering $1,540.00 Given to Strikers — Marvellous Spirit of Solidarity — Voluminous Decision to Continue Strike — Greatest Meeting in History of City.

What was easily the greatest meeting ever held in this city was held in Victoria Park on Sunday night. For three hours some 10,000 people at the Labor Church listened with rapt attention to a masterpiece address on the economic situation, from J.S. Woodsworth. The offering amounted to some $1,540.00 and was given to the strike fund to feed the striking girls and needy families. It was a truly marvellous gathering from start to finish. F.J. Dixon was the first speaker. He caught the crowd from the first moment. Ald. E. Robinson was also quite equal to the occasion. He outlined the situation to date and exhorted the strikers to stand fast. We will give a further report in next issue.

CITIZENS' COMMITTEE AND FINANCE

Monday, June 9th, was another red letter day in the history of Winnipeg. Great excitement was caused in the strikers' ranks when a comrade produced copies of letters that had been sent out to business men appealing for financial support, and a perusal of these letters will show the determination of the vested interests to break the strike at any cost. The following is from the "Strike Bulletin," of June 10th, 1919:

$1,000,000.00 TO CRUSH STRIKERS

Plan of Finance of Committee of 1000 Exposed — One Million Dollars Subscribed to Defeat Strikers — Volunteers Will be Compensated for Time Lost — Frantic Appeal for More Funds.
To prove to the workers that this is a fight to the death, we publish the financial side of the efforts of the Committee of 1000 to defeat us. We have our dollars and justice, they have their hundreds of thousands and injustice. The strike is costing them millions, we must stay with the game, and, if necessary, a plan must be devised to compel the 1000 to feed the strikers. A hungry multitude is a menace to our civilization. We shall not starve in spite of their millions. We shall fight on and win.

Here are the facts as taken from various communications sent out by the 1000 Committee:

Copy of Letters

"Dear Sir, — This will serve to acknowledge receipt of yours of even date, enclosing signatures to the compensation fund, totalling $249,000. On behalf of our Committee I beg to express their sincere thanks to yourself and those responsible for securing these pledges.

"Answering several enquiries you have received I am authorized to say that the Compensation Board of Citizens' Committee of 1000 will administer the fund in the following manner:

"No. 1. Whatever claims may be received will be fully investigated and, if found deserving, suitable compensation will be awarded and amount paid by Union Bank of Canada.

"2. The fund at this date is approximately $800,000 and in all possibility will be increased to $1,000,000.

"3. The object of this fund is to provide compensation for injury or loss to volunteer workers serving at the request of the Citizens' Committee during the present strike and on its termination the Board will assess to each signatory his or their share of the total disbursement made by the Compensation Board in the proportion of amount subscribed by him or them to the total amount pledged.

"We hope this will satisfactorily answer points mentioned in your letter and that you will be good enough to so advise under authority of this Board those making such enquiries. Yours very truly,

"W.H. McWILLIAM, Chairman."

One Million Dollars Not Enough

"Dear Sirs, — The Finance Committee of the Citizens' Executive of 1000 find it necessary to raise some further moneys to carry on in order to defray unavoidable expense at the present time. All commercial interests in the city are being canvassed to renew or increase their recent contribution. We have been asked to appeal to ———— for further contribution of $25 or $50. Can we ask you, please, to do the needful and send it down on behalf of the Citizens' Committee of 1000.

"H. BAIRD, and C. LILL."

These letters will give to the strikers the strength of the situation against them. Those who think the strikers are on strike just for fun will begin to grasp the significance of the strike from this million dollars to defeat us.

Where did their million come from? They robbed it from the workers. Now they use it to defeat them in the strike. We demand that the system that permits this shall be changed in the future. We demand today that we get a living wage through the right to collective bargaining.

After Gen. Ketchen and Canon Scott had spoken, resolutions were passed (and afterwards forwarded to the respective Governments concerned) calling upon the Federal, Provincial and Civic Governments to withdraw the "Ultimatum" submitted to their respective employees.

CITY COUNCIL, POLICE COMMISSION, AND POLICE LOCK OUT

Despite this resolution of protest, and pleading of strong delegations before the City Council, and later before the Police Commission, these bodies yielded to the pressure that was applied by the big interests as represented by the Citizens' Committee of 1000. Orders were issued to the Chief of Police, instructing him to call upon all members of the force to sign the agreement, which has well been designated a "Slave Pact." Each constable as he came off his beat was taken into the office of the chief and asked to sign, but despite his pleading, and his strong urging of every selfish reason why some of his old comrades should turn traitor to their fellows, every constable justified the high esteem in which the force was held, and refused to sign.

By 10 p.m. the entire force was locked out, and the City of Winnipeg was left without police protection.

In the afternoon a strong deputation from the returned soldiers waited upon the Police Commission to make a last plea that the Commission listen to the dictates of reason and common sense and not persist in the suicidal policy of dismissing the regular police force. At exactly 4 o'clock the chairman of the Police Commission informed **that** deputation that the matter was **then** under consideration by the Board and **no decision** had been arrived at.

In view of this statement of Ald. Sparling, chairman of the Police Commission, the deputation were amazed to find as they left the offices of the Board at 4.15 p.m., that newspapers were already on sale by the newsboys, stating in glaring headlines that the police were to be dismissed if they refused to sign the new agreement, and giving the decision of the Police Commission to that effect.

GENERAL KETCHEN AND CANON SCOTT

At the Labor Church meeting in Victoria Park the night before the appearance of Lieut.-Col. (Rev. Canon) Scott had excited much enthusiasm and as Brig.-Gen. Ketchen was invited to address the Soldiers' Parliament on Monday morning, an invitation was also extended to Canon Scott.

Gen. Ketchen arrived in the Park amidst the cheers of some thousands of returned men, hundreds of whom had served with him in France and Flanders. He is not a brilliant speaker, and was somewhat hesitant in giving replies to some of the questions put to him at the meeting, whether on account of his ignorance of the subject matter, or as a matter of diplomacy, it is hard to say, but there was no hesitation, but absolute sincerity in voice and manner when he said:

"I wish to compliment you, boys, on the orderliness and perfect discipline of your parades." After General Ketchen had spoken there were loud calls for Canon Scott.

In his opening remarks he told how he had served as chaplain with the First Canadian Contingent; how he heard in Quebec of the "war" that was raging in Winnipeg and felt that he should be with his "boys" in the new warfare; how despite the protestations of his family he had come all the way West to be with them and to use whatever influence he had to help effect a settlement.

The following clipping from the "Strike Bulletin" will show how he felt after he had been in the city a few hours, and had got a little insight and first-hand information:

CANON SCOTT SPEAKS

Pressed by the returned men to mount the rostrum, Canon Scott gave another of his characteristic good-humored speeches. He had been invited Sunday night to All Saints' Church, but had come to All Sinners. Perhaps some capitalist would hit him with a gold brick for doing that. He thought there was misunderstanding on both sides. It seemed to him that the initial mistake had been made when some men had been refused the right to form an organization that was quite legal.

Collective bargaining should not be objected to. Opposition to it was unconstitutional. Winnipeg was tame compared with what he had expected. The workers must be given an intelligent interest in industry and a share in the profits. They must stick until the workers got their just rights and those on strike were reinstated. The cheering was renewed as Canon Scott concluded, and many pressed forward to shake him by the hand. One veteran remarked: "The last time I saw Canon Scott was at Hill 70."

It would be interesting to know two things in this connection, but the facts are to this day withheld from the public knowledge. The first is: "Why did Ald. Sparling and other members of the Commission tell the deputation that **'No decision had been arrived at,'** if such a statement was not correct?" And the second: **"What was the conspiracy, and who were the conspirators** that were so sure of the operation of the machine that they dared to give the results of the deliberation of the Board to the newspapers before a decision had been arrived at?"

The feeling throughout the city was one of great indignation at this policy of the Police Commission, and the Soldiers' Parliament, the following morning, passed the two following resolutions:

ACTION OF THE CITY COUNCIL—GENERAL SITUATION

Whereas, we learn with regret that the City Council has shown by their attitude all through this trouble that they are not attempting to voice the will of the majority of the Citizens, but have lent themselves to further the ends of the financial interests of this city, who are a comparatively small minority; and by their actions have proven themselves in opposition to the true spirit of Democracy which we, the returned soldiers, have fought for on the fields of Flanders;

Therefore be it resolved, that we, the returned soldiers, call upon the Mayor and his Council to immediately take the necessary steps to have a plebiscite of the citizens taken, in order to demonstrate that our contentions are the wishes of the vast majority of the citizens of Winnipeg.

R.E. BRAY, Chairman,
F.H. DUNN, Secretary.

ACTION RE POLICE

We, returned soldiers of the City of Winnipeg, in mass meeting assembled in the Victoria Park, strongly condemn the action of the City Council and Police Commission in dismissing the members of the police force of the city, for their refusal to sign away the liberty and right of every British citizen.

We heartily endorse the action of the police force in refusing to sign a new agreement, and demand full reinstatement of all men so dismissed; failing which members of the City Council favoring such action immediately resign and appeal to the electors.

R.E. BRAY, Chairman.
F.H. DUNN, Secretary.

But the "interest" that was desirous of seeing violence and disorder on the streets had succeeded in their nefarious plans, they had applied sufficient pressure to have common sense and good judgement overruled and the way was open for the hirelings óf capitalism to get in their deadly work.

The Policemen's Union, totalling 240 members, of which nearly half had seen active service, fighting for the very principles for which they were now dismissed, passed the following resolution:

POLICE REQUEST HONOR ROLL BE VEILED

At a meeting of the Police Union yesterday, the following resolution was passed unanimously:

"That a delegation of returned soldier members interview the Chief Constable, Donald McPherson, requesting that the Roll of Honor situated in the Police Station be veiled, and the photographs of the men who gave their lives in defense of the Empire be taken from the walls until the police force is honorably reinstated to their positions without prejudice."

THE SPECIAL POLICE

After the dismissal of the regular police force, on Monday night, June 9th, the streets were patrolled by "Special Police," hired at the rate of $6.00 a day. It had taken the "Regulars," a well organized, well disciplined force, many years of hard fighting to get a living wage, but the forces of reaction were willing to pay 2,000 green hands a larger salary without hesitation.

In this connection it may be well to recall the report of a deputation of returned men who waited upon Mayor Gray on June 2nd, when the "slave pact" was first under discussion with him.

At that interview Mayor Gray repeatedly asserted that he had "inside information" of a well organized plan to take control of the city and that he was in receipt of letters from every part of the city stating that the regular police were not doing their duty. He stated, if the deputation only knew what he knew they would be shocked; that the "Bolshevists" fully intended to bring about a revolution, etc., etc.

To this Comrade A.E. Moore said: "If you will give us the information, and we think we are entitled to it, 10,000 returned men will clean up any organization with such foolish notions." Needless to say, Mayor Gray could not give what he did not possess. He further stated to this delegation that he "was credibly informed that it was the intention of the police force to come out on strike if asked again by the Strike Committee, **and he had reason to believe it was the intention of the Strike Committee to ask them to do so.**"

When the members of the deputation told him there was absolutely no ground for his fears, that there was no such intention either on the part of the Strike Committee or of the police force, he said:

"Will you guarantee me 200 men to maintain law and order in such an eventuality?" and he was immediately pledged, on behalf of the returned soldier strikers, the support of 2,000, who would serve "without pay" for the duration of the strike, if the police force came out on strike.

But after the arbitrary action of the Police Commission in locking out the regular force, instead of availing himself of the services of these men, which could have saved the city something like $225,000, men were hired at the rate of $6.00 per day.

These "Specials" appeared on the street on the morning of June 10th, armed with a "New Emblem of Democracy," in the shape of wagon neck-yokes sawn in two and about the shape of a baseball bat. These men, some mounted, some afoot, patrolled the city in sections of six. Instead of the one "man in blue" who had hitherto succeeded in directing and controlling all the traffic at Winnipeg's busiest intersection, there appeared at about 11 a.m. Tuesday, two of these imitation policemen, which number officially or otherwise, was doubled later in the day.

It was a lovely summer day, the streets were crowded with sightseers, men, women and children. In the absence of street cars, automobiles of every make and description thronged the streets, and the "green" pointsmen, whether from over excitement, or a new sense of dignity and importance, got somewhat muddled, and where one "blue coat" had been able to keep traffic moving, including a street car every two minutes, these two soon got hopelessly tangled, and at one o'clock there was every indication of incompetence and incapacity on the part

— Manitoba Archives
June 5 or 6. Winnipeg's city clerk, swearing in the special police who were to replace the regular Winnipeg police on June 9. Most of the specials were returned soldiers. Officers had been largely anti-strike from the start. Rank-and-file soldiers, more inclined to be neutral if not pro-strike, were persuaded by the red-scare propaganda.

— A. K. Gee, Public Archives
Portage and Main, June 10, about 2:30 p.m. An anti-strike alderman
later testified to the Robson royal commission on the strike that special
police were set out on the occasion shown in these photographs, to
"test" who had "control of the streets." The day before, Mayor Gray
had fired the city police force.

Two specials acting as traffic cops replaced the familiar "bobbies"
on this corner. They were heckled by pro-strike bystanders and men
from the nearby pool hall above the CV Cafe. After two hours, the
gathering crowd blocked all traffic. The cars shown here may well
belong to the Citizens' Committee headquarters just to the south of
the intersection — only the well-to-do drove cars, and they were used
to transport strikebreakers, RNWMP and army officers — or to Mayor
Gray, who rushed to the scene.

— Foote Collection, Manitoba Archives
June 10, about 3 p.m. One of the specials on point duty eventually
took refuge in Dingwall's store. Canon Scott, VC, the famous padre
of the Canadian Corps, pleaded with the crowd not to go after him.
Many were pro-strike veterans.

Meanwhile, Mayor Gray sent mounted specials to clear the intersection. Their leader later recalled how they charged thc crowd: "We
trotted into the mass, using batons where necessary in order to force
a way through ... The strikers, the mob seemed to back away on
to the sidewalks. A man called Coppins, a VC, who disobeyed my
orders by breaking rank and being hit over the head by a brickbat,
turned his horse into the mob and the side and, accompanied by another
trooper, was pulled off his horse and badly beaten up. We managed
to rescue him and get him back into line." Coppins denied this at
the later trials. The pro-strike *Citizen* screamed: "Aliens beat Victoria
Cross winner."

132

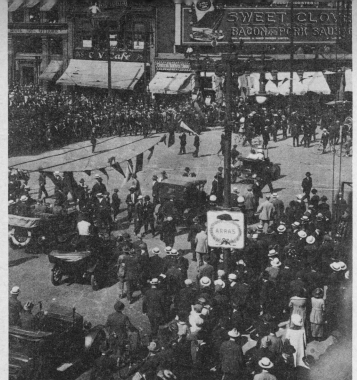

— A. K. Gee, Public Archives

The "riot" caused by the mounted specials around Dingwall's (out of frame to left) brought reinforcements of specials on foot, armed with clubs. Here they are seen entering the intersection from Main Street.

— A. K. Gee, Public Archives

June 10, between 4-5 p.m. Marching along Portage Avenue are some two hundred specials, armed with wagon yokes and baseball bats. Some of these clubs had been drilled out and filled with lead. They were advancing from city hall, clearing the streets. As the specials marched on crowds, "bats, fists, stones, bricks and broken bottles" began to fly. Mayor Gray had told the leader of the mounted specials that "he would shortly read the Riot Act, and that would enable the Royal Northwest Mounted Police to be brought in and firearms to be used if necessary." Thus he almost precipitated the bloodbath that would finally occur eleven days later.

of these two specials as pointsmen.

Their dilemma was the subject of many jocular remarks on the part of the passers by, but about 1.45 p.m. the situation got worse, the hundreds of people on the streets saw the amusing spectacle of these two pointsmen who should have acted in unison, so hopelessly out of harmony with each other that one was calling the traffic forward, whilst his partner behind was holding it back. Under these conditions it was only a few more minutes until the traffic was brought to a complete standstill.

The crowd started to ask embarrassing questions of the pointsmen, adding to their confusion: "Are you not afraid of being run over, standing in the middle of the street?" or "Are you lost?" "Does your mother know where you are?" The crowd was having a good holiday time. It increased in numbers until the front ranks were crowded off the sidewalk on to the road. Some of the "patrols" came along and clothed with their brief authority started swinging their new "Emblems of Democracy" amongst the crowd of sightseers, and when eventually a woman was struck on the arm, the real trouble started. A few returned men standing near resented the activity of the new guardian of the peace, and the last view of that particular "special" obtained by most of the crowd, was of a man, minus his hat, coat and half his shirt, seeking oblivion.

The mounted "specials" on their ponies (which it was commonly reported were the property of some of the large department stores of the city and lent for this particular purpose)* here appeared on the scene and assembling in squadron formation, proceeded to charge into the crowd. Their activities, and the ruthless manner in which they charged into the crowds of women and children aroused all the latent antagonism of both men and women, and soon the air was thick with flying missiles — bottles, bricks, and any other loose material being used.

These mounted men had little more control over themselves and their actions than they had over the horses they rode. Their methods are only comparable to those of the Cossacks at their worst. They deliberately charged into the crowds on the sidewalks, swinging their clubs. Mayor Gray, himself an onlooker, admitted that their actions were unnecessarily harsh and callous, and was so impressed with the brutality of one man in particular that he made notes of the man's description, but no steps, so far as can be ascertained, were taken to punish any of these men, and certainly none have ever been brought to trial for such violation of every law of decency and humanity.

The blame for the whole business lies entirely at the door of the

*This charge is repeated in Kenneth McNaught, *A Prophet in Politics* (Toronto, 1963), p. 117.

civic authorities, and the interests which dictated their action in dismissing the regular police and substituting such incompetents.

It was during this melee that a well known V.C. received his injuries. Notwithstanding the stories that appeared in the yellow press and which were spread broadcast through the world to the effect **"That a V.C. hero had been brutally attacked, dragged from his horse, and nearly kicked to death by aliens"** the same man has since sworn under oath, on three occasions, that he was never off his horse. So well did the papers play up this little episode, that it was believed that he was on the verge of death, while as a matter of fact, his injuries were only slight and it was at the hands of returned men and **not aliens** that he received his thrashing.

MAJOR LYLE, THE "SPECIALS" AND "THUGS"

The "Committee" of returned soldier strikers, realizing the possibility of serious rioting which might lead to bloodshed and the declaration of Martial Law, called upon the returned men in the crowd (which by this time numbered several thousands) to fall in at Victoria Park, the usual meeting place.

At that gathering a delegation was appointed to wait upon Mayor Gray with a request that the mounted men and the special constables be taken off the street in order that normal conditions would ensure.

To this request the only reply of the Mayor was an alternate thump on the palm of his hand and on his office table, accompanied by the expression: "By God, I am the Mayor of this city, and I will maintain law and order."

It was pointed out to him by the delegation that his position was not being disputed, but that it was the presence of the "mounties" and "specials" with their baseball bats that was directly inciting to disorder, but the delegation appealed to his common sense and reason all in vain for at least forty-five minutes, and then left his office with a reiteration by the Mayor as a farewell: "By God, I am Mayor of this city and will maintain law and order."

When the special police were hired, there appeared on the scene from somewhere (nobody seems to know where) one Major Lyle,* and this gentleman was waiting for the deputation in the Mayor's outer office and with pale face and evident great agitation said to the departing delegation: "Boys, I wish you would come up to my office, if you have time." The delegation readily consented, and after being seated, accepted cigarettes at the invitation of Major Lyle, as to use his own expression: "We can discuss things reasonably if we smoke." When all were settled and smoking, great was the astonishment of the delegation to hear Major Lyle say: "Boys, I want your advice." It was

*Appointed to command the "special police" on June 5, 1919.

quite a shock, after being maligned and vilified as the instigators of revolution, to be called upon for advice from the organizer of a force of special police.

The first piece of advice that was tendered by the delegation, was that the mounted men be taken off the streets, and to this Major Lyle answered that they were violating his instructions in leaving their patrols and produced a copy of typewritten instructions which he claimed had been handed to every man before going on duty that day.

That the first piece of advice of the delegation was acted upon there is good reason to believe, as Major Lyle apologized for leaving the room, as he wished to telephone, and ten minutes afterwards the mounted men were on their way to their quarters, and Major Lyle, re-entering the room, said to the waiting delegation: "Now, that's done, I am sorry to have kept you gentlemen waiting."

He then requested further advice from the delegation that would help him in his administration of the special force in such a manner as to minimize friction as much as possible. To this the delegation advised him to take away the clubs. To this he replied that he had issued instructions that the men should keep their batons concealed as much as possible. It was also pointed out that each constable should have a number, plainly visible for identification, in case some exceeded their authority. To this suggestion he readily agreed.

Then he was advised to send the men out singly or at most in two's and was promised the help and support of one or two thousand men, if necessary, in case of any infraction of the law. In answer to this suggestion he made a most astonishing and significant admission, as follows: "This force was recruited hurriedly, **and I know there are a number of thugs amongst them. I have not had time to select them yet. I had to send them out six at a time, as it was only one in six that I could rely on, and I sent them out in that manner in order that the one I did know could keep the others in order.**"

It was further suggested to him that the men be not allowed to carry fire arms as they were nervous and would be apt to shoot each other or the public, and he said he had definitely instructed every man to that effect.

But that his instructions were not carried out was demonstrated one or two days later when one of the special force shot his comrade on Main Street during an arrest.

CANON SCOTT AND THE "SPECIALS"

Whilst the disorder at the corner of Main Street and Portage Avenue was at its height and the Soldier Parliament were selecting their delegates to wait upon Mayor Gray, Canon Scott, in his Colonel's uniform was addressing the crowd, from the seat of an automobile at the corner of Portage Avenue, pleading with them to disperse in the interests of law and order, and this the crowd was more than willing to do, if the scab policemen were recalled with their obnoxious baseball bats.

But the activities of Canon Scott and his individual sympathy with the strikers had been noted and the proof of capitalist displeasure was soon to be visited upon him. During his short stay in the city, coming here with an open mind, he had made it his duty to seek and obtain first-hand information from both sides.

The Strike Committee placed at his disposal all the minutes and correspondence, besides spending several hours in conveying information, but on his application for information from the Citizens' Committee of 1000 he was peremptorily refused and told they had nothing to say.

The worthy Canon also functioned as chairman at a joint meeting of representatives of the Loyalist Soldiers' Association and the Strike Committee, and on that occasion had to remonstrate with the strikers' opponents for their ungentlemanly manner in handling their part in the debate. Shortly after this the word was issued to Canon Scott to report for duty and with many regrets he said good-bye to his many new friends and acquaintances, and after a sharp rebuke to the Military officials who accompanied him to the train for their reactionary attitude to organized labor and its demands, he said: **"I am getting old, but I am going to dedicate the rest of my life to fighting labor's battles."** And "I shall go back to the East and tell to all I can that after being on the spot, seeing and knowing all from the inside, my sympathies are all with the strikers."

In closing references to this episode we append copies of two short articles appearing in the "Strike Bulletin," of June 12th, 1919:

POLICE REPLACED BY INCOMPETENTS

In the fracas on Portage Avenue Tuesday afternoon, one of the strikers had his head split open with a murderous looking chain some 16 inches long, covered with leather to make it stiff, to the end of which is attached a short heavy clevice and bolt.

This chain is one of three that were seen last week in a meeting held under the auspices of the Committee of 1000. There was another loaded hose pipe also, and the four weapons were handled by what was nick-named "The Dirty Four."

These men were at that time volunteers in a fire hall near Broadway.

Today our streets are filled with such men who have replaced the police. They are not maintaining law and order, but are brutally attacking any person who voices any opinion favorable to the strikers.

Black Hand Gang

Two of these thugs are known to be hold-up men. They have robbed homes and held up small store-keepers within the past 48 hours. Their presence is a disgrace to our City Council. They are thugs placed on the streets for the express purpose of creating trouble. They are the last actors in the most damnable piece of viciousness ever perpetrated.

Our Little Grey Mare

"Man, proud man, dressed in a little brief authority, plays such fantastic tricks before high heaven as makes the angels weep."

To see the special police mounted on prancing ponies and to think that these are the men who are supposed to be keeping law and order is ridiculous. Many of them are but mere youths. The novelty of the thing catches their imagination. But they have no cause to defend. They are paid mercenaries facing men aflame with a passion for justice who next to ignore the existence of the puny paid private police.

Some of these special police stayed in the Gladstone school over the week-end; and so vile were their minds that the teacher on Monday morning had the disgusting task of erasing obscene drawings from the blackboards and destroying obscene books, etc. before the children could be admitted.

These are the men upon whom we are asked to expend $150,000.00 while our policemen, who nobly refused to become slaves after fighting for freedom, are dismissed from the force.

PERNICIOUS PRESS CAMPAIGN

A more pernicious press propaganda was never carried on than is being carried on at this time. The strikers for 24 days maintained such order that the police court record was lower than normal. The hospitals had no victims of violence to care for. Scarce a single doctor could find anyone who had been injured. But this was not satisfactory to the 1000. There had to be special police, and the regular force had to walk the plank. Then the trouble started.

The Tribune, on Tuesday evening, had a headline: "Mounted police charge huge crowds in streets." It was the first sign of disorder on any large scale. One would naturally expect the dailies to be averse to such disorders and the dismissal of the police force which was responsible for such. But no, no, no. Instead of this we find a full column editorial condemning the police who had refused to become abject slaves, and lauding "the Police Commission" which "acted wisely."

The statement is made that the city has been only "half-heartedly policed since the strikes began." Let us hope, then, that the Tribune is satisfied with the present state of affairs. It is asking for more disorder in almost every line. Its propaganda is pernicious.

When there was no disorder and no arrests the city was half-heartedly policed. When men's heads are broken and mounted police charge the crowd conditions are apparently satisfactory, what will it be when "we have normal police protection."

Coupled with the above is the renewal of the campaign against the leaders. Deport the leaders and all will be well. No need to remove the cause of the trouble. Just deport the agitators. Don't touch the profiteers.

ARRESTS AND RUMORS OF ARRESTS

After the incidents of Tuesday afternoon, the city was left practically without police protection, in many respects resembled the frontier town one reads of in "dime novels" and "penny dreadfuls." Whilst the melee was in progress, the most innocent and harmless individuals were arrested and several sentenced later to terms of imprisonment on the most flimsy evidence, none of which was absolutely reliable and all being given by the servants and tools of "big business."

But the general feeling of resentment on the part of the vast majority of the population at the methods used by the authorities, led the better element in the ranks of the specials themselves to refuse to be used longer for such miserable work, and more than one tore their armlets from their sleeves, and said they would not do such police duty for $60.00 per day.

On Wednesday morning it was reported that out of the boasted force of 2000 only something like 36 turned up for duty, and many of these, it is rumored, refused to go out on patrol. Many complaints were lodged with the Strike Committee of criminal acts on the part of the members of the special force; one to the effect that two men, returning from the lumber camps, B.C., staying at a city hotel, were approached by one man wearing the armlet of the special police, and armed with a six-shooter, who told them he had a warrant to search them and their room, and arrest them, but was willing to let them go on a payment of $10 each. After some argument they compromised by paying him $5 each to avoid a scene.

The following three clippings from the "Strike Bulletin," of June 11th and 12th, 1919, and also of June 13th, will give the reader some insight into the action of the authorities and their servants and show to what lengths capitalism will go to beat the workers into submission:

A HUNNISH ATROCITY

A returned soldier, Wm. H. Jacques, who has been gassed twice and is suffering from consumption, was thrown into jail last Monday without a charge being laid against him. His wife, who is in a delicate condition, becoming alarmed at his non-appearance communicated with some of his comrades who discovered him in jail on Wednesday. Although Comrade Jacques was in a very bad state of health owing to the treatment he had received, and notwithstanding the fact that no charge had been preferred against him, his comrades could not secure his release until $2,000 bail had been put up. This is a sample of the justice which is being meted out in Winnipeg in this year of our Lord 1919. It is part of the "Soldiers First" campaign.

PROSTITUTE JUSTICE

The record of our magistrates at this time is a travesty upon the very word justice. Gun men and thugs employed by, or friendly to, the Committee of 1000 and their servants the City Council, are released from the police station without so much as a charge being laid, while the wives of strikers are being held for a bail of $2,000.00. Strikers are held for $500.00; $1,000.00 or $2,000.00. It is just another dastardly attempt to "bleed 'em dry."

Surely wrong rules the land and waiting justice stands.

SPECIAL POLICE THUGS ARE HOLDING UP AND ROBBING PEOPLE

A Disgrace That Cries to Heaven

Residents of Barber Street report to us that city special police have called at their homes, and by threatening them with their clubs have extorted what cash they could get. In one or two cases $10.00 was secured. That is, they are daylight thugs paid $6.00 a day for their work.

These specials have been sworn in by the city irrespective of their character or nationality. The one qualification is opposition to the strikers. One man who was signing up these men said openly that he would take a bunch of Germans if they would help to smash the strikers. They were supplied with bludgeons and carry them in their hands at all times.

Imagine such men as these being paid $6.00 a day to maintain law and order. It is a disgrace to our city. It is time for it to end.

After Tuesday's disorder (the blame for which rests absolutely and entirely on the authorities) rumors were freely circulated that the many veiled threats of arrests and possibly deportation, under the Immigration

Act, of some of the leading spokesmen for the strikers were to be put into effect, and the men who were, according to these rumors slated for arrest were constantly appealed to not to go around alone, but to avail themselves of the protection of the many who volunteered their services as a bodyguard, whilst on the other hand, it was no uncommon thing to hear whispers from friend to friend on the part of those whose personal safety was the first consideration, to "keep off the platform or else be very careful of what you say." It was at this time that some of the officers and organizers of the A.F. of L. "packed up their tents like Arabs and silently stole away," only to be heard of later in distant fields, preaching docility and submission to the respectable, beneficent Government and employer recognized and blessed organization, the American Federation of Labor.

RUMOR PERSISTS

The following from the "Strike Bulletin," of June 12th, 1919, gives some indication of the extent to which the doings of our opponents were known to the Strike Committee.

It was this faculty of getting information from reliable sources, of the contemplated action of the authorities at the dictates of the Citizens' Committee of 1000, that was so exasperating to our opponents and so frequently brought their plans to naught:

UGLY ACTION CONTEMPLATED

Rumors of Martial Law and Wholesale Arrests of Leaders

If the information that reached the Strike Committee last night proves to be correct, then things will be doing shortly.

It is said that between 100 and 150 strike leaders are slated for early arrest. Provincial police are pouring into the city. Part are being put into uniform, and others are dogging the steps of the strike leaders. They are wholly at the disposal of the authorities. In addition to these, the military members of the Committee of 1000 and their friends are being mobilized. The special strike militia has been ordered to stand to. All soldiers in the city are confined to barracks. The mobilization headquarters and ordinance corps is Minto Street Barracks. Private automobiles are standing under requisition. Each man is ordered to pick up four passengers and carry them to the barracks. Martial Law is to be declared, and an armored car is ready for action.

The latter course is contemplated in view of the disorder that is likely to ensure when the leaders are arrested. Such, in a nutshell, is the word that reaches us as we go to press.

It is known that Mayor Gray is at his wits' end. He said on Wednesday to a deputation: "I'm in a ... of a fix. The Citizens' Committee has thrown me overboard. The strikers are against me. Even my old friend Knox McGee, has declared war on me because I refused to declare Martial Law." His only friends, he declared, were the returned soldiers in the camp of Labor, and he was not sure of them. He wanted to know if he could depend on their support at this stage. He was utterly dejected, and intimated that he had got to the point where he despaired altogether.

The solution is not in deportation or Martial Law. It is in getting the workers and the employers together. Up to date, the Committee of 1000 has made this impossible.

SOLDIER PARLIAMENT AND WOMEN STRIKERS

From the "Strike Bulletin," Friday, June 13th, 1919:

WOMEN ATTEND SOLDIERS' PARLIAMENT

Returned Men Jailed Without Charge — Woodsworth Speaks on Woman's Rights — Equal Pay for Equal Work — Dixon Exposes Tribune — Martin Denounces Telephone Buncombe — Rental Agents Threat Ridiculed — Committee Reports this Morning.

It was ladies' day at the Soldiers' Parliament in Victoria Park yesterday morning. At the invitation of the committee in charge a large number of women and girl strikers occupied seats of honor near the central platform. In the rear stood the returned men and a number of strikers.

Comrade Bray called attention to the fact that returned soldiers were being thrown into jail without a charge being made against them and then $2,000 bail demanded before they were released.

Law and Order

He read from a letter by Col. Wm. Morley the line of action to be taken by his men in case of serious disturbance. The audience cheered when Comrade Bray announced that the returned men would not be intimidated from doing what was just and right by any threats. He also related the facts of the shooting incident at the corner of Higgins and Main Streets, thus exposing the incorrectness of the press reports. The returned men, he said, were out to win this strike with clean hands. They would not be clubbed into submission. They would not go back to work as serfs or slaves. They would only go back as free men, when the strike was won. He intimated that there was a move afoot by the bosses to oust the elected head of the city and appealed to all returned men to be on hand this morning to protect their own interests.

Police Records of Special Police

Comrade Bray read the police records of some of the special police. One had been convicted of stealing an automobile and another of bootlegging.

Dixon Denies Tribune Report

F.J. Dixon requested all who heard him speak on Wednesday morning to hold up their hands. The great majority of the crowd complied. He then read an account of the meeting from the Tribune which reported that he had said "Coppins got what he was looking for when he signed up with the mounted police."

"Will those who heard me mention Coppins' name hold up their hands?" asked Dixon.

There was not a single hand. The speaker explained that he had never made that statement anywhere. "Go after them!" "Make them apologize," etc., shouted the crowd. Bro. Dixon explained that he was taking the matter up with the Tribune.

Women Will Fight Till the End

J.S. Woodsworth gave a historical review, showing how women had been drawn from the hearth into great modern industries by economic causes. The day of emancipation for women was yet to come. One of the provisions made at the peace conference was that men and women should receive equal pay for equal work. He pointed out that while the state had conscripted the boys whom the mothers had reared with infinite pains that the state had not made the financial outlay necessary to rear those boys. The day was coming when children would be considered the nation's greatest asset.

In the coming day women would take their place side by side with men, not as dependents or inferiors, but as equals. Thus there would be better relationships based on fundamental love and affinity. This strike was part of the great movement for the emancipation of women.

At the conclusion of the address many women and girls shouted: "We'll fight to the end."

Camouflage and Buncombe

Comrade Martin warned the strikers to beware of camouflage and buncombe. The civic and provincial authorities were working a scheme by which managers of departments telephoned up employees and told them that their chums had signed the slave pact and were back at work. This was only another cunning attempt at deception and it would fail to achieve its purpose. The rental agents, too, were threatening to eject workers from their homes if they were behind with the rent. "Well, they can't throw us all out," declared Comrade Martin, amid laughter and cheers.

The returned men will meet again in Victoria Park at ten o'clock this morning.

PRITCHARD ON THE JOB

The following brief account of Comrade W.A. Pritchard's* first appearance before a Winnipeg audience is from the "Strike Bulletin," of June 13th, 1919:

GOVERNMENT TREACHERY EXPOSED

Pritchard Unmasks Robertson — Emphasizes Political Aspect — Vancouver Backs Postal Employees — Must Be Reinstated — Borden Must Change His Mind — Workers Will Return Altogether — Cowley, Armstrong and Others Address Multitude.

The feature of Thursday's mass meeting in Victoria Park was an electrifying address by W.A. Pritchard of Vancouver, who was given more than the regular three cheers and a tiger when he concluded.

Appeals From Gideon Drunk to Gideon Sober

With telling emphasis Bro. Pritchard drove home the fact that the kind of collective bargaining demanded by the Metal Trades employees here, and repudiated by Senator Robertson, was exactly identical with the kind of collective bargaining contained in an agreement between the Metal Trades Council of Vancouver and the Shipyard employers. This, which was known as the Robertson agreement. The Government today was opposed to the workers of Winnipeg getting exactly the same kind of collective bargaining that the same Government had given to the Metal Trades employees of Vancouver one year ago.

Postal Situation Brought Vancouver Out

The action of the Government in discharging the postal employees, who had come out in support of organized labor because organized labor had supported their just demands last year, made the fight a political one. The extension of Government ownership, coupled with the fact that if this fight were lost, the loyal postal employees would be blacklisted from any job in the civil service, made organized labor in the West take the position that all the postal employees

*Head of the Longshoremen's Union in Vancouver, member of the Socialist Party of Canada, one of five people elected at Calgary to organize the OBU. He became one of the central figures in the subsequent trials.

must be re-instated without discrimination before negotiations could be opened.

Premier Borden had changed his mind many times to suit the exigencies of politics, he must be made to change it once more in the interests of the workers of Canada.

Daily Labor Paper Coming

Referring to the capitalistic papers as "detestable perverters of the truth," Bro. Pritchard emphasized the fact that the only way to overcome their pernicious influence was by the establishment of a daily labor paper.

Let Us Rise!

Complimenting the strikers on the splendid manner in which law and order had been preserved through four trying weeks, the speaker went on to say that this strike would be won by their intelligent self-sacrifice of the mass. The workers would not be saved by any great man but by themselves. "The great," quoted Pritchard, "appear great to us because we are on our knees. Let us rise!"

Labor Cannot Lose

Bro. Cowley drew hearty applause when he suggested that the strikers should wear a badge bearing the inscription: "Labor Cannot Lose." Such an emblem would show our strength. The street cars were not running because the men "did not deem it advisable to accede to the request of the management." A medal for meritorious conduct should be given to the returned soldiers who had so splendidly supported the strike. Bro. Geo. Armstrong is speaking as we go to press.

On a previous occasion, when dealing with the interview with Major Lyle, we referred in brief to a shooting incident that took place on Main Street during the attempted arrest of a striker. The following account, taken from the "Strike Bulletin," of June 13th, can be vouched for by a score of witnesses. In spite of this and in direct violation of the facts the police authorities, through the columns of the daily press, professed ignorance of the identity of the man who fired the shot, and went so far as to advertise the payment of a reward of $50.00 for information which would identify the criminal and lead to his conviction.

Surely the ruthlessness and viciousness of capitalism has a strangle hold on "Constituted Authority" when such methods must be adopted:

THAT SHOOTING INCIDENT
Facts From an Eye-Witness

Sharper than a serpent's tooth is base ingratitude. This was never more clearly exemplified than by the reports in the daily papers of the shooting incident which occurred at the intersection of Higgins and Main Streets onWednesday last.

About 4.30 a passerby noted a special constable displaying his baton and passed some remark. Whereupon the constable struck him across the forehead with his baton. This incensed the bystanders who started to jostle the constable. Two returned men, who are on strike, defended the constable. While they were doing this a car driven by Capt. Drewry arrived. Another special constable in the car fired a gun into the crowd, narrowly missed one of the returned men, who was assisting the constable, and hit the constable who immediately dropped to the ground.

The two returned men jumped upon the footboard of the car and insisted that it be driven to the police station. There they requested that the man who had done the shooting should show his authority for packing a gun. They were told that they (the specials) did not have to show their authority to everybody. As a matter of fact, the man who did the shooting wore no mark to indicate that he was a special constable. He carried his badge inside his coat. The constable on duty refused to take the names of the occupants of the car and an individual, apparently a member of the One Thousand attempted to lay a charge of mobbing the automobile against the two returned men who had accompanied it to the police station. This is a bare recital of the facts, which speak for themselves.

The number of the car from which the shooting was done is 7578. It is apparently owned by Capt. Drewry. He was in the auto with one other man, if men's eyes are to be believed, and, either he or his companion fired the shot. They were both taken to the police station, and were sent away again by the authorities without any charge being laid against either. To pretend that strikers did the shooting, or that it is not known who did it is erroneous.

In addition to all that has been written in preceding pages and all that follows, there are thousands of most interesting incidents that for lack of space must be either omitted altogether or only touched on very briefly in these pages. If time and space would permit, a two or three thousand page history of the Winnipeg Strike could be written and every page be full of matter of vital importance to the reader and to the working class all over the world. Perhaps at some future date it may be possible to issue a more imposing work than this, wherein the "Little things with the great potentialities" may be enumerated.

Space forbids to go into details of the organization of the Newsboys' Union — of their thousands of copies of the "yellow press" that littered the streets of the city; of "Society" ladies stepping from their luxurious limousines on to the sidewalk to sell or give away the "Sifton Press" or the "Winnipeg Telegram" or the "Winnipeg Tribune" — the organs, respectively, of the Liberals, the Tories and the Opportunists; of the inglorious exploits of the Millionaire Volunteer Fire Brigade, using their hands to break glass instead of using their hatchets; of members of the "parasitic" class, having to walk up eight and ten flights of stairs to their offices in the sweltering heat of 86 degrees in the shade; of intimidation and assault of women and little girls who were selling the "Strike Bulletin" or peacefully picketing the warehouses and stores.

Of the profiteering of the champions of "Law and Order" in raising the price of the necessities of life, of the efforts of individuals, organizations, and public bodies to effect a settlement — of the delegations that waited upon the Mayor and the chief of police, on behalf of the North-End residents of foreign birth, to protest against the incitement to violence and to massacre, through the paid advertisements of the Citizens' Committee of 1000 — of how that delegation, including in its personnel a leading lawyer and a prominent doctor, met both the Mayor and the chief of police who advised them to interview the Citizens' Committee — how this delegation protested that such an interview would be tantamount to acknowledging the Citizens' Committee as a "Constituted Authority" — how they were refused admittance to the Committee meeting by W.A.T. Sweatman, K.C. (afterwards one of the prosecuting counsel for the Crown) and told "that the alien residents had nothing to fear," the committee were not particularly concerned about the "alien" but they wished to divert the issue and that they were out to smash collective bargaining — of how one leading luminary on the Committee of 1000 blamed free education for all the discontent and unrest, and stated that on account of said free education "the workers know as much as we do ourselves" — of reports brought in and afterwards verified of the Federal Government paying charwomen at the Tuxedo Military Hospital the miserable pittance of 1.16 per day — of restaurant girls getting $15.00 per month, out of which they had to pay their laundry bills and maintain a certain standard of dress — of the conspiracy of certain restaurant keepers, headed by a notorious strike-breaker from the U.S.A., to close up their business in order to inconvenience and starve their employees into repudiating their union — of the driving out of the volunteers from one suburban fire hall in the city, by the enraged women of the district, whose men folk were on strike — of the cheerful endurance by wives and mothers, of privation and suffering in order that victory might be achieved in this fight for liberty — of how foreign-born citizens were picked up by police and charged with being strikers and union men and when no union card was found on their person being offered jobs at the rate of $1.00 per hour if they would only "scab" — of how young lads were approached by their bosses and asked if they were in favor of "Law and Order," and then being asked to sign a card, not knowing that they were signing on for the emergency Strike Militia — of how the mothers of some of these boys spent weary anxious hours when they did not return home for supper and found out afterwards that they were "confined to barracks."

These and thousands of other incidents and episodes of a like nature have to be touched upon briefly, but if dealt with in detail are of sufficient import, and reveal such a depth of infamy on the part of our boasted guardians of "Law and Order" and upholders of "Constituted Authority," as to fill any man or woman, in whose veins flows good red blood, with anger and resentment.

Of the secret meetings and "conspiracies" of leading lights in our city pulpits — of attempted bribery by bottles of whiskey — of these things we could write at length, but space and the editorial committee forbid — but don't despair, dear readers, perhaps in the quietness and seclusion of Manitoba Penitentiary we may write other and interesting accounts of what took place during May and June of 1919* — unless the workers of this Dominion rise to their glorious opportunities — and we have faith enough in them to believe they will do so — unless they make their protest heard to such effect that our "despotic" and "Prussianized" Government will step out of the way, and make room for men who can and will handle the present economic situation in a statesmanlike manner.

THE LABOR CHURCH AGAIN
8,000 IN ATTENDANCE AT LABOR CHURCH

Addresses by J.S. Woodsworth, W.A. Pritchard and Rev. A.E. Smith — $1,000 Offering for Strikers' Relief Fund — Splendid Band — Great Enthusiasm — Members of 1,000 Committee Seen.

The stifling heat did not prevent the teeming crowds from once more flocking to the Labor Church last night in Victoria Park (now renamed Liberty Park). The trees in their new covering of beautiful green formed a magnificent background for the improvised pulpit. The Committee of 1000 has prevented the Labor Church from procuring the Industrial Bureau for these services, consequently several women fainted from exhaustion due to the heat and the prolonged

*This interesting reference would suggest that all or some of this book was written by the strike leaders in 1919 while in Stony Mountain penitentiary, awaiting either bail or deportation hearings.

standing. One man also collapsed.

An excellent band opened the services with appropriate music, and the hymns were rendered with great enthusiasm.

Mr. J.S. Woodsworth, the first speaker, drew attention to the representative nature of the congregation. He had endorsed the principle of the One Big Union for the industrial fight, he endorsed the principle of the One Big Church as well. The real test was brotherhood. The one requisite was the forward look.

The pioneers of such new movements had always been persecuted, but the movements could not be stopped by persecution. The time had come for a forward march economically, and the old forms of religion were inapplicable today. The trouble with theologians was that they had insisted that they had found the ne plus ultra. The world today wanted forms that expressed the spirit of the hour.

Rev. A.E. Smith,* ex-President of the Manitoba Methodist Conference, was the second speaker. He stated that the time had come when it was next to impossible for a preacher to preach the genuine gospel of Christ in the churches. The Methodist Church at its last General Conference had declared for a radical reconstruction of society, and the substitution of the co-operative system for the competitive system. The result of this had been that rich men had threatened to leave the Church. "Let them go," he said. The Church that thought more of real estate than of principles had no place in the life of today.

He described the Bankers' Association as a One Big Union. The same was true of the Committee of 1000, yet these same men opposed any effort of the workers to organize a similar movement.

The sympathetic strike was just as religious a movement as a Church revival. It was just as ethical as the fight in Flanders. Those who opposed this strike did so because they were individualists; the workers supported it because they put society and the interests of others ahead of their own interests. The individualist has no programme, hence he attacks the man or the body that tries to work out a programme.

Lying back of all the unrest was the profit system and private ownership. The individualist was spending all his strength in defending a system that was passing rapidly. It has been tried and found wanting. The great common mass was aware of this, and so the heart of the workers of the world was one heart. When the worker

---

*Elected to the Manitoba legislature in 1920, he later moved to Ontario where he was elected president of the Ontario section of the Canadian Labour Party. He later became a member of the Communist Party of Canada, and was arrested in 1934 on a charge of sedition for a speech at Massey Hall in Toronto denouncing Section 98 of the Criminal Code. He was defended by Hon. E. J. McMurray, who had been defence counsel for some of the Winnipeg strikers, and was acquitted.

stopped working it was like the heart of a man stopping its beating. It meant death. The solution of the unrest of this hour is the greatest task we have to face. It is a religious problem. The only way to find a solution is to put service in the place of profits.

He made it clear that there is a large body of thought in Winnipeg that is not finding voice in the Committee of 1000, though they call themselves the Citizens' Committee. These men, and those on the City Council do not accurately express the mind of a very large section of the community. These people do not approve of the continued attempts of these men to get the city under Martial Law. They are sick to death of the fooling being put over in the name of patriotism. A way must be found for this vast body of people to express its convictions.

Pritchard of Vancouver

Pritchard, of Vancouver, was given a rousing welcome, and as he spoke it soon became evident that the vast crowd had not misjudged its man. He is an orator and a thinker of the first water.

He referred in scathing tones to the vicious attack of the Winnipeg press upon his character. They were described as cesspits from which nothing clear could be expected.

He gave a brief review of history, pointing out how he was taught the Magna Carta meant liberty and justice at a time when his father, a British miner was on strike, and he was punished because he could not pay the school fees.

Every great change in history had come because classes of men were rising to a consciousness of their power. Luther was a product of the change from feudalism into capitalism, while he stood for a measure of religious liberty, he was no democrat, for he urged the cruel suppression of the peasants.

Existence is the only thing common to all things. Understanding is the cement that binds together. Hence the great need for this hour is understanding. When men understand, no thunderings or threatenings can shake their faith.

The world moves forward, but there is a section of humanity that insists on standing still. They live in the dead past. Such a body is the Committee of 1000.

The truly educated person is he or she who can correctly understand the nature of economic crises as they approach and act accordingly. This the 1000 had failed to do.

The speaker paid a tribute to the workers as the natural supporters of peace and law and order. He drew attention to the fact that the editors of the three daily papers and the Committee of 1000 have used every power they possessed to create disorder and introduce

Martial Law and bloodshed, but the intuitive sense and good judgment of the workers had foiled every attempt. The workers produce everything that is useful; the only thing the other side ever do produce is trouble. That is the game.

This was no accident, he averred. He had, in England, met on the job, Italians, Slavs, Frenchmen, Englishmen, Scotchmen and other savages. They had discussed economics and philosophy, and in the university of experience had got down to the root of the matter. Because of this, the workers were able to act intelligently in a crisis while their masters became panic-striken.

The workers did not ask that anything they said be taken for granted. Take the word of nobody, he said, but test out every proposition, and see for yourselves.

Describing the condition of Scotland, Lord Roseberry had said there were two kinds of Scotchmen: "Scots who hae, and Scots who hae not." In Britain there were those who produced all and possessed nothing, and those who produced nothing and possessed all. In Canada there were those who live and do not work, and those who work but do not live. This condition must be changed. This was the fundamental cause of the unrest.

Vancouver was now tied tight, and it would stick until every striker was reinstated, and until collective bargaining was fully guaranteed. When Ottawa acted to crush labor, then Vancouver struck to help labor. If you are whipped we are whipped. If you go down we will go down in the same boat. But if you are to be victorious we must help you. And we will. (Thunderous applause.)

The boys of the bulldog breed never had a job to do like the present job. If they had not lost all their teeth hanging on to a job, this was the time to bite and hang on.

Ottawa had had a chance to put out a little fire at the first, but they had tried to put it out with coal oil and it had spread. Borden believed in collective bargaining in Versailles, but not in Winnipeg.

People talked of democracy, the strike was not democracy, but he maintained that when four old men got together behind closed doors and secretly settled the destinies of all mankind that was the very antithesis of democracy. Labor wanted none of it. The workers stood for open discussion and decision by ballot. That was how this strike was called.

The following account of the meeting of the Soldiers' Parliament on Saturday, of June 14th, 1919, taken from the "Strike Bulletin," of June 15th, is inserted because of its valuable information, which is well worthy of more than passing notice:

THE SOLDIERS' PARLIAMENT

Labor Party Mooted — Raids in North Winnipeg — Sensations Promised — Precautions Taken — Bathie Answered — Bribe Refused — Telephone Operators get $110.00 — Another Meet this Morning.

"Business as usual" was the slogan at the Soldiers' Parliament in Victoria Park on Saturday morning.

Comrade Bray reported for the committee and promised something extra interesting for Monday morning.

The press has shouted through its headlines that something big was to have happened in the last 24 hours. Whatever had been contemplated had not eventuated. He pleaded with the returned men to keep off the streets and continue to preserve law and order.

North Winnipeg Raids

Information had leaked out that an order had emanated from Kennedy Street that several cars, manned by Provincial Police, were to raid the north end and arrest any one who might be shooting craps. If they could not catch anyone· violating the law, they were to "get them anyway."

Forty to One, and that One a Woman

Information was to hand that a body of forty, purporting to be special police, had broken into several houses in the North End about 3 o'clock on Saturday morning. They had a warrant for the arrest of one man. In one of the houses the sole occupant was a woman. Nevertheless the house was broken into and furniture smashed.

Something in the Wind

There was something in the wind. Imported spies were on the streets asking returned men if they were "strikers or citizens." Booze was being liberally supplied at the special police headquarters and the strike militia were confined to barracks. Provincial police. were also being concentrated in Winnipeg and members of the Soldiers' Committee were being shadowed.

Fifty-Fifty Answered

Attention was called to a letter signed by Comrade Bathie, which had appeared in the press. It was doubtful if he had written it. The statements it contained were a flat contradiction of the statements made by Comrade Bathie before the G.W.V.A. and on the floor of the Provincial Legislature.

The Unseen Hand

A certain slippery politician had offered money to soldiers to assist in the formation of a Political Organization, but this had been indignantly refused. The Committee was, however, considering the formation of a permanent organization in the nature of a Soldiers' Labor Party. It was not yet ready to report.

The High Cost of Living

A document was quoted showing that Premier Borden had $9,500.00 worth of stock in the Manitoba Cold Storage Company. Members of the Committee of 1000 also had stock in that and other cold storage companies and yet they prated about reducing the cost of living.

Spontaneous Offering

A Committee moved among the crowd and sold $50 worth of tickets for the ball game next Tuesday afternoon on Wesley Grounds, the proceeds to go to the aid of the striking telephone operators. At the conclusion of the meeting someone started a volunteer offering for the same purpose, which netted $60.

A fine spirit prevailed and after listening to a final plea for the preservation of law and order under all circumstances, the assembly dispersed to meet again this morning.

THE STRIKE COMMITTEE AND THE MEDIATORS

In the meantime, whilst the events we have chronicled were taking place outside, what of the work of the representatives of the thousands of strikers, who were sitting, two and three sessions daily on the General Strike Committee?

At this time the last body to offer themselves as "mediators," were the Grand Lodge officers of the Railroad Brotherhoods.

These men held daily sessions with the ironmasters, submitting propositions, receiving counter propositions which, in turn, were submitted first to the Central Committee and through them to the General Committee. There they were discussed at great length and such amendments suggested as the collective knowledge of that Committee thought desirable.

Many times the Brotherhood officers were on the verge of giving up in despair of ever being able to convince the upholders of industrial autocracy that new times demanded new conditions; but they were asked to continue their efforts and went to their task with greater energy and zeal, as they realized that a great tie-up of the great railroad systems was imminent unless a satisfactory agreement could be reached.

In the "Free Press," of June 15th, was a report to the effect that "the men who had gone out were mostly firemen and switchmen. Last night the C.P.R. issued an official notice that all passenger trains had been dispatched. There would be reduced freight service," and the following from the same paper and same date explains the situation of other railroads:

FREIGHT YARDS AFFECTED

The running trades walk-out is creating considerable difficulty in the railway freight yards. The C.N.R. Fort Rouge yards and the Paddington yards in St. Boniface are most seriously affected. The Union stock yards are still in operation, the shunting engine remaining at work to handle livestock.

In the Fort Rouge yards practically all enginemen, firemen and switchmen of the Canadian National Railways are out. C.P.R. engineers have stayed with their engines almost to a man, it is reported, but a number of firemen and switchmen joined in the strike movement. Office help and yardmasters are replacing them.

The train and yard men in the C.P.R. had taken the ballot and it was circulated on the lines West of Winnipeg, and the sentiment, so far as could be ascertained, was overwhelmingly in favor of striking in sympathy with Winnipeg, notwithstanding the fact that James Murdock, Vice-President B.R.T., gave a lengthy statement to the press denying the accuracy of the strikers' contention, and in the issue of the "Strike Bulletin," for June 17th, there appeared the following:

RUNNING TRADES REPUDIATE STATEMENT

A statement appeared in last evening's issue of the "Tribune" claiming that the strike vote recently taken of men in train and yard service on the C.P.R. was taken under misrepresentation. The statement was attributed to Jas. Murdock, International Vice-President of the Trainmen's Brotherhood. The undersigned Committee representing men in train and yard service wish to say that this is nothing but a glaring falsehood. They believe it was issued by Murdock for the apparent purpose of discrediting the men active in the movement; and, also, for the purpose of attempting to stampede some of the men back to work.

Every man who voted was acquainted with the fact that the ballot was to be used locally in a progressive strike.

This is only one of the many fruitless attempts made by Murdock to gain a following by the employment of illegitimate methods.

(Signed) RUNNING TRADES
PUBLICITY COMMITTEE.

Running Trades Mean Business

Members of the Running Trades assert that the whole of the West is alive to the strike situation, and will likely be out in large numbers within a few days. Brandon, Dauphin, Saskatoon, Vancouver, etc., are right on the job. Dauphin foremen walked out this morning.

On Monday, June 16th, there appeared in all the Winnipeg daily papers a lengthy letter from Metal Trades employers, signed on behalf of the Vulcan Iron Works, by E. G. Barrett; Manitoba Bridge and Iron Works, by H.B. Lyall, and Dominion Bridge Company, by N.W. Warren.*

This letter purported to outline to the citizens of Winnipeg their position and definition of the term "Collective Bargaining." This letter and definition of collective bargaining was followed by letters from, first, Senator Robertson (whose endorsation, in view of his record during the strike, caused the strikers to look for the proverbial joker); second, the members of the Railroad Brotherhoods who had been acting as mediators, signed by: Ash Kennedy, B.L.E.; George K. Wark, B.L.F. & E.; James Murdock, B.R.T.; H.G. Barker, O. of R.C.; D. McPherson, O. of R.T.; A. McAndrews, M. of W. Employees; and lastly, by the resident Winnipeg managers of the three railroad systems: D. C. Coleman, C.P.R.; A. E. Warren, C.N.R.; W. P. Hunter, G.T.P.R.

THE DUPLICITY OF THE HOLY TRINITY

This definition of collective bargaining on the part of the ironmasters was not satisfactory to organized labor as represented on the General Strike Committee.

In further proof, if it were needed, of the contentions of the strikers that neither the ironmasters nor the Citizens' Committee of 1000 (who had arrogated to themselves the right to make a settlement) were sincere in their profession of seeing a settlement made, and as an exposure of the deceit and duplicity and prevarication during the whole course of the strike, we append the following cutting from the Winnipeg "Tribune," of June 17th, 1919:

ASSERTS IRONMASTERS DID NOT ACCEPT COLLECTIVE BARGAINING UNTIL AFTER MEDIATORS HAD QUIT

Running Trades' Board Reviews Attempts to End Strike

Refusal of the Ironmasters to recognize the Metal Trades Council

*This letter appeared to indicate that the metal-trades employers were prepared to accept the principles of collective bargaining, and that the onus was on the strike leaders to settle. But it is interesting to note that the evening of the day on which this letter was printed, the police began to round up and arrest these leaders, before they had even had an opportunity to discuss the "offer"!

was the rock on which the mediation ship was wrecked, according to a statement issued today by the mediation board.

The statement reviews at great length the proceedings of the board.

It concludes with the assertion that the ironmasters' letter, published Monday, was their first acceptance of the principles of collective bargaining as practised by the railway organizations. The board declares that no such proposal was made by the ironmasters while the mediators were in session.

"We desire to point out," reads the statement, "that during the period of mediation no proposition was submitted by the employers which could be endorsed as being identical with the practises of the train service organization."

In the report they draw attention to the ironmasters' refusal to accept the various proposals made to them, each containing the definition of collective bargaining as in operation between the various railroads and their employees.

As further evidence of conspiracy and collusion and determination to break the strike by undermining the morale of the strikers, is the fact that two or three days after this, there appeared in the daily press a full and complete definition of the term, with all the necessary details, together with a signed statement signifying the willingness of the ironmasters to accept their definition therein contained as a basis for a settlement.

But they stated that a copy of this same document had been forwarded to the Strike Committee for acceptance, whereas in fact it was a few days after their insertion in the daily press, that copies were received from Senator Robertson, who had in his possession a reproduction of what appeared in the papers.

By such despicable tactics they hoped to stampede the strikers back to work, and bring discredit upon the strike leaders, for not accepting a definition of the term in accordance with their own specifications.

PRUSSIAN ESPIONAGE

Whilst the Strike Committee were giving close attention to these matters of such great moment to organized labor, what of the busy world outside?

The rumors that had been in circulation for over a week, later confirmed by reliable information, were gradually developing into facts. Strange, mysterious noises were heard under the window sills of men's homes as they conversed with their families — hurrying footsteps revealed the presence of eavesdroppers — speakers at strikers' meetings saw faces with singular persistence and regularity at the different meetings at which they spoke — strangers adopted all the familiarity of intimate acquaintances — strange shadows dogged the footsteps of the men afterwards arrested — with stealthy tread strange forms appeared from under verandahs and vanished in the darkness — veiled threats were made that "we will get you yet" — all reminiscent of what we have read of the Prussian spy and the Agents Provocateurs.

Some of these gentlemen had an unpleasant experience in St. John's Park where Comrade Bray was addressing a meeting. At the close of his speech some half dozen of these spies said: "We'll get you yet, Bray," and much to their chagrin and disappointment, some twenty women in the crowd immediately caught them by the arm and coat lapels, and invited them to "come and get him now," but they beat a hasty and very shame-faced retreat in the high-powered cars in which they had arrived.

THE COWARDLY ARRESTS

Monday, June 16th, 1919, like all the days that preceded it, had been a strenuous one for many. Strike business in the morning, including a general view of the situation, a hurried lunch, an hour in the Strike Committee, away to address the awaiting crowds, pass along the information available, back to the Strike Committee till 6 o'clock — a hurried supper, away to all points of the compass, within the city, and outside, to talk to other waiting crowds; back to the Strike Committee, until the "wee sma' hours"; a weary tramp homewards, except to such as owned a "bike" or could beg a ride in some auto. Such was the daily round.

The weary workers for a better day for the whole of mankind had hardly closed their eyes in sleep when a rap on the door, followed by another and still another, reverberated through the quiet of that lovely summer's morning, and a voice of command: "Open the door or we shall break it open." Something new in the experience of all to whom the summons came, but as the doors were opened, in marched a stalwart guardian of the law, and the first intimation of his errand was conveyed to the astonished householder, when the first intruder was followed by two, and in some cases three or four red-coated members of the R.N.W.M. Police, each packing his gun and loaded riding whip, bedecked in sombrero, top boots and spurs, whilst in the first light of early dawn could be seen a big high-powered car in charge of a chauffeur, who kept his engine running, and footsteps betokened the presence of other servants of constituted authority guarding any possible means of escape from the rear of the house; though why such precautions should be taken, when the intruders each packed a gun, and the poor victim was clothed only in pyjamas or nightshirts, it is hard to understand.

Simultaneously, at a few minutes to three, these high-powered cars, with their armed occupants started on their errand; simultaneously nine families were roused from their sleep by these minions of the Law

— and many and varied were their experiences.

Arriving at the home of George Armstrong, on Edmonton Street, they knocked and demanded admission, but no admission did they get until Mr. Armstrong had telephoned the police station and made sure from the Chief of Police that they were there on the King's (?) business.

Then the door was opened and armed with a blank search warrant, they proceeded to investigate every nook and corner of the house — gathering up books, papers and periodicals — the valued sources of knowledge — knowledge of the truth, which shall eventually set men free.

At the same hour, a similar knock resounded on the door of the home of Ivens, the terrible, whose unpardonable crime was that he had told the truth as editor of the "Western Labor News" — who loved mankind better than the worn-out creeds and rituals of a Church which existed only to cover the nakedness of the exploiters of his fellow-men. Here the same search for incriminating letters, papers, books or documents.

It is hardly necessary to give him the prefix and affixes to which he is entitled, as so many know him and of him, but in case some reader does not, he is the Rev. William Ivens, M.A., B.D., a Minister of the Methodist Church, and today the pastor of the largest Church in Winnipeg, with more adherents than any other church in the continent of America, the "Winnipeg Labor Church."

The press, of course, and all his enemies insist that his last affix signifies "Bad Devil," but many a good laugh was had at "Bill's" expense when he was trying to convince Serg. Reames (head of the spies' department of the R.N.W.M.P.) that the men who had arrested him and searched his house "were not gentlemen." Whilst Ivens was being arrested and searched, other parties were arresting R.B. Russell, out at Weston. If there is a man in Winnipeg who is dearer to the heart of the workers, or who has fought harder on their behalf, the workers would like to know him.

At the same time another party was at the home of R.E. Bray, who, when told by the first intruder that he had a warrant for his arrest and a search warrant to look over the premises, told them to go ahead whilst he got dressed. But the three men followed at his heels and despite protest entered into the bedroom and proceeded to turn over the bedclothes and mattress before his wife was allowed to dress, even going so far as to search the bedroom of his sleeping children, "looking for seditious literature or concealed firearms," as though a child's bed was the place to find either. The Mounties nosed around and seemed very disappointed at not being able to find anything of an incriminating character.

Simultaneously the home of Alderman Heaps was visited. It so happened that Alderman John Queen, whose family was staying at Gimli for the Summer, was spending the night with his brother alderman, and these two, who were the elected representatives of one of the largest wards in the city, were handcuffed together like a couple of common criminals. On the same warrant, charged with some offences, were the names of R.J. Johns who, since the middle of April, had been attending sittings of the National Railway Board in Montreal, as the elected representative of all the Machinists on all the Railways in Canada, and that of W.A. Pritchard, who had been sent by the Trades and Labor Council of Vancouver (of which body he was an Executive member) to look over the situation in Winnipeg, and was at the time the others were arrested speeding home to his wife and bairns, anxiously awaiting his home-coming.

To add "color" and for "theatrical effect" there also appeared in the self same warrant the names of the five foreign citizens, whose homes were visited by the guardians of the Law: M. Charitonoff, editor of the "Working People," a weekly paper published in Russian, suppressed during the war, but for the publication of which he had in his possession, at the time of his arrest, permission from the Federal authorities at Ottawa; M. Almazoff, a student of the Manitoba University, a writer and thinker who had come to Canada from Russia at the age of 23; Sam Blumenberg, a delegate to the Winnipeg Trades and Labor Council, formerly a member of the Socialist Party of Canada; and, lastly, the name of one Davieatkin, also of Russian birth, but who had been away on his farm for nearly two months prior to June 17th, and it is in connection with him that one of the greatest outrages ever committed in a British Dominion in the name of justice was perpetrated. This man had left in charge of his home a Russian youth by the name of Verenchuck, who had retired to bed leaving the inner door unfastened and only the screen door hooked on the inside. According to Verenchuck's own story minions of the Law did not trouble to knock but made a hole through the fly screen, unhooked the door, and without the formality of turning on the light and waking the sleeper found the way to his bedroom by means of a flashlight, threw back the bedclothes, grabbed him by the feet and flashing the flashlight in his eyes whilst two of the red-coats pointed their guns at his head gave him five minutes to get dressed.

Never a mention of a warrant, never asking his name, but at the point of the guns compelling him to dress and go with them. This was brutal and inhuman even for a hardened criminal, but here was a boy who in 1915 volunteered to help "make the world safe for democracy"; was wounded and recovered and passed through all the stages of hospitals, convalescences, retraining and another draft for

France, where he was wounded the second time and shell-shocked on the Somme in those terrible days of 1916. Back to Hospital, Blighty, and home to Canada, where he was honorably discharged in 1917. **And his name was not on the warrant and in fact no warrant was issued for him until he had been in the Penitentiary 36 hours.**

But there was worse to follow for him, which will be told on a later page.

NORTH WINNIPEG POLICE STATION

The cars started from their station in time to make the arrests simultaneously and the only thing that prevented simultaneous arrival at the North End Police Station, was a difference in the time taken to search the different homes, and as it was there was only twenty minutes between the first arrival and the last. On arrival there the thing that was most noticeable was the evidence of panic which was written on every countenance of those in authority and which manifested itself in the "jumpiness" of all the officials; and it is safe to say that could the few hours' work have been done there, it would have saved the "powers that be" much worry and many dollars.

By the irony of fate (or perhaps with malice aforethought) Armstrong was placed in one of the cells that he himself had built and with his characteristic humor he remarked that he had often heard Ivens talking about "they that build fine houses shall live in them," but he hardly expected to live in the cell he himself had built.

A cursory examination for firearms and the arrivals were placed in the usual cells and the doors locked, and with the refinement of cruelty that is a product of our vaunted civilization and vulgar curiosity the tools and servants of a corrupt Government wandered around from cell to cell, gazing upon the outcome of their infamous raid, as they would at animals in the Zoo. "Where's Ivens! Where's Bray! Where's Russell!" and the poor ignorant boobs would gaze and grin at their victims who were guilty of what? Trying to make the world what it should be.

THE TRIP TO STONY MOUNTAIN

Less than thirty minutes from the arrival of the first "prisoner" a pompous individual bedecked in all the trappings of the R.N.W.M.P., his arm gaily decorated with three gold braid stripes, appeared at the door of the cell, took out the prisoner and placed him in charge of two "subordinates" each armed with gun and loaded whip, and anything in the nature of human treatment and ordinary civility called forth his strongest condemnation. "Take hold of that prisoner both of you," he bawled to the two privates who were leading Bobby Russell outside to the waiting car.

The "nine" were led to the two high-powered cars waiting outside, the chauffeurs were at the wheels, seated beside them was one of the city's special constables. The prisoners were placed in the rear seats, with a Mountie on either side, and in that sweet fresh summer morning, the cars sped over the prairie to the place where lie buried so many hopes, to that living tomb, where all that is best and noblest in human nature is stifled, where the laughing voices and the rippling laughter of little children is never heard, where the angelic presence, the sunny smile, and the gentle touch of a woman's hand is unknown. Arrived outside those grim forbidding walls, over twenty feet high, smooth as glass, atop of which an armed guard kept watch — there was none to open until the warden was wakened from his slumber.

Was it through the dwelling on the possibility of the execution of the threat of arrest, or was it some intuitive sub-conscious knowledge that led Ivens, on the night before to set out the headline of the "Strike Bulletin"? However it may be, it was most appropriate and very significant that the headline of the issue for June 17th, 1919, should be:

"COMRADES! HOLD THE LINE."

As was both title and subject matter of the leading article of the same issue:

THE MORNING DAWNS?

It looks as if a settlement of the strike is approaching — so says the man on the street. Maybe yes, maybe no. Many a battle has been lost by over-confidence. Now is the time for boys of the bull dog breed to hang on." Don't let go. Don't be too optimistic — the fight isn't won yet. We are still carrying on trying to get others to come to our help. Hold the line. Keep quiet. Do nothing. If the other fellow is wavering, lend him a quarter to buy ice cream to cool his fever, or to buy a roll of wool to keep his feet warm. Don't let the enemy fool you with over-confidence. It is his last card. Don't be fooled. The "Western Labor News" will announce the settlement when it comes. Till then, hold your horses and do nothing.

Remember that over twenty cities are out in sympathy with you, so you must hold the line till the battle is won. Negotiations are entered into whenever an opening appears, but the Strike Committee will make no settlement that is not honorable and worthy of the fight. At present we must "Carry on."

STONY MOUNTAIN PENITENTIARY OUTSIDE
AND INSIDE

Stony Mountain is the highest ground around Winnipeg, and it was

— Manitoba Archives
Strike leaders in a photograph taken at Stony Mountain penitentiary.

to this spot the early settlers fled in time of flood when the surrounding prairie was one vast lake.

The district itself is similar to any other prairie settlement, with the exception that here one sees the quaint buildings of some of Manitoba's early settlers, in strange contrast to the modern buildings where dwell the wardens and guards of the penitentiary. Outside the walls on that Summer morning, all looked so quiet and restful, the white-washed houses and barns, the cattle in the pasture and the meadow larks singing; it seemed as if the big city was in another land with all its noisy traffic, its jostling crowds, and its bitter strife. The green of the prairie grass and the leaves of the trees gently rustling in the morning breeze, accentuated the evil that was being done by man to his fellow-man, and the red-coats and the shining spurs of the "Mounties" made each feel more deeply the great injustice that was being done in the name of the Law.

Ten men, whose one object in life, whose one ambition it was to make all the world as restful, as contented and as happy as their surroundings, at that moment were being led into that living tomb before them, because, forsooth, their activities were stopping the profits of the exploiters and slave drivers.

The warden appears and the massive steel-barred gates are opened and the "prisoners" are marched in and the door "clangs" behind them. Inside the gravelled courtyard they are lined up in a row, until the order is given to pass into the building proper — how dark and forbidding it looks, only those who have passed through its portal know. Through four or five of these steel-barred doors they are led and the doors are closed and locked behind them; into the office, where they are searched from the crown of the head to the toe of the boot, pockets turned inside out and every vestige of tobacco dust shaken from the corners; every piece of paper, watches, rings, tie pins, all taken and stored in canvas bags with the name of the owner on a slip of paper; names entered in a register, and they pass out through other steel-barred doors, ceasing to be human beings, becoming things designated by a number. Up a flight of stairs into a big room with rows of cells each about nine by five feet with a bedstead, stool and table, brick walls two feet thick, the only opening a steel-barred door so situated that no two prisoners can see each other, and all that can be seen of the great world outside is the blue sky by day and the stars by night. Such is the place they send human beings into to "reform" or "remake" them. A typical criminal factory, a model product of capitalist society and "Christian" civilization.

It was to this same penitentiary that the millionaire was committed for two years, after a jury had found him guilty of defrauding the Province of Manitoba of something over $1,000,000 in connection with the new Legislative buildings; but who never entered a convict's cell, never wore a convict's suit, never submitted to the regulation hair cut, never ate the penitentiary fare, but was supplied from outside with the best that money could buy, on orders from the Government at Ottawa.*

This was the statement given under oath by warden Graham.

The men arrested for helping to "make a new world" thought they would at any rate get decent fare, at least until they were convicted, but when the jailer came around at seven o'clock the first morning it was to hand in a bowl of porridge, minus both milk and sugar, but decorated and flavored with cooking molasses, one round of dry bread, about one and a half inches thick, minus even the despised Margerine, then the door was locked again. Shortly after there appeared a man in the black and brown striped suit of the convict, with close cropped head, bearing a watering can with a yard long spout, and in a voice that would wake the dead, yelled: "Want any tea," and poking the long spout of tin can through the bars of the cell door filled up the little enamel mug with colored water, minus milk and sugar. This was breakfast; dinner, tasteless boiled beef, with all the nutriment boiled out, potatoes mashed with skin, eyes and all, and more dry bread; supper, hash, dry bread and more colored water. This was the fare for three days, with the exception of soup one day for dinner and radish and dry bread one day for supper.

COURT SITS IN THE PENITENTIARY

In the afternoon there appeared at the penitentiary the leading and chief mouth-piece of the Citizens' Committee of 1000, in the person of A.J. Andrews, K.C., this time in the role of Deputy Minister of Justice, an office conferred upon him, according to Senator Gideon Robertson, by the acting Minister of Justice, Honorable Arthur Meighen, on the recommendation of the Senator. With him was a police magistrate, and when the "boys" were lined up, this gentleman arose from his seat at the table in this improvised courtroom, and mumbled in a typical police court style something which afterwards turned out to be the charges that had been laid against them. When he had finished Andrews got up and asked for a remand for eight days. That was the first intimation the "boys" had that they were in a court of justice. Of course, protests were made that the prisoners had not seen their counsel and they were informed that the solicitor for the Trades and Labor Council had started, but that his car had got mired, **but they had no need to worry, they**

*This is a reference to the notorious scandal involving fraudulent payments to the contracting firm constructing the Manitoba legislative building. The contractor went to the penitentiary, and Sir Rodmond P. Roblin, premier at the time, retired to Florida.

would, in all probability, be on the Atlantic homeward bound to the land of their birth inside of 72 hours. Further protest was made and application for bail, but Mr. Andrews said **he was instructed to refuse bail under any consideration and of any amount, but that the special Immigration Board was on its way from Ottawa and they would be tried either Wednesday or Thursday with their wives and families.** It was at this time that it was discovered that there was no warrant for Verenchuck and Warden Graham also swore later that there was no warrant for Armstrong.

The daily paper came out on Tuesday with glaring headlines in red ink that ten strike leaders were in jail, and the following account appeared in the afternoon "Tribune," of June 17th, about the same time the "boys" were in court in the "pen":

GOING TO KINGSTON FOR TRIAL, IS REPORT; MORE MAY BE NABBED

Labor and Ukrainian Temple and Liberty Hall Raided by Royal Police, Assisted by Special Constables

Ten men, including six who have been prominent as leaders in the Winnipeg strike, were arrested early this morning by Royal Northwest Mounted Police, assisted by special city constables.

The ten were taken in automobiles to the penitentiary at Stonewall. From there, it was reported this afternoon, they may be taken to the penitentiary at Kingston, Ont., within a day or two, for arraignment and trial.

Those arrested are:

Rev. William Ivens, editor of the "Western Labor News," pastor of the Labor Church and chief orator of the strikers.

R.B. Russell, Secretary of the Metal Trades Council.

John Queen, Alderman from Ward Five and business manager of the "Western Labor News."

A.A. Heaps, Alderman from Ward Five.

George Armstrong, street car motorman.

Moses Almazoff.

R.E. Bray, leader in strikers' parades and "Chairman of the Soldiers' Parliament."

Mike Verenchuck.

S. Choppelrei.

F. Charitonoff, editor of the Russian "Working People."

Raids were made simultaneously on the Labor Temple, Ukrainian Temple, Liberty Hall and homes of the arrested men by about 50 Royal "Mounties" and 500 special city police. The police had a warrant for each of the ten. No resistance was offered by any of them.

According to Acting Chief Newton, charges of seditious conspiracy are to be preferred against the prisoners.

A. J. Andrews, K.C., will represent the Government as special prosecutor in these cases, Crown Prosecutor R. B. Graham announced. It is understood that Mr. Andrews swore out the warrants on instructions he received from Ottawa Monday afternoon.

Mr. Andrews, in an interview this afternoon, said he was acting on instructions from the Federal Department of Justice.

"Federal officers have been investigating for two weeks and the action taken is the result," he declared.

It is reported that the Dominion Government contemplated arresting alleged agitators simultaneously in all Western cities where strikes are in progress. Latest dispatches from Vancouver, Regina, Brandon, Edmonton, Moose Jaw, Calgary, and Saskatoon this afternoon were that no arrests had been made in any of those cities.

The raids and arrests came as a dramatic climax to a long period of inactivity on the part of Federal, Provincial, and Civic officials, during which rumors that such action was contemplated were circulated everywhere.

The fact that the responsibility for the raids and arrests rests entirely upon the Federal Government is attested by statements made by Premier Norris and Mayor Gray, in which they declare that they had no previous knowledge of the plans.

A delegation from the Strike Committee called upon the Mayor shortly before noon and asked whether the city had ordered the arrests.

"We have just come from Senator Robertson," they said. "We asked him who ordered the raids and he referred us to you."

The Mayor asserted that he knew nothing about the matter.

Premier Norris was equally emphatic. When asked what he knew about the affair, he said: "Just leave us out of it." Other members of the Provincial Cabinet said they knew nothing about it whatever.

Warrants for the arrest of several more men were issued this morning on orders of A. J. Andrews, K.C., prosecutor for the Dominion Government, it was stated at the police station. Their arrest, it was said, would be only a matter of a short time.

Included in the charges of seditious libel are the following allegations:

"That the men did conspire against his person, King George V."

"That they conspired with intent against the constitutional Government of Canada."

"That they conspired with intent to oppose the authority of constables appointed by the City of Winnipeg."

"That certain articles published in the 'Western Labor News' were published with intent to ridicule the constitutional Government of the Dominion.''

The charge of seditious conspiracy, along with an innuendo of considerable length, reads:

''That these men did conspire with intent to overthrow the constitutional Government of the Dominion of Canada.''

More than 500 special constables and 50 members of the Royal North West Mounted Police were used in the raids.

Automobiles which were mobilized on Broadway, near Main Street, and in the vicinity of the R.N.W.M.P. headquarters, at Smith Street and Assiniboine Avenue, were used to visit the homes of the men taken into custody.

The first auto left police headquarters at 2 o'clock this morning with a warrant for the arrest of Alderman Heaps. Twenty other cars followed, each loaded with mounted and special police. At 4 o'clock the round-up was complete.

At the same hour, the Labor Temple, Ukrainian Temple and Liberty halls were raided. Quantities of literature were seized and loaded on a truck, which was taken to the police station.

Books and literature in connection with the Calgary convention also were seized, it is understood.

The biggest haul in literature was made at the Labor Temple, where the truck was more than half loaded.

Literature printed in Ukrainian, English, German, and Polish, was found in the two other places raided, police said.

Draw Cordon Around Temple

While the squad of North West Mounted Police and special constables raided the Labor Temple, more than 400 constables drew a cordon around the building, to prevent interference. The men were armed and had instructions not to allow anybody to approach the building.

Inspector Henry Green was in charge of the squad.

''Open in the name of the Law,'' he shouted, after rapping on the door of the place.

No one replied.

He then tried the door. It was locked.

The plate glass in the window was then smashed, and the door opened. No one was found in the building. The janitor, who, according to police, is on duty there all night, was not to be seen.

Desks were opened and literature and documentary evidence seized.

Safes Are Sealed

Safes were sealed and guards placed over them. On the second floor, which was occupied by Mr. Russell, and the Cloak and Garment Makers' Union, police found copies of the "Red Flag," an organ published at Vancouver.

Copies of literature endorsing the Soviet Government as the one body approaching perfection, were also found on this floor, according to constables.

The office of the Trades and Labor Council, on the main floor, was then raided. A large quantity of literature was found there.

Heaps First Arrested

Alderman Heaps, from Ward Five, was the first man arrested. He was in bed when special constables, and two members of the Royal North West Mounted Police arrived.

He protested vigorously, and is said to have told the constables that they should have waited until later in the morning. He did not attempt to resist, however, and when the warrant was read to him, he dressed and accompanied the policemen to an automobile and was conveyed to the Central Police Station.

"Wait, that's all," Alderman John Queen is said to have told the two constables who apprehended him. He dressed and quietly accompanied the officers.

R. B. Russell, Rev. William Ivens, George Armstrong, F. Charitonoff, and Moses Almazoff made no statements when apprehended.

Mrs. Armstrong, however, is said to have protested, when officers attempted to arrest her husband.

"You cannot get him out of this house until Chief Newton tells me you have the right to," she told the policemen.

The officers waited while Mrs. Armstrong ran to the North-End police station. She telephoned Chief Newton from the station.

"They have a warrant to arrest George," she told Mr. Newton.

"I guess it's all right, then," Chief Newton replied.

Mrs. Armstrong then went home and "formally" released her husband to the officers.

R. E. Bray, leader of the strikers' parades, fainted when policemen woke him up, according to constables who were in the house when he was arrested.

He was revived, but wept all the way to the station, constables said.

City Officials Ignorant of Raids

Civic officials were ignored by the Dominion Government

authorities in connection with the arrest early today of strike leaders. They declared they knew nothing about it and did not know it was to take place.

"I don't know anything about it," Mayor Gray said. "I have nothing to say except that I was asleep at Elm Park when the arrests were made."

Alderman J. K. Sparling, Chairman of the Police Commission, was equally in the dark.

"I knew nothing about the arrest until I came down town this morning," he said. "It was carried out entirely by the Dominion authorities."

The arrests were the chief topics of conversation around the city hall.

Alderman John Queen, one of those arrested, is a member of the Civic Food Committee, but he had attended only one meeting since the city established food depots in schools.

Mayor Gray said he knew nothing about the possibility of Martial Law being declared. Other Council members said they also knew nothing about any action along that line.

Say Constables Swiped Cigars

"A lot of special constables are smoking union made cigars today," according to men at the Labor Temple, who said the cigar stand had been more thoroughly ransacked than any other part of the building.

Every room of the building was searched. Even cartoons were taken from the windows and carried away as evidence.

Two hundred special police and North West Mounted men were in the group that carried out the actual raid on the Labor Temple. About 400 others were held in reserve.

The streets about the temple were lined with machines, each one loaded with special police.

Every way one might turn there were police and still more police.

Some of the specials were in their shirt sleeves although the morning air was chilly. They had been called hurriedly out of bed without warning.

"Come on, there's something doing," was all the orders that some of them received. But they showed up at once.

According to specials in the party only the officers knew of the plans to raid the Labor Temple and arrest the leaders.

And on Wednesday, June 18th, the following two choice articles appeared, confirming Andrews' statements to the "boys" in the penitentiary, and, incidentally, proving the "conspiracy" that led to the infamous amendments to the Immigration Act on June 6th, at Ottawa, at the instigation of U.S.A. financial magnates. This was the result of what General Ketchen described to the meeting in the Arena Rink on June 6th, as "the steps that were being taken **at this instant**, to enable the Government to handle all **undesirable agitators, British-born and otherwise:**

DEPORTATION ORDERS COME FOR REDS HERE
Action Will be Taken Under Amended Immigration Act.

Ottawa, June 17. — Comment here today dwelt much upon the arrest of strike leaders that orders for the deportation of the men arrested were sent to Winnipeg by the Minister of Immigration yesterday afternoon. Action was taken under the amended Immigration Act calling for the deportation of persons who strive for the overthrow of constituted authority by forcible means. The act as first amended this session referred only to aliens in this regard and it was found unworkable as applied to men of British birth; as it now stands it may apply to anyone who is not a British subject by birth in Canada or by naturalization therein and will, therefore, include in its scope nearly all British-born who have declared themselves as being for the forcible overthrow of constituted authority. From present indications it is the intention of the Immigration authorities to proceed at once with the other formalities necessary to the carrying out of the orders issued.

The above despatch from Ottawa confirms information received locally by the Free Press that the arrests are preliminary to deportation proceedings in the case of these leaders, who are not of Canadian birth. Meanwhile they are also facing charges of seditious conspiracy.

TRIAL OF REDS TO BE BEHIND CLOSED DOORS

Special Board Will Hear Allegations on Deportable Charge — Immediate Action is Prosecutor's Decision — Accused May be En Route Across Atlantic in 76 Hours, Says A. J. Andrews, K.C.

Red leaders arrested in Winnipeg early yesterday may be on their way across the Atlantic within the next 76 hours, it was announced today.

They will be tried at Stony Mountain tomorrow, provided the board coming from Ottawa to hear the charge against them, arrives in the city tonight.

This board, it is stated by A. J. Andrews, K.C., who is conducting the case for the Crown, has the power to deport them right away. If they are not deported they will be dealt with under the criminal code. Bail will not be allowed, if Mr. Andrews can possibly prevent it, according to his statement.

The public will not be admitted to the hearings which are expected to start at Stony Mountain at 10 a.m. tomorrow.

Coming From Ottawa

Three members of the board are coming from Ottawa. Their names were not available.

Also eligible for membership of the board are Col. Stearns, of the R.N.W.M.P., Commissioner A. A. Perry, and Thomas Jelley, acting Commissioner of Immigration in Winnipeg for the Federal Government.

Counsel for the accused has been given permission to appear for them. The press may be admitted by a permit from the Chairman of the Board.

T. J. Murray with Mr. Andrews met Senator G. D. Robertson at the Royal Alexandra at noon today. Following a conference lasting more than an hour, Mr. Murray was the first to leave. He declined to make any statement at this juncture.

Immediate Deportation

"Under the amended Order-in-Council the Board will have power to deport the accused immediately," said A. J. Andrews. "If they do not come under this amendment they can be dealt with under the criminal code on all the charges named. The Board may not consider the charges sufficiently serious for immediate deportation, in which case criminal proceedings will be immediately instituted."

More charges, in addition to those already laid, may be preferred against the accused, counsel for the Crown intimated.

"LAW AND ORDER" AT THE LABOR TEMPLE

Whilst the homes of the men were being visited and the men themselves being whisked away to Stony Mountain, some hundreds of "Special Police" and "Mounties" were raiding the various meeting places of the strikers and headquarters of organized labor.

At the Labor Temple on James Street, the large plate glass doors were broken and every room broken into and searched. In room 14, the office of the Machinists' Local, No. 122, the headquarters of Brother R.B. Russell, a desk was deliberately smashed open and in addition to the papers and documents there was between $50 and $60 in cash, dues paid in by members after banking hours the previous day; and when these minions of the Law left, after their search, this money as well as the papers and documents were missing.

The show case on the ground floor was liberally stocked with cigars, cigarettes, and tobacco, but without specifically charging the searchers with theft, it is a fact that after they left there was hardly so much as a cigarette paper left.

On a subsequent visit the three safes in the building were opened in a most expert manner, and despoiled of their contents. The Ukrainian Labor Temple was visited and suffered wanton destruction in the same manner. Type already set in the printing machine in the basement was scattered all over the floor and machines wilfully damaged.

About $38 worth of chocolate and candy were taken from the show cases here, as the cigars, etc., from the Labor Temple.

A DISCREDITED GOVERNMENT AND AN ERSTWHILE RESPECTED FORCE

One of the charges laid against the men arrested is that "of bringing His Majesty's Government into contempt and ridicule," but this charge could lie more properly against the Government itself, for its own policy and action have earned the contempt of 85% of the population; and never in the history of Canada has a Government been held in such contempt by the mass of the people as the present Union Government.

By wholesale disfranchisement, by the manipulation of the "floating" vote of the soldiers,* by intimidation, they rode into power, and disgusted the entire electorate by their policy of Government by Order-in-Council. All this was bad enough, but when they use the members of what was looked upon as one of the best constabulary forces in the world for such base purposes as stool pigeons and common spies, it shows to what lengths they are prepared to go to bolster the crumbling reign of despotism.

HOLDING THE LINE

After the arrests, meetings were held to protest against the Prussian methods adopted by our "Democratic Government," but there followed no unseemly demonstrations, only a quiet firm determination to carry on "till the fight was won." "Hold the Line!" was the rallying cry, and hold the line they did.

The "Strike Bulletin" came out as usual, with J.S. Woodsworth as editor, and as evidence of fearless courage and undaunted enthusiasm, we append the following article from the issue of Wednesday, June 18th, 1919:

*This is a reference to the notorious Wartime Elections Act of 1917. Meighen piloted that act through Parliament in preparation for the coming federal elections, which would be fought on the conscription issue. This act disenfranchised all citizens from what were then enemy nations who had been naturalized since 1901. It also enfranchised wives, sweethearts, mothers and grandmothers of men on active service, as well as the soldiers themselves, regardless of their age. It permitted balloting overseas with wide latitude given to election officials to assign soldiers' votes to constituencies at their discretion. This "floating" vote gave the Union government the opportunity, which they used, to distribute soldiers' votes to constituencies where the government candidates needed them most.

FOOLS AND KNAVES

"Whom the Gods would destroy they first make mad." When the knaves on the Committee of 1000 started the villainous campaign which has resulted in the arrest of six of the most devoted men who ever served the cause of labor, they fondly and falsely imagined that by securing the arrest of these men they could break the strike. During the early part of the strike the plutocratic 1000 expected to starve the workers into submission in two weeks. When the workers refused to submit they said:

"The fact that these workers can live more than two weeks without working shows that they are getting too high wages. We must grind them down." Later the Committee boasted that its position had been endorsed by the Civic, Provincial and Federal Governments. Then came thundering the ultimatums of the various Governments and corporations. These failed of their purpose, which was rank intimidation.

While the old police force was on the city streets, peaceful and law-abiding citizens could sleep quietly in their beds without fear of molestation. Citizens could walk the streets unafraid of gunmen, because they could rely on the old city police to administer the Law without fear or favor. This was not to the liking of the 1000, so they maligned the loyal police until the Police Commission was induced to lock them out.

Then followed a Cossack-like attempt to club the workers into submission.

All the miserable tactics of the 1000 have failed of their main purpose. They have failed to break the strike. They have failed to prevent the strike from spreading.

After a month's campaign of vilification, misrepresentation and intimidation, unparalleled in this country in its intensity, there are more men and women on strike in Winnipeg than there were a month ago. The Committee of Knaves realizes this and as a consequence they have gone stark raving mad.

We thought their last card was played when they ousted the men who were the embodiment of law and order from the streets. But they had another card up their sleeve, namely, the brutal arrest of strike leaders. Perhaps they have another card yet. Let them play it. They will find that the strikers can give them cards and spades and then beat them. It is impossible for that infamous Committee to descend much lower, but let them go the limit; we have no intention of following them. Whatever foul tactics may be indulged in by the opposition, the strikers will continue calm and strong, resolved to win by lawful and orderly methods those righteous principles which are at stake. It is not the fact of this or that man that will decide the issue. It is the firm resolution to win that will overcome and cast down the greedy tyrants from the pedestal on which they have placed themselves. The actions of the Committee of 1000 indicate that its policy is dictated by mad knaves and carried out by credulous fools. They will find out, however, that the brains of the labor movement are not all contained in the heads of six men; that the determination of the labor movement is not confined in six hearts. They will be taught that 35,000 brains and hearts are united and that these brains and hearts will in the long run rise victorious through all the nefarious machinations of the 1000, secure the objects for which this strike is being waged and vindicate the men who were arrested on Tuesday morning.

DOMINION WIDE PROTESTS

Meantime, while the "boys" in Winnipeg were determined to close the ranks and carry on, protests were being sent from every point of the Dominion to the Trades and Labor Congress, as the following clipping from the "Free Press Bulletin," of June 18th, will show:

LABOR HEADS KEEP OUT OF CITY TROUBLE

But Dominion Congress May Intervene if They Are Appealed to

Ottawa, June 18. — The Dominion Labor Congress is ready to back the Winnipeg strikers with all necessary assistance as circumstances may demand, but it is up to the Winnipeg strikers or their Committee, or the arrested leaders themselves, to ask the Congress to take action.

Until the Winnipeg labor men resume communication with the Congress, President Tom Moore holds that it would be indelicate and uncalled for on his part to interfere. For this reason he has so far given no answer to a score or more of telegrams, from labor councils all over Canada demanding that the Congress call anything from a Dominion wide one-day strike to an indefinite general strike lasting until all the grievances of the Winnipeg men are remedied.

Labor councils all over Canada are standing by the Winnipeg strikers, and are up in arms over the arrest of the leaders, their telegrams to Ottawa are said to show.

Vancouver Men Silent

Vancouver, B.C., June 17. — Up to a late hour this evening recognized labor leaders here had no comment to make publicly concerning the arrests this morning in Winnipeg of radicals and agitators. There were no new developments locally in the strike situation.

"The World," which is now the only regularly published daily newspaper in Vancouver, commenting on the Winnipeg strike, says:

"The Dominion Government has at last acted with vigor in Winnipeg; it has ordered the arrest of the strike leaders and the seizure of evidence. The leaders are now under detention and a raid on the Labor Temple has yielded up many documents.

"The Government in directing these arrests and this seizure is acting under process of law. It is acting in the name of the citizens of Canada, and it is clothed with the authority to do what it has done.

Must be Established

"The conclusion does not follow, however, that because the strike leaders have been arrested that they are necessarily guilty or that they have been plotting to 'overthrow the Government.' Nor because documents have been found in the Labor Temple are they necessarily incitements to break the Law. The facts relating to these matters have yet to be established in a Court of Law and they can be satisfactorily established in no other way.

"The strike leaders will receive a fair trial. They are entitled to it and must receive it. If they have broken the Law by act or word they must meet the consequences. If they have not broken it and their deeds or language are merely irresponsible and not illegal, then the public, which has foreseen so many calamities impending in the last week or two, may be reassured."

Proof Required, Says Moore

Ottawa, Ont., June 18. — "The Trades and Labor movement will not stand for strong arm methods for the suppression of legitimate labor demonstrations, and if the proof is not sufficient to show the Winnipeg labor leaders were plotting danger to the State, the Government will be held strictly accountable," said Tom Moore, President of the Dominion Trades and Labor Congress, when speaking of the arrests of the Winnipeg labor leaders.

"The news of the arrests came as an absolute surprise to me," Mr. Moore continued.

Welcomes Arrest of Reds

Edmonton, Alta., June 17. — The arrest of ten of the so-called strike leaders in Winnipeg early this morning has caused considerable of a flutter in local strike circles. No action under the new Act in Edmonton is expected. But strike leaders here, nevertheless, are keenly interested in Winnipeg developments.

"If these arrests are confined solely to Winnipeg and strike leaders

there are arrested wholesale, it will only have the effect of making
the strikers more determined,'' said one strong union man who is
not on the Strike Committee. ''On the other hand, if the real 'Red'
agitators throughout all Canada are gathered in it would be a good
thing. There is really one such man in Edmonton now. Vancouver
has one or two, also.''

Karl Berg, Vice-Chairman of the Central Strike Committee,
declared that the arrests in Winnipeg would only ''inflame'' the
strikers and make them more determined than ever to stay out until
they get what they are fighting for.

Locally, the strike situation remains unchanged. No trainmen, firemen or switchmen in Edmonton have gone out on strike, and the
railway situation is as it was a week ago.

Want Dominion Strike

Calgary, Alta., June 18. — Request that a Dominion wide strike
in protest of the arrest of the strike leaders in Winnipeg be called
by the Dominion Trades Congress, has been made by the Trades
Council here in a wire sent last night to Tom Moore, President
of the Dominion Congress. Strike leaders here do not discuss the
Winnipeg stiuation except to say that their cause is a just one and
that they have nothing to fear.

Pritchard Disappears

Brandon, Man., June. 17. — Quite a mystery surrounds the complete disappearance of two prominent labor men from this city tonight.

A mass meeting of labor had been called to take place in Rideau
Park at 7.30 this evening, at which time close on 400 people were
present. W.A. Pritchard, of Vancouver, and H.M. Bartholomew,
of this city, were scheduled to be the speakers. After waiting for
about an hour and a half, part of which time was taken up with
impromptu speakers, Chairman Ayers announced that he feared something had happened to them, hinting that the same fate might have
befallen them as that which befell the leaders in Winnipeg.

The meeting shortly afterwards broke up.

Such of the Mounted Police as could be interrogated denied any
knowledge of the affair, and up to the time of writing no trace
of the men had been found.

Demand Winnipegers' Release

As the result of the arrest of the labor leaders in Winnipeg, a
resolution was passed this afternoon by the Brandon Trades and
Labor Council to this effect:

That the meeting assembled protests against the summary arrest of six labor leaders at Winnipeg and calls for their immediate release and places itself on record that the workers of Canada refuse to discuss a settlement of the present strike until their leaders be released and reinstated. Further be it resolved that this resolution be sent Premier Borden, Premier Norris and Mayor Gray and copy of same to every Strike Committee.

Toronto Strikers Protest

Toronto, June 17. — General indignation is expressed by local labor men over the arrests made at Winnipeg. The most pointed intimation of how they feel about it came from the striking Metal Trades Council, who framed a telegram which was sent to Sir Robert Borden. The telegram reads:

"The Metal Trades Council of Toronto representing several thousand workers on strike in this city, recognizing that the Dominion Government is evidently assisting the employing class in Winnipeg with the intention of destroying the labor movement of the West and in Canada, demand that your Government take steps that will assure the release at once of representatives of labor arrested in the City of Winnipeg.

"We further demand that the recent act intended to be used for the purpose of injuring the working class movement be repealed immediately. We declare that the connivance of the Government with the employing class is inexcusable and criminal and invites grave trouble over the whole of Canada."

Coast Situation Better

Vancouver, B.C., June 17. — The fifteenth day of the Vancouver strike finds the city undisturbed in its domestic life and very little affected in its business life. The strike is marking time. The Strike Committee has "nothing to announce." Secretary Cavanagh merely remarking, when he heard the news of the Winnipeg arrests, that the strike would now spread to unorganized labor.

Some of the strikers in different industries are going back to work in ones and twos. Some of the longshoremen have gone back, and are working alongside of volunteer longshoremen, who are unloading an occasional boat in the harbor. There has been not the smallest approach to rioting anywhere.

Naylor Not Wanted to Speak

Nanaimo, B.C., June 17. — The Retail Clerks' Association of this city at a meeting here tonight repudiated the action of their Executive in asking Joseph Naylor, organizer for the One Big Union, to address them on the question of affiliation with the O.B.U., and voted by a large majority not to permit Naylor to address them.

Would Purge Winnipeg

Toronto, June 18. — Regarding the arrest of strike leaders in Winnipeg, The "Mail and Empire" says:

"The Government must not stop half way or listen to the Counsels of the solemn owls who undertake to utter clap-trap in the name of the citizens. The citizens want to have Winnipeg purged of the gang who did their best to throttle it and set up a rebel Government. Riel was hanged for resorting to arms to do what they were attempting.

"Those who insist that the smoking out of anarchists will be resented by labor are slanderers of labor."

The "Globe" editorially says:

"As to the wisdom or unwisdom of the Government's action at this time, the details so far to hand do not afford ground for decision, but having assumed responsibility for so drastic a step, it is incumbent upon the Federal authorities to satisfy the public that it is justified. If the arrests are part of a plan to railroad the strike leaders out of the country without trial, under the terms of the amendment to the Immigration Act, they should be abandoned now."

New Westminster to Strike

New Westminster, B.C., June 18. — The General Strike Committee appointed last week by the New Westminster Trades and Labor Council issued a call this morning for a general strike of union workers in this city, to take effect at 1 o'clock this afternoon.

A telegram has been sent to Ottawa declaring that the strike order is made as a protest against the arrests of the Winnipeg strike leaders.

Retail clerks and drivers of milk and bread wagons are exempted from the stop work order. Printers and postal employees will ignore the call, it is said. More than 400 street car men probably will quit work, however, and tie up all suburban lines to and from Vancouver, with the exception of the Fraser Valley line. These suburban routes have not been affected by the Vancouver strike.

No Arrests in Calgary

Calgary, Alta., June 18. — No arrests of strike agitators have occurred here yet. Shopmen remain at work on receipt of instructions from R. J. Tallon, at Montreal, that the strike has been indefinitely postponed.

BRITISH LABOR PROTESTS

But perhaps the most interesting news is as follows, taken from the "Telegram," showing that beyond the confines of this continent, the working class had their eyes upon Winnipeg: Telegram, June 26th:

BRITISH LABOR WANTS CANADIAN GOVERNMENT TO AVOID DEPORTING

LONDON, June 26. — The Labor Party Conference at Southport has passed a resolution protesting against the attempt of the Canadian Government to secretly deport British-born leaders of labor for participation in recent industrial disputes in the Dominion and urging the British Government to use its influence to prevent the Canadian Government from proceeding with such a step.

PRITCHARD ARRESTED IN CALGARY

As the ten prisoners in their solitary cells at Stony Mountain awaited news of the world outside, the following dispatch was received in Winnipeg from Calgary, telling its own story, of frustrated hopes and anxious hours for a lonely wife and waiting bairns:

PRITCHARD IS ARRESTED ON CALGARY TRAIN

Calgary, Alta., June 20. — W. A. Pritchard, prominent organizer of the One Big Union, and one of its officials, is a prisoner in the Calgary city jail, awaiting transportation to Winnipeg on a charge of having knowledge of seditious conspiracy.

Pritchard was taken from the westbound C.P.R. train at Calgary at 6.40 o'clock last night by Staff-Sergt. Hall, of the R.N.W.M.P., who have been watching all trains on the lookout for the fugitive. The prisoner was brought before Police Magistrate Sanders, D.S.O., this morning and was briefly informed that he would bè held pending the arrival of an officer from Winnipeg.

"Do you know what the charge is against you?" inquired the police magistrate of Pritchard.

Knew About Charge

"Yes, I know," responded the prisoner briefly, which was the extent of his remarks while in the dock. He was removed again to the cell and the case remanded until Monday pending the arrival of a Winnipeg officer.

In spite of the screaming headlines in the kept press, to the effect that the arrested men would be deported without the formality of a civil trial: "That in 76 hours they would be on the high seas," and despite the statements of A. J. Andrews that: "Bail would not be granted under any conditions," on Thursday evening, June 19th, as the various members of the Strike Committee, who had been out addressing meetings returned to the Labor Temple, it was seen that something was in the air. Little groups stood around discussing earnestly some information that had been handed out, whilst others were laughing and flinging their caps in the air and when it was finally announced that arrangements had been made for the release of the British-born prisoners, the greatest enthusiasm prevailed. The amount of bail was a personal bond of $2,000 from each man, and two sureties of $1,000 each, and when this was announced by T. J. Murray, of Murray & Noble, Solicitors for the Trades and Labor Council, there was a great scramble for the honor, and even at that late hour there would have been little difficulty in securing bondsmen for ten times the amount needed.

Mr. Andrews, for the Crown, demurred when informed it was the intention to go after the men at this hour (midnight) on the ground that the warden and the guards would be abed, but was promptly informed that if the "boys" could be taken out of bed to go in, the officials could be called out of bed to let them out. So a hunt was made for a police magistrate, and secured in the person of E. A. Andrews, who, in company with T. J. Murray and about 40 or 50 strikers, started out on the long trip over the prairie. It was a weird procession and must have caused surprise to anybody seeing it pass.

Owing to the severe electric storm of the previous Saturday, the electric lights in the upper portion of the penitentiary were out of commission, but after waking up the warden, and getting him out of bed to issue the necessary orders for admittance, the guard on duty went around to the cells wherein the prisoners were confined and with some difficulty wakened them, with the information that they had to go to the city.

The first thought was that it was the intention of the authorities to move them in the night, in order to have them on hand for the Immigration Board, as each man had been shaved that morning in order to be presentable, should the Board arrive at the "Pen." Great was their surprise on arrival in the office to see the smiling faces of their friends and to receive their hearty handshakes. Soon the formalities of signing were gone through and the men who three days before had passed through the gates into this "tomb of the living" escorted by armed men, who had suffered all the indignities of convicted criminals, were led out escorted by their friends.

Outside the gate, old friends and comrades crowded round them, men and women, baskets of food and fruit were brought out and under the black and forbidding walls of the prison, in all their repulsive hideousness, they ate the first good meal they had tasted for three days. Three days! It seemed to those men like three years — to men who physically and mentally, for the past few weeks had been keyed to the highest pitch, the three days of solitary confinement and inactivity had seemed half a lifetime.

In reluctantly consenting to bail, however, the agent for the Crown had insisted, like Shylock of old, in having his "pound of flesh" and the men were compelled to sign an agreement to the effect that they: "Would take no further part in the strike, that they would not address any other meetings, nor give any interviews to the press," which agreement, in spite of much provocation, the men kept both in letter and in spirit. For what purposes such an unprecedented condition was put will be told in another page.

As was to be expected, as soon as the "boys" appeared on the streets the following day, they were the recipients of the hearty congratulations of their fellow-workers, and the heartiness and multiplicity of these congratulations gave the "Spies" and "Stool Pigeons" much upon which their imagination could play in making their reports to their superiors.

The one disheartening feature to the British-born prisoners who were released on bail and to the whole body of strikers was the fact that the five foreign-born, arrested on the same charges were refused their liberty.

The following is from the "Strike Bulletin," of June 21st, 1919:

FIVE MEN TO COME OUT

Six of the strike leaders are out on bail. Five men are still in Stony Mountain penitentiary. They must come out.

The eleven men were all arrested on the same information. There were two charges; the one, seditious conspiracy, the other seditious libel. According to the first these eleven men did conspire and agree with one another and with other persons ... and were thereby guilty of seditious conspiracy. The second charge is based on an article which appeared in the "Western Labor News" with regard to the special police. — All eleven are held responsible.

As a matter of fact none of the five men had anything to do with the strike, were not on the Committees or did not address any meeting. Some of them were not even known by some of the strike leaders.

M. Charitonoff who was arrested some time ago and released has taken no active part in public matters since his release. He was about to publish a newspaper with the full knowledge of the authorities who raised no objections. He cannot be tried again on the previous charge. Apparently he has a clean sheet.

S. Almazoff is a student at the university. He has been taking a course in philosophy and economics. Three days before he was arrested he finished writing on his examinations.

M. Berenczat is a returned soldier. He enlisted in the Second C. M. R., at the beginning of the war and returned in April, 1917, after being twice wounded.

Oscar Schappellrei is American-born and is still in uniform.

Sam Blumenberg was put out of the Socialist Party of Canada five months ago for not being sufficiently "Orthodox" and "scientific." When he learned that a warrant was out for him he voluntarily surrendered himself.

The British-born men are now out on bail and are to be given a civil trial. The foreign-born — though they include two men who fought for Canada — are to be proceeded against under the amended Immigration Law. This will mean trial by an ordinary Committee, though it is understood that legal forms will be observed and the men will be represented by counsel. The only appeal is to the Minister in charge of the Department of Immigration.

Surely if these men are guilty they, too, might be tried under the ordinary process of law and not kicked out of the back door as undesirables — two of them returned men!

In any case why cannot they be released on bail as is the ordinary procedure? The Government can have no fear that they would not be forthcoming at the time of trial. Why should they not have a chance to prepare their defense? If the Government saw fit to release six why not release the remaining five arrested on the same charge? Should not men irrespective of birthplace enjoy British justice? What political purpose has the Government in keeping them in confinement?

British justice and constitutional Government are on their trial these days. We believe the soldiers are prepared to back the workers in insisting that all men are given fair play. Organized labor protests against the detention of these men, who, although not connected with the strike, were arrested on a charge of being parties with the strike leaders to seditious conspiracy and responsible with them for alleged seditious libel.

The following article is also taken from the "Strike Bulletin," of June 21st:

IN AGAIN — OUT AGAIN

"Once there was a King of France. He had ten thousand men. He marched them up a great big hill and then he marched them down again!"

Two days ago six desperate characters were seized by our soldier-police force. Their houses were violently broken open; their wives and children seriously frightened; their private papers ransacked — they were handcuffed, placed under heavy guard in automobiles and drove at top speed to the penitentiary at Stony Mountain. They, though British-born, were to be deported "without the formality of a civil trial" and by this time were to be on the deep, blue sea.

But a cog slipped; in fact several cogs slipped, and now these desperate Red leaders of a frightfully red revolution — Canadian-wide in scope and engineered from Moscow and backed up by unlimited Bolshevist funds from the United States — these dangerous characters are peacefully resting in their own homes with their wives and children.

Surely the whole world's a stage; life is still full of dramatic interest; ambition is not the only creature that o'er leaps itself with disastrous results. (Haven't time to consult my Shakespeare.)

If the authorities have such overwhelming evidence in their possession, the defenceless citizens of Winnipeg may well claim that the officials responsible are derelict in duty if they allow these men the possibility of escape.

The statement issued by A.J. Andrews, K.C., is a choice bit of reading. Remember that there have been all sorts of negotiations going on; that there have been sharp differences of opinion between the Provincial and Federal authorities; that there has been great pressure from public leaders and influential private citizens; that there have been threats from large bodies of men whom the authorities dare not antagonize. — Remember all this and read Mr. Andrews' statement.

"As representing the Department of Justice, in order that no citizen should have any cause to complain that the Government was disposed to deny the following persons, namely, R.B. Russell, W. Ivens, John Queen, A.A. Heaps, George Armstrong and R.E. Bray **a fair trial by jury if they so desire**, the Government is very gracious. — (We extend our heartfelt gratitude for their unparalleled generosity to British citizens.) I have decided to postpone any proceedings for their deportation until the charges against them have been heard."

"I have decided" (and who is Mr. Andrews that he should hold in his hand the right to decide whether a British-born citizen should have a fair trial by jury or whether he should be summarily deported) — what right have any group of men to postpone proceedings or proceed to deport men **"until the charges against them have been heard?"**

This article may be interpreted as tending to discredit authority. It is intended to discredit any individual or group that would deprive us of the fundamental rights of Canadian citizens and British subjects.

But the conditions under which the strike leaders are released are interesting and very significant. The first condition, which does not appear in Mr. Andrews' statement, but which was definitely stipulated in the negotiations with the Committee, was that there should be no "victory parade" on the part of the strikers. Of course the ostensible reason is the danger of the enthusiastic crowd becoming excited and breaking bounds. But at the same time the authorities, doubtless, have no desire to have the victory of the strikers heralded to the world. They know the psychological value of dramatic action. They know more of the psychological effects of certain actions than they did two days ago. They are by no means disposed to admit how complete the back down of the authorities has been.

But after all, they have been able to snatch victory from defeat. The strike leaders are released on bail on the express understanding that they will take no further part in the strike. — That, after all, appears to have been the purpose behind the arrest. Dangerous revolutionaries would not be allowed at large on $2,000 bail. The farce is evident to all. The employer-capitalist group have used the processes of the Law and created unheard of extra-legal machinery to fight the workers now on strike. By a sudden and unscrupulous coup the leaders have been removed from the field.

"Constituted authority," indeed! The workers will never forget its meaning.

Fortunately other men have stepped into the vacant places and the fight goes on with greater determination.

Whatever the immediate issue the workers have learned the measure of their opponents.

THE "SILENT PARADE" AND "BLOODY SATURDAY"

On Friday evening of June 20th, the returned soldiers' Committee (who had elected another Chairman after the arrest of R.E. Bray, and were prepared to "Carry on") called a meeting in the Market Square at which many strongly worded resolutions were passed at which it was decided to call a "Silent Parade" of returned men for the following day, to march to the Royal Alexandra Hotel, and demand of Senator Robertson an account of his activities during the strike.

It was on account of the speeches they made at this meeting, at which were present some five or six thousand people, that Comrades Martin, Grant, and Farnell were afterwards arrested on charges of "Uttering seditious words."

The Grand Jury later brought in "No Bill" against Martin and Grant, but a "True Bill" against Farnell.

The following account of the Parade and what happened on Saturday, June 21st, one of the blackest chapters in Canadian history, is taken from the "Strike Bulletin," of June 23rd, 1919:

BLOODY SATURDAY

R.N.W.M.P. Make Gory Debut — Peaceful Citizens Shot Without Warning — City Under Military Control — Returned Men Incensed — Strikers More Determined.

One is dead and a number injured, probably thirty or more, as a result of the forcible prevention of the "silent parade" which had been planned by returned men to start at 2.30 o'clock last Saturday afternoon. Apparently the bloody business was carefully planned, for Mayor Gray issued a proclamation in the morning stating that "Any women taking part in a parade do so at their own risk." Nevertheless a vast crowd of men, women and children assembled to witness the "silent parade."

The Soldiers' Committee, which had been interviewing Senator Robertson, had not returned to their comrades when the latter commenced to line up on Main Street, near the city hall.

No attempt was made to use the special city police to prevent the parade. On a previous occasion a dozen of the old regular city police had persuaded the returned men to abandon a parade which had commenced to move.

On Saturday, about 2.30 p.m., just the time when the parade was scheduled to start, some 50 mounted men swinging baseball bats rode down Main Street. Half were red-coated R.N.W.M.P., the others wore khaki. They quickened pace as they passed the Union Bank. The crowd opened, let them through and closed in behind them. They turned and charged through the crowd again, greeted by hisses, boos, and some stones. There were two riderless horses with the squad when it emerged and galloped up Main Street. The men in khaki disappeared at this juncture, but the red-coats reined their horses and reformed opposite the old post office.

Shooting to Kill

Then, with revolvers drawn, they galloped down Main Street, turned, and charged right into the crowd on William Avenue, firing as they charged. One man, standing on the sidewalk, thought the mounties were firing blank cartridges until a spectator standing beside him dropped with a bullet through his breast. Another standing near-by was shot through the head. We have no exact information about the total number of casualties, but there were not less than thirty. The crowd dispersed as quickly as possible when the shooting began.

Some Citizens Applaud Man-Killers

When the mounties rode back to the corner of Portage Avenue and Main Street, after the fray, at least two of them were twirling their reeking tubes high in the air in Orthodox Deadwood Dick style.

Text continues on page 205.

— Foote Collection, Manitoba Archives
June 21, about 1:45 p.m. A crowd gathers on Main Street to watch
the "silent parade" called by pro-strike returned soldiers in defiance
of Mayor Gray's ban on parades. A noisy meeting had been held at
city hall (just out of the frame, top and right) the night before. The
mayor feared the violence that might erupt if specials and this parade
fought, since there were soldiers on both sides. The demonstrators
declared that they would hold the parade "at whatever cost." It was
exactly the potential catastrophe the Strike Committee had been trying
to avoid since May 22.

— Foote Collection, Manitoba Archives
June 21, about 1:45 p.m. The same scene, showing the Union Bank
building from which other photographs of these events were taken.
No attempt was made to use specials to prevent the silent parade,
although a dozen regular police had on a previous occasion been sufficient to halt a parade already underway. Note women and children
in the crowd. Specials had been held in readiness at the nearby Rupert
Street police station since 10 a.m.

— Foote Collection, Manitoba Archives

June 21, about 2:30 p.m. Fifty-four Mounties under Inspectors Proby and Mead ride north on Main Street, near the Citizens' Committee headquarters. Note that men towards the rear are still wearing army uniforms. Technically, they had been transferred from the military police to the RNWMP so that Arthur Meighen could later deny that he had allowed troops to be used against civilians. The use of "yellow-hat" Mounties in khaki was especially galling to veterans. Many returned men had a cordial loathing for military police. Some forty-five minutes before this photograph was taken, Mayor Gray had rushed to Osborne Barracks and, in the presence of General Ketchen and the attorney-general of Manitoba, formally requested Commissioner Perry of the RNWMP to come to "the aid of the civil power."

— Foote Collection, Manitoba Archives
The RNWMP reach Portage Avenue on their way north on Main Street. Note the streetcar. Running the streetcars was a provocation to the strikers since the street railwaymen were on strike. The streetcars were manned by Citizens' Committee volunteers and armed militia, drawn from middle-class office workers of large Winnipeg companies.

— Manitoba Archives

June 21, between 1:45 and 2:45 p.m. An eyewitness recalls: "A streetcar with two men came from the North End. It was said by some they were officers. They got as far as the city hall, where the crowd was gathering, and one fellow took a flying leap and pulled the trolley off." Shortly after 2:30 p.m., leaving some trucks with machine-gun squads at Portage and Main, the fifty-four Mounties rode north to clear the crowd. They broke into a trot as they passed the Union Bank (shown here, top right), but were slowed to a walk in the crowd around the streetcar, and beat their way through with baseball bats. About this time, Mayor Gray read the Riot Act. His voice was "drowned in bedlam." The Mounties rode on another six blocks up Main Street.

— Manitoba Archives

This picture probably shows the crowd closing in again as the Mounties complete their first charge up Main Street.

— Foote Collection, Manitoba Archives
"A bunch of men got together, most of them teenaged boys, and heaved," recalls an eyewitness to this attempt to topple the streetcar on its side. The streetcar's fender was ripped off about this time.

— CBC Winnipeg, Public Archives

Mounties returning south along Main Street — probably from the first charge. When they got near the crowd at City Hall, there was "a rain of stones and bricks." Some of the boys stood "about one hundred feet" away; older men would "go up about six feet away from a policeman and let him have it in the face," reports an eyewitness. "When this happened, almost every man in khaki lost control of his horse."

— Foote Collection, Manitoba Archives

The second charge of the RNWMP, galloping north on Main. This time, all the men in khaki were left out. Note the clubs in their hands. The crowd was throwing stones taken from a construction site (out of frame to right). A number of Mounties were hit; two fell from their horses and were dragged to safety — one in city hall, the other into a funeral parlour on the left where Sir Samuel Steele, one of the original "redcoats" of the ride West in 1876, lay in state.

— Manitoba Archives

The third charge. This time the Mounties returned with clubs in the left hand and .45 revolvers drawn. Behind them were assembling "fellows in civvies, three deep, with wagon spokes," and the militia "with rifles and fixed bayonets." As the Mounties turned left on to William Street, as shown here, charging into the crowd, they fired a volley. Later they were to claim that this was aimed "over the heads" of the crowd. However, at least one onlooker, an old man standing by the Union Bank, was hit. As the crowd broke and ran, the Mounties fired at the legs of the "rioters." Note the broken streetcar fender lying on Main Street, upper right.

— Manitoba Archives

The Mounties are now behind the City Hall, and one man is lying on the sidewalk, apparently shot. Another is kneeling at the curb. As the text notes, many people in the crowd thought the RNWMP were firing blanks until they saw men falling down shot. Many people are running away, and a few are coming to help the stricken men.

The Mounties slowed to a walk in the market behind city hall, and prepared to charge the crowd which had been throwing stones around the streetcar.

— Manitoba Archives

The return of the third charge. The Mounties had charged the crowd around the streetcar. Reports one eyewitness: "They were running out of stones ... and another fellow — he was a real fanatic — ran up to pick up half a brick — it was only fifteen feet in front of a Mountie. He had just straightened up when — he got it." He was probably Mike Sokolowiski, "who stood in front of the Manitoba Hotel ... killed instantly by a shot in the heart."

Note that in this photo one man is lying on the curb, and the Mounties are all turned around looking at him.

Onlookers reported that, as the Mounties rode south on Main after this third charge, some were "twirling their reeking tubes high in the air in orthodox Deadwood Dick style."

— Foote Collection, Manitoba Archives
As special constables armed with clubs marched out to clear the streets, some members of the crowd set the streetcar on fire. "A fellow went in the front door — he was wearing what we called blue serge [a working man's Sunday best]. He took out a knife and slashed the seats and put a match to it."

Hand-to-hand battles between specials and some of the crowd raged in back alleys.

— Manitoba Archives

June 21, about 3:45 p.m. Special constables are thrown across the street to prevent the crowds from returning, and to guard the volunteer firemen trying to put out the fire in the streetcar. One former special recalls, ''There were several hundred university students who had been recruited as night watchmen ... and we got drawn into this. The specials were kept in the Rupert Street police station until after the Mounted Police had formed up. The Mounties were well ahead of us, and had already shot. We could see them coming back, about two or three blocks towards Portage and Main from us ... We came out, and marched from our building clear across Main Street to the City Hall.''

— Foote Collection, Manitoba Archives
Mounties at ease, just after the charges, on Main near Portage. The
government's violence in breaking the strike has never been forgotten
or forgiven. James Winning called it "another Peterloo," referring
to the Manchester massacre of Chartists in 1819. Fred Dixon, editing
the *Western Labor News* after Ivens's arrest, called it "Kaiserism in
Canada" and "Bloody Saturday."

— Foote Collection, Manitoba Archives
June 21, about 3:45 p.m. Specials across Main Street at Market Street, just north of the city hall. They are carrying their clubs, and their white armbands read "CITY S.P." Note the metal frame on the sidewalk in the top right-hand corner, perhaps the streetcar fender which had earlier been lying on the street.

— United Church Archives

After the RNWMP charge, Canadian Army Service Corps trucks carrying Lewis machine guns were brought out on the streets. The Lewis guns were from the Flying Corps. They were sent to Winnipeg during the early part of the strike, as Heenan notes in his 1926 speech, in cases marked "regimental baggage." This photo was taken in the Market Square area behind the city hall.

— Foote Collection, Manitoba Archives
Mounties with rifles and militia, after the charges, on Main Street just south of the city hall. Top right, the Union Bank building which stands across William Street from the city hall. On the left, Ashdown's hardware store which supplied "thousands" of wagon spokes for clubs for the specials. Technically, these police and troops were acting under and "in aid of" the civil power.

— Public Archives

Mounties on the streets, clubs in hand.

— Manitoba Archives

The scene from the corner of Portage and Main, looking north towards the city hall. This is long after everything is over, and the streets are completely empty of people. According to the Winnipeg *Tribune,* Mayor Gray rode in an open car at the head of a line of vehicles which drove through the city after the events of the early afternoon ''to show civil law was still in force.''

''Crowds,'' reported the anti-strike *Tribune,* ''cheered.''

Some individuals, apparently opposed to the strike, applauded the man-killers as they rode by.

Special Police Appear

Lines of special police, swinging their big clubs, were then thrown across Main Street, and the intersecting thoroughfares. Dismounted red-coats lined up across Portage Avenue and Main Street declaring the city under military control. Khaki-clad men with rifles were stationed on the street corners.

Public Meetings Abandoned

There were no open-air meetings on Saturday night, but the Central Strike Committee met as usual and resolved to "carry on" with redoubled vigor. If the city remains under military control meetings will likely be held outside the city limits.

Soldier Strikers Incensed

Indignation at the action of the authorities was forcibly expressed by returned men. They feel that the prevention of the parade was an infringement of the human rights they have fought to defend, and they are especially incensed by the murderous assault of the mounties upon an unarmed crowd. One man, recently returned, said: "They treated us worse than we ever treated Fritzy."

The returned men assumed full responsibility for the "silent parade" proposition, making a special request that the strikers should not join them. "This is our affair," they declared. Had they intended violence they would hardly have invited their wives to join in the parade.

THE WINNIPEG "YELLOWGRAM" AND CONSTITUTED AUTHORITY

The following article is taken from the Winnipeg "Telegram" of June 20th, and provides somewhat startling confirmation of the strikers' contention, that the Citizens' Committee of 1000 had usurped authority and arrogated to themselves the function of Government:

RED, BLUE AND ALL YELLOW

The Federal Government's badge is blue. The badge of the Bolshevists is red. The Government is supposed to be a true blue Government. Those revolutionaries who were arrested and sent to Stony Mountain the other morning boast of being "Reds."

Sandpaper both of these worthy bodies, and their true color is revealed — a brilliant yellow!

After making a theatrical display — which is only revealed as theatrical because of the farcical aftermath — after arresting the ringleaders in the attempted rebellion and spiriting them away to the penitentiary, the Government has entered into negotiations with the very men that it accused of some of the most serious crimes of which anyone could be guilty — negotiations by which six of them are given their liberty on paltry bail, and on their personal undertaking not TO INDULGE IN ANY FURTHER UNLAWFUL CONDUCT, and not even to exercise their undoubted right to resume participation, directly or indirectly, in the general strike!

This is such a pitiable farce, such a miserable fiasco, that one is in doubt whether to curse or to laugh at it.

There is no doubt whatever how those citizens that have been working like slaves as private soldiers in barracks in this almost insufferable weather, those that are doing the work of special policemen in a broiling sun, those who spend their days and nights in a fire hall, and those who render other public services that they should not be expected to do in a well-ordered country feel about this betrayal of their interests.

They are indignant beyond the powers of expression — and their indignation is quite justified.

There never has been finer service rendered in any community, that has been so spontaneously and generously given by the citizens of all classes who rallied to the defense of the State, of our institutions and of our very lives when the call was made for their services.

For five DREARY weeks they have endured hardship, annoyance, monetary loss and loss of the right to associate with their families, that they might render public service for which they could never adequately be compensated.

They did all this in the firm conviction that it was necessary for them to do so in order to maintain British Government here and to sustain in a great trial constituted authority. They did all this, also, in the conviction that constituted authority was worthy of their sacrifices, would not be ungrateful, but would stand behind them in the front line and do its duty by them to the end.

The citizens of Winnipeg have not failed, and they will not fail. The Federal Government has failed abjectly — and failed because of no lack of understanding of the trickery of political expediency.

There is a tendency today for every man to turn from his self-appointed task in disgust. He feels that he has been betrayed by the politicians, and he asks himself why he should be true to men who are untrue to him.

This is a natural attitude — but it is an attitude that ought to be avoided.

Because others fail, furnishes no adequate reason why you should fail. Because a Government, for selfish reasons, desires to hasten the end of this strike by a deal rather than by a decision, furnishes no adequate reason why private individuals, who have made enormous sacrifices, should permit their good work of five long weeks to go for nought in a quite natural passion of disgust.

It is nothing common or ordinary that the organizations of patriotic citizens have accomplished up-to-date. Therefore, to be true to their record, they should continue to stand steadfast and refuse now to adopt a common, ordinary, or expected course.

They, not the authorities, have won this strike. Let them, therefore, resolve that they, and not the authorities, shall dictate the terms of peace.

Let them stick to their posts; let every one of them who have any influence with an employer of labor bring every pressure to bear to compel those unlawfully on strike to return to their work without obtaining any advantage from their unlawful adventure.

This can readily be accomplished if the Citizens' Committee, the volunteer soldiers, the volunteer firemen and other volunteers engaged in public service will take a new resolution from this betrayal, and adopt a course that will convince the authorities that even "good politics" will make it necessary in this case to get back into line with sound public opinion by the shortest route available — even though that short route should involve the turning of another handspring, at which the authorities of today have developed an expertness that is as inimitable as it is undignified.

Let our motto be "Carry On!"

J. S. WOODSWORTH ARRESTED

After the arrest of Rev. Wm. Ivens, editor of the Western Labor News, and the "Strike Bulletin," J. S. Woodsworth stepped into the breach and filled the position to such good effect that he called down upon his head the wrath of the powers that rule, with the result that the following letter was sent to the Winnipeg Printing and Engraving Co.:

"Winnipeg, June 23rd, 1919.
"Winnipeg Printing and Engraving Co., Ltd.
"Gentlemen:
"Certain numbers of the Winnipeg Western Labor News Special Strike edition have contained objectionable matter in that it is seditious, inflammatory and inciting to riot, and this publication must be discontinued.

"No more issues of this publication must be printed or circulated.
"Yours truly,
"(Signed)   ALFRED J. ANDREWS,
"Agent, Department of Justice."

Government by professional politicians, controlled by "big interests" was bad enough; Government by Order-in-Council was worse, but this was Government by means of dictatorship.

Passing down Main Street in company with F. J. Dixon, M.L.A., for Centre Winnipeg, Mr. Woodsworth was accosted by a man who informed him that he had a warrant for his arrest. Surprised and rightly indignant, he offered no demur, but left Mr. Dixon to continue on his errand and inform the Strike Committee of what had occurred.

He was taken to the police court, and thrown into a cell like an ordinary criminal, and taken from there to the Provincial gaol, where he was detained from Monday to Friday and refused bail.

Imagine, reader, if you can, the infamy of such proceeding and the cruel suffering and anxiety imposed upon his wife and children away on the Pacific Coast.

The following portion of the indictment will show two of the articles which are charged against him, the third being one published in the "Strike Bulletin," of June 23rd, entitled: "Is there a way out."

The jurors aforesaid, do further present:

4.   That J. S. Woodsworth, on or about the month of June, in the year of our Lord one thousand nine hundred and nineteen, at the City of Winnipeg, in the Province of Manitoba, unlawfully and seditiously published seditious libels in the words and figures following:

"Woe unto them that decree unrighteous decrees, and that write grievousness which they have prescribed; to turn aside the needy from judgment, and to take away the right from the poor of my people that widows may be their prey and that they may rob the fatherless.

"Isaiah."

"And they shall build houses and inhabit them, and they shall plant vineyards and eat the fruit of them. They shall not build and another inhabit, they shall not plant and another eat; for as the days of a tree are the days of my people, and mine elect shall long enjoy the work of their hands.

"Isaiah, II."

The jurors aforesaid do further present:

6.   That J. S. Woodsworth, in or about the month of June, in the year of our Lord one thousand nine hundred and nineteen, at

the City of Winnipeg in the Province of Manitoba, unlawfully and seditiously published seditious libels in the words and figures following:

"THE BRITISH WAY"

"Apparently a good many of our local business men have the idea that after the strike things will go on again as usual. The war was to them merely an interruption in the smooth current of events — an opportunity for piling up greater profits. It is true that a few months ago we heard considerable talk about 'Reconstruction,' but the matter was not taken very seriously. In fact reconstruction for the Canadian business men was conceived as construction on a larger scale along the old lines.

"The general strike came somewhat as a shock, just as the business man thought things were beginning to get back to 'normal' — the blankety-blank labor people upset everything, housing schemes and all. To say that the business man was angry is putting it mildly. He didn't see that the strike was an inevitable outcome of the industrial and financial conditions brought on by the war. Then some one whispered the dread word "Bolsheviki" and he became positively hysterical. The strike was sort of a carefully concocted conspiracy to overthrow constitutional Government in Canada. Five dangerous 'Reds' were responsible for the whole miserable business — off with their heads and we will have peace and prosperity again.

"Now, instead of thinking so much about the dreadful things that are happening in Russia, suppose we consider the remarkable changes that are likely to take place in Great Britain. Within the last few days several men, prominent in civic affairs and in the Citizens' Committee, have confessed that they know nothing of the platform of the British Labor Party. Yet this party is now in opposition in the British House of Commons, and it is generally conceded will before long become the Government of Great Britain. Their policy is then a matter of practical politics and may, in the not distant future, be carried into operation. Either this, say the students of social movements, or the deluge.

"The draft report on reconstruction has already appeared in full in the "Western Labor News," so we touch only on the outstanding points.

" 'The view of the Labor Party is that what has to be reconstructed after the war is not this or that Government Department or this or that piece of machinery, but, so far as Britain is concerned, society itself.'

" 'Revolutionary! Certainly. But the exponents of this view are not persecuted as British and Scotch Anarchists. A goodly number of them have been elected to Parliament . . .'

" 'The individual system of capitalism, based on the private owner-ship and competitive administration of land and capital, with its reckless "profiteering" and wage slavery; with its glorification of the unhampered struggle for the means of life, and its hypocritical pretense of the survival of the fittest, with the monstrous inequality of circumstances which it produces and the degradation and brutaliza-tion both moral and spiritual, resulting therefrom, may, we hope, indeed have received a deathblow.'

"Sounds like a Socialist soap-box orator, eh? 'And does that really mean the doing away with private ownership of land and capital?' Precisely. 'Why, that is Bolshevism.' Oh, no, it's only the policy of the party in opposition in the British House of Commons.

" 'We must insure that what is presently to be built up is a new social order, based not on fighting but of fraternity — not on the competitive struggle for the means of bare life, but on a deliberately planned co-operation in production and distribution for the benefit of all who participate by hand or by brain — not on the utmost possible inequality of riches, but on a systematic approach toward a healthy equality of material circumstances for every person born into the world, not on an enforced dominion over subject nations, subject races, subject colonies, subject classes, or a subject sex; but, in industry as well as in government on that equal freedom, that general consciousness of consequences and that widest possible participation in power, both economic and political, which is charac-teristic of democracy.

" 'Anarchist, Internationalist, Pacifist, and Pro-German, off with him to the penitentiary. We would subvert constituted authority! In England, he is called into the Councils of Government.'

"In the pamphlet which explains the draft programme, a solemn warning is given: 'Whether we like it or fear it, we have to recognize that in the course of the last three and a half years people have become habituated to thought of violence. They have seen force employed on an unprecedented scale as an instrument of policy . . . We may be warned by a perception of these facts, that if barricades are indeed likely to be erected in our streets, they will be manned by men who have learned how to fight and not by ill-disciplined mobs, unversed in the use of modern weapons, likely to be easily overcome by trained troops.'

"This is not incendiary writing. It comes from the Right Honourable Arthur Henderson, who sees some of the dangers ahead if the legiti-mate aims of labor are fought.

"But what is this new Social Order, and how is it to be brought in? The Labor Party insists, first, on a minimum standard of living.

Each family must have sufficient to supply for a decent living —
good food, clothing and shelter, opportunities for education, recreation and culture, insurance against accidents, sickness, unemployment, old age. The State assumes responsibility for finding men
work and providing for all their needs.

"This is not continental Socialism, it is not an Utopian dream.
Today England is paying millions of pounds in unemployment
benefits. In the second place the Labor Party stands for a democratic
control of industry; this means the progressive elimination from the
control of industry of the private capitalist, individual or private
stock; it means a genuinely scientific reorganization of the nation's
industry, no longer deflected by individual profiteering on the basis
of the common ownership of the means of production (Rank
Socialism); it means the immediate nationalization of railways, mines,
and electric power. It means that the worker has a voice and a share
in the industry in which he is engaged.

"But how is all this to be financed? How provide for the means
of all? How buy out railways and factories? The Britisher does not
like the word 'confiscation,' so he has worked out a little scheme
to accomplish his end in another way. He is not hot-headed like
the Russian, he goes more slowly, but he is just as thorough.

"He proposes that all revenues should be raised from two sources:
(a) an income tax, (b) an inheritance tax.

"The capitalist says he will not engage in industry without the
incentive of profit. 'Very well,' says the Britisher, 'Go to it. Make
all the money you like, but remember the State will take most of
it back in taxes.' The Labor Party proposes to exempt from taxation
all income above that necessary to maintain a good standard of living.
After that there will be a steeply graded tax rising from a penny
in the pound on the smallest assessable income up to sixteen or
even nineteen shillings in the pound on the highest income of the
millionaire ...

"With regard to inheritance there will need to be a complete reversal
in the point of view. Today we go on the assumption that a man
has a right to say who will inherit his property. The State claiming
merely certain inheritance taxes. The Labor Party goes on the idea
that naked a man came into the world, naked he will go out again.
At a man's death, all over what is necessary for the needs of his
immediate family will revert to the State. Thus in the course of
a generation all the great estates will revert to the common people
of England from whom they were filched by the 'enclosing' of the
'common lands.'

"This is the British way, and, remember, it is absolutely constitutional!

"The surplus which will accrue from these national enterprises and large revenues will be used for the common good. Such is the programme of the British Labor Party, regarded by radicals as rather temporising and altogether too slow.

"Do our Canadian business men suppose that with revolution going on all over Europe and with its programme offered in England as a substitute for sudden and perhaps violent revolution that we in Canada are going to be permitted to go with undisturbed step along the accustomed way?

"No! We, too, must face the new situation. Whether the radical changes that are inevitable may be brought about peaceably largely depends on the good sense of the Canadian business man who now largely controls both the industry and Government of this country.

"We confess the prospects are not over bright."

DIXON FILLS VACANT POST

The strikers' paper is dead — long live the strikers' paper. If the authorities thought they could break the lines of communication by suppressing the "Strike Bulletin," they had a rude awakening.

After the arrest of Woodsworth a worthy successor was found in F.J. Dixon, and the following morning there appeared the "Western Star," which gave a detailed account of the raid on the "Strike Bulletin" and the arrest of Woodsworth, and bore in large type the motto: "ON TO VICTORY" and an article which is given below:

WITHOUT PREJUDICE

When the soldier-strikers offered to give their services to the city in order to preserve law and order, Mayor Gray told them that if they thought they could act without prejudice they might turn their names in to the organizer of the special police force. They offered their services, but they were not accepted. Now A.J. Andrews, one time spokesman for the Committee of 1000 before the City Council, has been appointed agent for the Department of Justice. Mr. Andrews, of course, can act without prejudice. One instance of his fairness and impartiality is shown by the fact that one sheet, that purports to be a newspaper, can counsel the wiping out of half the population of Winnipeg in order that the will of the class it represents may prevail and it is not suppressed. On the other hand, the "Labor News," which has always counselled the strikers to "Do Nothing," to be lawful and orderly and all that, has been suppressed. A man who can mete out such impartial justice must be without prejudice. Mr. Andrews is to be congratulated upon the way in which Mr. Andrews, representative of the Citizens' Committee, is subjugated by Mr. Andrews, agent for the Department of Justice. Greater is he who conquereth himself than he who conquereth a city.

It also conveyed to his striking comrades, the inspiring message of "Bobby" Russell's aged mother in Glasgow, who, when she heard her boy was arrested sent a cablegram of just two words: "Have courage."

If she had sent a thousand words, they could have said no more. "Have courage."

The "Western Star" had but a short existence, but was followed by the "Enlightener," still under the editorship of Dixon, for whom a warrant had been issued. In the enforced absence of Ivens and Woodsworth, it was imperative that Dixon keep out of the clutches of the law until such time as the "Western Labor News" could resume publication, and Ivens receive permission to proceed with his duties as editor, and for three days, from the seclusion of his hiding place, Dixon kept the iron hot, until Friday evening about 7 o'clock, when Ivens returned to his post, the genial "Fred" walked down to the police station and said to the sergeant in charge: "I believe you have a warrant for my arrest," to which the sergeant replied in the affirmative and "Fred" was put in the cell, where he remained for about two hours, being then removed to the Provincial gaol, where he was detained for a further twenty-one hours before being granted bail.

To most readers Fred. J. Dixon will need no introduction, but there may be some readers of this history in the far away corner of the world who do not know and for their benefit, the following brief account of his activities is given:

In the Provincial election of 1915 he had the largest majority of any candidate in Manitoba, and took his seat in the Legislature as member for Centre Winnipeg. He is one of, if not the best known Single-Taxer in Canada, and few progressive organizations have not heard him. A fluent speaker, he is never dry, even when talking on a dry subject, but can chase away the "blues" with a timely joke.

A man of strong convictions, and better still, with courage to uphold them. He was the champion of "No conscription of man power without the conscription of wealth," and on this account was black-balled by his erstwhile friends and associates in the Legislature, chased by an angry mob of returned soldiers — when he spoke in the Legislature, the other members became engrossed either in animated conversation with each other or with the daily papers, even the Premier on one occasion deliberately turning his back upon him whilst he (Dixon) was advocating the retention of the natural resources of the Province for the benefit of all the people, instead of distributing them to the friends of the Government.

The kept press had bitterly assailed him, but he was true to his convictions and in contrast to the mealy-mouthed politicians, when the testing time came, he was the ONLY ONE in the Provincial House to stand squarely behind the strikers in their demands, and whereas, in January angry mobs had sought his life, in May and June he was in great demand as a speaker, both with soldiers and civilians, and when his name was mentioned in the Legislature at the time the returned soldiers' delegation was waiting upon the premier, some of the men who had sought his life six months previously, led such cheering as has never been heard in that building before.

DIXON'S INDICTMENT

The jurors for our Lord the King present:

That F.J. Dixon, in or about the month of June, in the year of our Lord one thousand nine hundred and nineteen, at the City of Winnipeg, in the Province of Manitoba, unlawfully and seditiously published seditious libels in the words and figures following:

"KAISERISM IN CANADA"

"What shall the sacrifice profit Canada if she who has helped to destroy Kaiserism in Germany shall allow Kaiserism to be established at home?

"Whoever ordered the shooting last Saturday is a Kaiser of the deepest dye.

"The responsibility must be placed and the criminal brought before the bar of justice.

"There may be those who think that the blood of innocent men upon our streets is preferable to a 'silent parade.' There may be those who think their dignity must be upheld at any cost. But we fail to see the slightest justification for the murderous assault which was committed. Whoever ordered it acted in the spirit of Kaiser Wilhelm when he said: 'Recruits! Before the altar and the servant of God you have given me the oath of allegiance. You are too young to know the full meaning of what you have said, but your first care must be to obey implicitly all orders and directions. You have sworn fidelity to me, you are the children of my guard, you are my soldiers, you have surrendered yourselves to me, body and soul. Only one enemy can exist for you — my enemy. With the present Socialist machinations, it may happen that I shall order you to shoot your own relations, your brothers, or even your parents — which, God forbid — and then you are bound in duty implicitly to obey my orders.'

"The events of last week show to what lengths the opponents of labor will go in their efforts to fasten despotism on this city and this country. The midnight arrest of men whose only crime seems to be that of 'lese majeste' against the profiteers, and the shooting of innocent and defenceless citizens mark the depths of desperation to which the Kaiser-like crowd at the Industrial Bureau are prepared to go in order to turn their defeat into a temporary victory.

"But they must not be allowed even temporary satisfaction. Organized labor must continue the magnificent fight of the last five weeks until its just and moderate demands are granted. It were better that the whole 35,000 strikers languished in jail; better, even, that we all rested beside the men who were slain on Saturday, than that the forces of Kaiserism shall prevail.

"There have always been those who imagined that 'a whiff of grape shot' would stop the cry of the people for justice. There are those in Winnipeg who think the shooting on Saturday taught labor a lesson. The parade was attempted and the blood of innocent men spilled 'without permission of the Strike Committee.' Labor already knew that two dozen men on horseback, shooting to kill, could disperse a crowd of several thousand unarmed men and women.

"The Committee of 1000 has, however, many lessons to learn — among other things the members of that Committee must be taught that ideas are more powerful than bullets. The blood of the martyrs is the seed of the church. We shall 'carry on,' in spite of hell, till the victory is won.

PRITCHARD OUT ON BAIL

On Friday afternoon, after an imprisonment of six days, Pritchard was released on bail from the pen, and the following day Dixon and Woodsworth were each released.

Pritchard at once proceeded to his home in Vancouver until the preliminary hearing should take place.

SYMPATHETIC STRIKE CALLED OFF

"The Enlightener," of June 25th, bore in large type on its front page the words: "Sympathetic Strike Called Off" for Thursday, June 26th, at 11 a.m., to the great surprise of a large body of strikers, who, for the most part were very angry and much opposed to the action of the Strike Committee in calling off the strike until the different unions had had a chance to vote on the question. The Labor Temple was beseiged with inquiries as to the reason for this sudden action of the Strike Committee, and for over a week thousands of strikers refused to give in.

The reasons given for their action by the Strike Committee were to the effect that as the funds had run out, owing to the meetings being banned, thus closing them as a source of revenue for the relief fund, many workers were finding it impossible to stay out any longer, as their families were suffering and near to starvation. Then the publication of what purported to be the acceptance of the Metal Trades Employers of collective bargaining, had had the desired results and provided an excuse for some of the waverers to go back to work, and it was feared that there was a possibility of a stampede unless the strike was officially called off. This and the undertaking of the Provincial Government to appoint a Commission to go into the causes of the strike and effect the reinstatement of all strikers, had much influence in leading the Strike Committee to its final decision. And so ended the Winnipeg general strike of 1919, when all the forces of capital, Church, and State combined to block the path of progress.

The end was acclaimed as a glorious victory for "Law and Order" and "Constituted Authority," and the kept press, the Citizens' Committee of 1000, and every organization of boodlers, shameless profiteers and professional politicians joined in the chorus and chanted the requiem, the while the blood of innocent, law-abiding men, the tears of the widows and the wailing of orphaned children cried out in judgment against them.

Poor, blind fools, they thought to match their puny strength against the forces of progress — they are either ignorant of all the lessons of history, or else, like the ostrich, they were satisfied to hide their heads in the sand and ignore the danger they could not see.

But such a "victory" for reaction, history has proved, is always in reality a victory for progress, and this was no exception.

It demonstrated the nature of the class struggle, the ruthlessness and brutality of imperialist capital, the humbug of "Christianity," the real purpose of military and semi-military bodies. It proved the futility of Craft Unionism and the need for an industrial organization to meet the changes brought about by machine production. It started men and women to think and to study, to realize the power they possessed if they could use it unitedly and to what extent it was used is proven by the election of three radicals out of seven candidates to the City Council, whilst the Labor Candidate for Mayor was only defeated by "repeater" votes and vacant lots. The coming Provincial and Federal elections will see a Labor candidate in every constituency where Labor predominates over the farmers, and vice-versa, a farmer candidate, backed by Labor in agricultural constituencies.

There are many who are enjoying better wages and working conditions directly resulting from the strike and there are many who are black-listed not only in Winnipeg, but throughout the Dominion.

This is little to be wondered at, in view of the campaign through the press, of which we submit a sample, taken from the Winnipeg "Telegram," of June 28th, 1919:

LET US REASON TOGETHER

Now that the strike is officially over, let us make all reasonable haste to see that it becomes actually over at the earliest possible moment.

There ought to be no spirit of exultation manifest or felt on the part of those who were instrumental in defeating the attacks made upon our democracy and our British institutions by some thousands of our citizens who were misled by a handful of revolutionaries and anarchists.

The loyal citizens of Winnipeg have won a hard-fought fight. They naturally feel gratified with their victory — but the manly victor never kicks the body of his fallen foe, nor cheers his own triumph.

The spirit of hate and the harboring of a desire for revenge are foreign to a really manly spirit. Hatred and revenge can only flourish in a withered soul, on which they feed until the soul itself vanishes.

The employers of Winnipeg have suffered great loss. They have endured much undeserved annoyance and inconvenience. They have been unreasonably provoked to the point that would justify extreme exasperation. But they must remember that they are big men, who ought to look at things in a big way, and ought to banish from their hearts any sentiments that might be cherished by meaner spirits.

One thing that should be borne in mind on all occasions is that probably ninety per cent of those who were on strike went on strike unwillingly, or at least not for the purpose of promoting any revolutionary movement. They were misled, deceived and stampeded by windy oratory. They were also, in thousands of cases, cruelly intimidated into adopting a course of action detrimental to their interests and abhorrent to their sentiments.

Let this idea be firmly established in the mind of every employer, and he will find himself possessing a mental attitude that will not only stimulate his self-respect as a man of generosity and justice, but will also lead him to a course of action that will be profitable to him and highly beneficial to the community.

It has come to the attention of The Telegram that some employers have refused to employ any person who has been on strike without a grievance. This might be a natural position for one to adopt in a moment of extreme irritation. But it is not the position that big men will adopt after calm reflection.

The business of the city must be re-established. It must proceed. We have endured five years of adversity. We must now take steps that promise to ensure us five years of prosperity.

We cannot be prosperous, we cannot carry on, if thousands of our citizens, merely because they have been fantastically deluded by designing tricksters, should be kept permanently out of employment, rendered permanently useless to the community, become permanently unproductive and a charge upon charity.

Every one must work if we are to succeed. Therefore, every one must banish from his mind every idea of punishing the deluded because they were the victims of betrayers of their own class.

Heaven knows these poor people, irritating as their conduct was, have been punished enough to teach them a lesson that will make further punishment unnecessary. The unpardonable sin is a hideous doctrine, impossible to obtain the endorsement of a normal man with a charitable spirit. Let us recognize this fact, and let us treat those misguided strikers as if they were bad boys and girls returning repentant to the discipline of our laws and institutions.

This charity that The Telegram earnestly advocates ought not to be applied to those who deliberately and knowingly precipitated our catastrophe. They deserve deeper punishment than they have brought down upon themselves — a deeper punishment, even, than they are likely to suffer.

They should be permanently black-listed. They should be made to wander abroad.

It should be a standing rule of all employers that no agitator, known as such, should find work in this city. This will be simple justice. It would also be patriotic — for it would protect us against the machinations of conspirators in the future.

But this just punishment ought not to be applied to the dupes of these men and women who have already suffered as victims and who are doomed, even under the most charitable attitude that the public can adopt towards them, to suffer still further consequences of their folly during many months to come.

"BRITISH JUSTICE" AND "FAIR PLAY" AND THE "ALIEN"

After several remands, Ivens, Russell, Heaps, Queen, Bray, and Armstrong appeared before Magistrate Sir H. J. McDonald, in the police court, July 3rd. They had given notice to the crown agent, A. J. Andrews, that on that date owing to the campaign carried on in the press, they would cease to recognize the agreement they had been compelled to sign as a condition for being released on bail, owing to the campaign carried on in the press, where they were tried, evidence submitted, convicted and sentenced in the most shameless manner, that could not fail to prejudice their chance of a fair trial. On these grounds Mr. A. J. Andrews asked that the bonds be increased to $10,000 each, and Magistrate McDonald eventually fixed upon $8,000, $4,000 personal bond and two sureties of $2,000 each.

Despite the fact that he had taken part in discussions before the Railway War Board and has addressed public meetings in Montreal, R. J. Johns had not been arrested, and his appearance in court when his name was called, caused evident surprise to the authorities. He was out on bail before he had gone through the formality of arrest.

Following the reading of the names of the eight British-born accused, counsel for the Crown proceeded to read the names of the foreign-born (who were still held prisoners, being removed that morning, July 3rd, from the Stony Mountain Penitentiary to the Immigration Hall in the city) and when the name of Verenchuck was read, Mr. A. J. Andrews stepped forward to the magistrate and said: "Your Worship, counsel for the Crown finds it has not sufficient evidence to proceed with the charges against this man under the Criminal Code and being naturalized British subject, we cannot deal with him under the amended Immigration Act, **but we have great reason to doubt his sanity and propose to hand him over to the Military authorities to take care of him.**"

The murmur of dissent increased to a howl of execration as counsel for the Crown made these statements, as the eight who had spent three days in the penitentiary with him knew that he was as sane as Mr. Andrews or any one of them.

Counsel for the defense immediately demanded his release, but this was opposed by Andrews, and it was then demanded that he be examined by a board of alienists and this was done the following day and the man declared quite sane and he was released.

Does the reader get the full significance of the foregoing? Here was a man who volunteered to help fight for liberty, freedom, and justice, which he was told were in danger — twice wounded in that fight, back to Canada, honorably discharged in 1917, and who had **been refused bail in any amount or on any condition, had been kept in the penitentiary under convict conditions, eating convict food in a convict cell, with only twenty minutes exercise, in solitude each day for seventeen days. Taken there in the first place without any warrant the Dominion of Canada raked over with a fine-tooth comb and no evidence against him, and to save the face of the authorities and the corrupt discredited Government at Ottawa, Mr. Andrews, in the name of Law and order and constituted authority appeared willing to railroad a perfectly sane and innocent man to a lunatic asylum.**

After many delays the other four foreign-born were brought before the Immigration Board and one was let go on the understanding that he got out of the country as soon as he had settled up his business, for which purpose he was allowed two weeks.

Almazoff made a strong plea on his own behalf, in which he pointed out that he would have no serious objections to being deported if assured of a safe conduct to "Soviet Russia," but that if he or any others that are deported with the undesirable tag of the Government of Canada upon them and they came into the hands of Kolchack, it was equal to a death sentence. He was released.

Charitonoff, editor of the Russian Worker, was ordered deported, but this case was appealed to Ottawa and the verdict of the Board reversed and he was set free. Of the five, one only, Oscar Chapelroi, who was in uniform at the time of his arrest, was deported, and only then on the ground of some irregularity in his papers when entering Canada, and not for any activities during the strike.

THE DOMINION WIDE RAIDS

The action of the authorities established a precedent in any British Dominion in that men were arrested and railroaded to the penitentiary and afterwards a search was made from Halifax to Vancouver to secure evidence, much along the same lines that were followed in pioneer days on the frontier, when a suspected horse thief was first hanged and then tried. On the evening of June 30th and during the early morning of July 1st, Labor Temple, offices and headquarters of Socialist speakers were raided from the Atlantic to the Pacific, and letters, documents and literature were seized. Homes were broken into, women were compelled to submit to the search in their night clothes, such a thing as was not done under the Czarist regime in Russia, where a woman was always sent if women, or women's apartments had to be searched. After this travesty of justice and British fair play, Mr. A. J. Andrews, K.C., chief spokesman for the Citizens' Committee of 1000, son of a Methodist Minister, himself a pillar of the Methodist Church, acting Deputy Minister of Justice, told the reporters **"that in view of the tons of literature seized we felt confident of securing a conviction of the men accused."**

Fellow-worker, this was all done in your name by men who claim to be your representatives. Is this possible? If it is, then you have been guilty of criminal negligence in the discharge of your duty as a citizen, and it is up to you to do your duty in future, as the only reparation for the sins and folly of the past.

It is your move.

PRELIMINARY TRIAL

Ordinarily we would be inclined to take the position that the less said about the preliminary hearing the better. This incident of the dispute between the masters and the workingmen of Winnipeg might never have received the distinction of a place in recorded history were it not for the fact that the prosecution presented a vast stack of documents, consisting of pamphlets, books on Social Science, etc., together with evidence of alleged utterances of the accused at various meetings held at different times and different places.

The usual objection against much of this matter on the ground of its irrelevancy, was always over-ruled, on the ground that, "If it be relevant it should go in, and if it be irrelevant it won't hurt the accused anyhow."

On one occasion when the Crown counsel stated that the evidence already in was sufficient to warrant asking for a commitment, that it proved a conspiracy, the defense counsel objected on the grounds that no connection had been shown between it and the accused, whereupon the Trial Judge interpolated with a remarkable statement to the effect that it is now the business of the accused to show that there is no connection, and that these men must prove their innocence.

We have not the space nor the inclination to wade through the monotony of those four weeks taken up by the preliminary hearing, in which the aforesaid documents, speeches, etc., together with the general strike and all its incidents and accidents, were played up so prominently, but it was from all this mountain of matter that the grand jury drew its charges for the "True Bill" on the indictment.

A DIGEST OF THIS INDICTMENT APPEARS BELOW

We here give a digest of the indictment only, as the document is so lengthy that the clerk of the court took 52 minutes to read it out to the accused, when they were arraigned:

Summary of Indictment Against Eight Strike Leaders

COUNT ONE — Charges seditious conspiracy in a general form.

COUNT TWO — Charges seditious conspiracy with the following overt acts:

1—Walker Theatre meeting, December 22, 1918.
2—Majestic Theatre meeting, January 19, 1919.
3—Arrangement to form O.B.U.
4—Calgary Convention, March 13, 14, 15, 1919.
5—Publication and distribution of seditious literature.
6—General strike, Winnipeg, May and June, 1919. Effects and intentions of strike are given, including statement that a number of various classes of employees broke their contracts of service and some went out contrary to Industrial Disputes Investigation Act. Statement is made of formation of Strike Committee, purporting to usurp the functions of the Government. "Western Labor News Strike Bulletin" was aided and assisted by accused, it is charged.

COUNT THREE — Charges conspiracy to carry into effect a seditious intention, to wit.: unlawful general strike.

COUNT FOUR — Charges seditious conspiracy to organize an unlawful combination or association or associations of workmen and employees to get demands by unlawful general strikes which were intended to be a step in a revolution against the constituted form of Government in Canada.

COUNT FIVE — Another charge in connection with the O.B.U., alleging intention to undermine and destroy the confidence of citizens in the Government and to bring about the formation of an unlawful combination or association for the purpose of controlling all industries and of obtaining property belonging to others, and of compelling compliance with the demands of such association by unlawful general strikes.

COUNT SIX — Charges of conspiracy to unlawfully bring about changes in the constitution and to enforce the "soviet" form of government in Canada through means similar to those used in Russia.

COUNT SEVEN — Charges committing a common nuisance because of the alleged unlawful general sympathetic strike brought about by assistance of the accused in which various employees walked out illegally and which endangered the lives, health, safety, property and comfort of the public and obstructed the exercise and enjoyment of rights common to all of His Majesty's subjects.

The eight men charged with seditious conspiracy are:

1. R.B. RUSSELL, at time of arrest, Secretary District No. 2, Machinists (all machinists on all railroads in Canada). Member of Strike Committee.

2. R.J. JOHNS, during the whole period of Winnipeg strike, down at Montreal as representative for all machinists on all Canadian Railroads on negotiations before Railway War Board.

3. WM. IVENS, formerly Methodist Pastor at McDougal Church, Winnipeg, which he was compelled to vacate on account of pronounced pacifist proclivities. Founder of Winnipeg Labor Church, and at time of arrest editor of the "Western Labor News."

4. JOHN QUEEN, labor alderman, and fearless fighter on labor's behalf. Since his arrest re-elected to City Council as representative of Ward 5 by overwhelming majority. Advertising Manager of the "Western Labor News."

5. A.A. HEAPS, also labor alderman for Ward 5, City of Winnipeg, and speaker at some of the mass meetings during strike. Was member of Upholsterer's Union. Member of Strike Committee.

6. GEO. ARMSTRONG, one time organizer for United Brotherhood of Carpenters, of which organization he is still a member; well known in Winnipeg as speaker for the Socialist Party and exponent of Marxian Economics. Member of Strike Committee.

7. R.E. BRAY, chairman of returned soldier strikers, returned from England to Winnipeg on December 31st, 1918. Member of Strike Com-

mittee.

8.   W.A. PRITCHARD, Socialist writer and speaker, and Executive member of Vancouver (B.C.) Trades and Labor Council. In Winnipeg for four days as representing Vancouver on Strike Committee.

In addition to the above two other men have also been indicted on a charge of "Seditious Libel."

1.   F.J. DIXON, labor member of the Provincial Legislature who undertook the publication of the "Western Labor News" after the arrest of J.S. Woodsworth, who had taken over the editorship following the arrest of Mr. Ivens.

2.   J.S. WOODSWORTH, who became editor of the "Western Labor News," as already indicated; had been a social worker and lecturer for many years and happened to get into Winnipeg during the strike while on a lecture tour through the Canadian West on behalf of the Labor Church movement. Graduate of Manitoba University, former Methodist Minister, Secretary of the Canadian Forum movement, Secretary of Bureau of Social Research for Governments of three Prairie Provinces. Superintendent of "All People's Mission," and author of several books on "The Alien in Canada."

Three returned soldier strikers were also charged with "seditious utterances." They were J.A. Martin, J. Farnell, and James Grant.

The Grand Jury found "No Bill" against Martin and Grant, but an indictment was returned against Farnell, who is to appear early in January, 1920.

THE CROWN'S CASE

It would indeed be the height of folly to attempt to give a correct and comprehensive view of the case for the prosecution in a nut shell, for its most significant evidence embraces all and sundry who have had anything to do with the accused, or who have been acquainted or associated with any who have been acquainted or associated with them.

Commencing with the attempt of Western labor delegates to the Canadian Trades Congress of 1918, held in Quebec city, to have resolutions passed in favor of the repeal of Orders-in-Council, by which certain scientific and religious publications had been banned, the withdrawal of troops from Russia, etc., down to meetings held in Winnipeg under the auspices of both the Trades and Labor Council and the Socialist Party of Canada, Labor conventions of Miners, and meetings in Calgary and other points where similar resolutions were passed. Of course, it has nothing to do with this case apparently that also similar resolutions have been passed at the Trades Congress in Britain and also conferences of the British Labor Party.

Russell was a member of the Winnipeg Local of the Socialist Party of Canada. All correspondence, therefore, between any member and any other person who may write for information, etc., is considered part of the Crown's case. Speeches made by the accused, together with speeches made by people whom the accused did not know and had never seen, in places where he had never been, are all considered admissible. Riots staged by returned soldiers and directed in chief against aliens, whom the soldiers considered were holding jobs to which the soldiers were entitled are also thrown in as responsible acts of the accused. Happenings at Labor conventions at which none of the accused were present have also been produced as evidence. Places and people unknown to the defendants crop up in rich profusion as evil spirits refusing to be exorcised, all pointing the accusing finger at the indicted men. According to the evidence of the Crown most of the damning utterances and actions took place mainly in regions not altogether remote from the Canadian Rocky Mountains, but strange to say, no one from that portion of the earth's surface was arrested, except Pritchard, of Vancouver, who came to Winnipeg for four days during the strike and was on his way home to the Pacific Coast when his arrest took place.

The whole of the position of the Socialist Party of Canada, together with its literature, dealing with Sociology, History, Economics, and Philosophy; the Winnipeg Labor Church, with its speakers and their actions and utterances, and even its hymn sheets, despite the fact that these two organizations have nothing in common, one being a political party, and the other a socio-religious body, are all brought in as evidence against Russell, the first of eight men to be tried.

It were an extremely wearisome process to describe in detail the matter introduced as evidence of a conspiracy. The holding of a convention, to which any member of the public was welcome, the sending for a Government court stenographer to take a verbatim report thereof, the printing in Winnipeg of 20,000 copies of the proceedings of such convention, all form very interesting details in the evidence introduced by the Crown to prove a "seditious conspiracy."

In short, the purpose of the Crown is to show that the Winnipeg Labor Church, the Winnipeg Trades and Labor Council, together with other Trades and Labor Councils throughout the West, the Socialist Party of Canada, and ordinary and usual conventions of Trades Unionists, and a whole assortment of other things more or less remote, were parts of one grand great conspiracy. Special detectives, secret service men, manufacturers, and merchants have all been called to give their little "bit" of evidence to fit into the picture.

The position of the Crown on many of these points can only be made clear in light of the position taken by the defense, respecting the Winnipeg strike and the position of the accused to the several matters put in as evidence. Of this we propose to give a partial synopsis.

LITERATURE PRESENTED AS EVIDENCE

One remarkable feature of the trial now proceeding against the eight men arrested during the Winnipeg general Strike, and charged with seditious conspiracy; one which the labor movement would do well to take cognizance of, as being indicative of the nature of the prosecution throughout, is the production, as evidence, of leaflets, pamphlets, standard works, etc., most of which have been freely circulated throughout the labor and socialist movements in Britain for the last thirty years, and are still being circulated there, and have been, to our knowledge, circulated in Canada for the last fifteen years.

Realizing the importance of the case, and in order to give a correct idea as to its character, we beg briefly to enumerate some of the pamphlets herein referred to. For the purpose of convenience we will classify them as follows:

SCIENTIFIC—
>Wage Labor, and Capital; Value, Price and Profit; Capitalist Production (Capital) by Karl Marx.
>Communist Manifesto, by Marx and Engels.
>Socialism, Utopian and Scientific, by F. Engels.
>Marxism and Darwinism, by Anton Pannekoek.
>And many similar works.

DESCRIPTIVE OR NARRATIVE—
>Pamphlet published first in Glasgow, containing John McLean's speech under trial, entitled "Condemned from the Dock."
>"Bolsheviks and Soviets," by Rev. A. Rhys. Williams.

PACIFIST—
>Many pamphlets, leaflets, etc., which are purely pacifist in character.
>There have also been put in as evidence the following:

Many issues of the Winnipeg "Western Labor News," (official organ of the Winnipeg Trades and Labor Council); Winnipeg "Socialist Bulletin," and "Red Flag," of Vancouver, B.C.

"The Slave of the Farm," by A. Budden (pamphlet dealing with Canadian Farmer from Socialist standpoint).

"Political Parties in Russia," by Lenine.

"The Liberator," Radical paper published in New York.

The New York "Nation," paper somewhat similar to weekly edition of "Manchester Guardian."

The New York "New Republic."

The Buffalo "New Age."

The following pamphlets and books:

"The Church, the War, and Patriotism."

"The Profits of Religion," by Upton Sinclair.

The Manifesto of the Socialist Party of Canada, published first in 1908.

The History of the Seattle General Strike.

The Russian Constitution.

"The Right to be Lazy," by Paul Lafargue.

"The Class Struggle," by Karl Kautsky.

"Anti-Patriotism," speech by Gustave Herve.

"Socialism and Religion," pamphlet published by Socialist Party of Great Britain.

In addition to this papers published in this country, quoting articles from old country papers, which, in Britain, would scarcely cause a ripple on the smooth running waters of master class diplomacy, are taken and put in as evidence to prove a "seditious conspiracy," whose object is the overthrow of the Government. For example, a paper published under the title of "The Red Flag," at Vancouver, B.C., republished in its columns an article by Bundock in "The Labor Leader," in which the writer refers to the ownership of land and machinery by the whole community as being Socialism and concludes: "This is our proposal. We will work for it. We will vote for it."

This paragraph has been marked as an exhibit by the prosecution and put in as evidence of the "conspiracy." We are mentioning this one item as being typical of hundreds connected with this case.

Any labor paper which refers at all to the Russian situation is diligently scrutinized, marked off, and "put in," as though some exceptionally reprehensible matter had been "discovered."

Were we to have papers, giving all kinds of valuable news and comment, such as the Glasgow "Forward," the London "Daily Herald," the Manchester "Guardian," or "The Labor Leader," it would be pretty certain that a much more serious charge would have been preferred.

THE SITUATION FROM THE ARRESTS UP TO THE COMMENCEMENT OF THE JURY TRIAL

Following the nocturnal visitations of bodies of armed men into the homes of labor men in the City of Winnipeg, June 17th, 1919, by means of which these men, ruthlessly torn from bed, from the midst of their families, were taken to the Manitoba Penitentiary at Stony Mountain, a storm of protest from people in all walks of life broke out from the Atlantic seaboard to the Pacific slope. We are pretty well convinced that the volume and character of this protest was, if not entirely, at least in the main, responsible for the fact that some few days afterwards the men were released on bail and permitted to return to their homes. For, at the time of these "Cossack-conducted" arrests, the present leading Crown counsel, who had then been appointed by the Department of Justice at Ottawa as Deputy Minister of Justice for the Dominion Government for Winnipeg, and who, during the strike, was the foremost spokesman for the self-constituted alleged "Citizens' Committee of One Thousand," made a public statement that these men would have neither bail nor jury trial, but would appear, in camera, before a specially created Board of Inquiry, and shipped overseas, with their wives and families to follow, if necessary.

However, as we have stated, the men were released. The few foreigners, who were arrested and indicted together with them, have since that time been disposed of, but, strange to say, not one has been sent out to the land of his nativity. The general public conception is that these latter were arrested along with the English-speaking accused, in order to give the much desired foreign coloring to the case. Labor unions here, for years, have fought the Government of Canada on the matter of wholesale immigration of peoples from Central Europe, brought in by large corporations for the purpose of breaking strikes, and generally to reduce the standard of living of the Canadian worker, but all to no avail. Consequently, they were ultimately forced to the point where they had to turn round and organize the foreign speaking workmen for their own welfare and advancement, and now refuse, and rightly, to turn against these men at the behest of the same powers and interests that were the most active in bringing the so-called alien into the country in the first place.

Following the release of the arrested men from Stony Mountain Penitentiary, the Workers' Defense Committee sprang into existence in the City of Winnipeg and has now grown in scope and character. The arrested men themselves were despatched throughout the country in order to tell some little of the abominable story to the rest of the workers, both East and west. The consequence of all this is that everywhere, wherever workers can be found, there can also be found a Defense Committee acting in conjunction with the head office in Winnipeg. The mind of the working class has been awakened as a result of the ruthless action of a Government which has perpetuated its existence by manoeuvering the Franchise to suit its purposes, and Orders-in-Council to carry out its wishes. Often Parliament has not been consulted on many things, and Cabinet rule, purely and simply, has been the order of the day in Canada for some few years past.

At the preliminary hearing, staged about the middle of July last, which was the longest preliminary hearing of any case in the history of Canada, all kinds of matters, in no way connected with the accused were allowed to go in as evidence. Behind it all one purpose appeared clearly to us. By means of as corrupt a press as can be found anywhere in the world, all this mass of "evidence" could be delightfully distorted and colored and spread broadcast throughout the land, in the hope that by the very power of suggestion probable jurors might become afflicted with pre-dispositions. Remarkable as this procedure was, and disgusted as many honest-minded citizens were, at the tactics thus pursued by the Crown, a still more remarkable and disgusting incident was to break, like a bolt from the blue, upon the astonished minds of Canadian workingmen and women.

The order to commit had been given, when it was discovered that the usual application for bail, concerning which no one for a single moment had any apprehension, was refused and the eight men were trotted off, under the escort of Mounted Police, to the Manitoba Provincial Gaol. Here they were allowed to remain for four weeks, denied bail upon a bailable offense. Once again a storm of protest raged. The Miners of Nova Scotia and the Lumberjacks of British Columbia together with many of the varied tradesmen in the intervening territory held mass meetings of protest. In Winnipeg 8,000 labor men and women paraded in the rain on September 2nd, while the accused were yet in jail, many of the returned soldiers taking part (in fact, the Soldiers' and Sailors' Labor Party had a section of the parade to themselves) and wound up with mass protest meetings. As an upshot to all this, the eight men were again released on bail and allowed to proceed to their homes and their families. Again they went forth throughout the country and redoubled their efforts in agitating for strong and effective defense being erected.

(The End)

The Heenan Disclosures

After the strike, attempts were repeatedly made in and outside the House of Commons for full disclosure of the strike documents, particularly those relating to the dispatch of troops and the arrest of the strike leaders. On May 11, 1926, Mr. Peter Heenan, a former Labour member of the Ontario legislature and newly elected Liberal member of Parliament for Kenora-Rainy River, hinted in the course of the budget debate that he had seen the documents and now knew why the Conservatives wanted to keep them secret. They showed, he said, that the activities of the government at the time, particularly of its minister of Labour, prolonged the strike; further, they revealed that, by sending troops into Winnipeg, the minister had provoked the resulting bloodshed.

These charges were hotly denied in the Senate by the ex-minister, Gideon Robertson. The Toronto *Star* called on Heenan in an editorial either to prove his charges or to withdraw them. On June 2, Heenan rose on a point of privilege and asked for the unanimous consent of the House to present the documents that would substantiate his earlier statements. This was denied him, but later in the day he found an opportunity to present the documents without requiring the unanimous consent of members present. Heenan's speech of that day is reprinted here in full.

In the heated debate that followed, Meighen did not deny the authenticity of the documents that Heenan presented. He did deny, however, that troops were "ordered in" from the outside. They were already there, he said, but were never used. The troops that were used were local militia of citizens who "enlisted voluntarily" under the command of "the permanent officer of that unit." He estimated that the number of men involved was somewhere between two and three thousand. But he then read a letter from an unnamed person whom he could identify only as "one high in authority." This letter confirmed that no troops were sent in, but it also stated that regular troops of the Winnipeg garrison were used on June 21 against the silent parade, in addition to the RCMP and the militia.

Meighen did not refer directly to the other documents, although he was challenged to do so by A. A. Heaps, MP. But he did defend his actions, and the main point he made is contained in the following passage:

> Winnipeg was in charge of a strike committee; not a child could have milk to drink except by permission of that strike committee. The regularly constituted authorities were no longer in control in connection with the distribution of necessities. If that is a state of affairs to be sneered at and considered quite the incident of a day, well and good; but I would never care to be a member which so regarded anything of that importance.[1]

Heenan later became minister of Labour in the King government. There can be little doubt that he acted with the full consent of that government in revealing these documents, without which he would never have had access to them.

1. House of Commons *Debates*, 1926, vol. 4, page 4010.

Address of Peter Heenan to the House of Commons, June 2, 1926

Mr. PETER HEENAN (Kenora-Rainy River): Before the motion is carried I should like to have from the government a statement of its policy in relation to the despatch of troops into strike areas. In this connection I want to relate some of the circumstances that attended the strike in Winnipeg in 1919. On May 11 I stated on the floor of this House that troops had been sent into Winnipeg at the time of that strike, that shots were fired, and that a person was killed; and I added that had the then Minister of Labour exercised a little horse sense that strike could have been settled without any bloodshed. Now I desire to prove these statements.

I notice that the ex-Minister of Labour, speaking in another place, lamented the fact that he had left the files behind him when he left the department, but I want to assure him that the files are all right. They are intact and to refresh his memory I shall quote several of his own telegrams and communications as taken from those very files. The strike occurred on May 15, 1919 and I find that on the previous day, May 14, General Kitchen, the commanding officer in Winnipeg, communicated with the secretary of the military council at Ottawa, advising that the mayor of Winnipeg had communicated to him his intention of calling upon the military authorities to take steps to protect property. So that we have evidence there that it was the intention of the mayor to seek the assistance of the military authorities.

On May 19, four days after the strike was declared, General Kitchen wired from Winnipeg to Military Headquarters at Ottawa:

> At the request of the mayor and on his written statement that he anticipated disturbances beyond the powers of civil authorities to deal with, a percentage of the active militia has been called out.

In that communication he enumerated the different battalions, eleven in number. So that right at the outset we have evidence that the militia had been called out. On the 15th of the month, the day the strike took place, instructions were sent for a squadron of the Northwest Mounted Police returning from overseas, to be demobilized at Winnipeg and handed over to Commissioner Perry. Later this was done. Consequently during their term of duty in Winnipeg they were members of the mounted police and not of the Canadian Expeditionary Force. In other words, Mr. Speaker, the authorities were camouflaging and pretending that these men of the Canadian Expeditionary Force were members of the mounted police because of the fact that they had been demobilized — and for a purpose.

On May 20 General Kitchen wired for authority as to the source of pay for the militia units that he had called out or of the portion of the units that might be used in the course of the strike. On the same day he was advised that the pay would come from the military authorities.

On May 22 the Adjutant General sent a message to General Kitchen that the Hon. Mr. Meighen and Senator Robertson were convinced by the Citizens Committee of Winnipeg that a certain officer at the head of the militia should be relieved and his place taken by some other officers whose names they suggested. On the same date a message was sent by General Kitchen to the acting prime minister and the military authorities at Ottawa reporting that everything was quiet in Winnipeg, that there were no signs of disturbance, but asking that extra Lewis guns be furnished and forwarded to Winnipeg under guard. It rather looked as if everything was not so quiet.

On May 23 General Hill was ordered to go to Montreal to meet the 27th battalion, explain the situation at Winnipeg, and ascertain whether the whole or a portion of that battalion would consent to remain on duty during the period of emergency in Winnipeg. He was also advised that an officer would report to him at Turcotte yards, near Montreal, at 3:30 a.m. on the 24th instant with eight Lewis machine guns packed in ordinary packing boxes and marked regimental baggage, 27th Battalion. These were to be placed on the first train carrying that unit and delivered to the officer commanding military district No. 40 on arrival. The message continued:

> An officer will deliver twelve Lewis guns similarly packed and addressed at Smiths Falls on arrival of the first train. It is desired that these guns reach Winnipeg without anyone being the wiser.

If the then Minister of Labour did not know what was going on he should have known, because his government was doing this.

On May 25 Senator Robertson wired for the information of council that in his judgment:

> This is not an opportune time to make a declaration in favour of principle collective bargaining as it would be grasped as an excuse by strikers to claim they have forced the government and thereby proved success of sympathetic strike.

In the same message he added:

> I anticipate that the general strike will either be called off very shortly or a last desperate move made to make it successful. If it proves a failure the One Big Union movement intended to be launched at the Calgary convention on June 4 —

That is, about ten days ahead,

> — will I think also fail. These are my personal views expressed in Mr. Meighen's absence and for the information of council.*

I said the other day, Mr. Speaker, that had the then Minister of Labour used a little horse sense the strike could have been settled without bloodshed. The strike was called on May 15, and everyone that had anything to do with it said that it was for the purpose of maintaining the principle of collective bargaining. Yet on May 25 — ten days afterwards — it appears that some of his colleagues in council here had been advising him to make a declaration in favour of the principle of collective bargaining, but Senator Robertson at the time apparently put his own views before those of some of his colleagues and said that this was not the proper time to make such a declaration. His only excuse was that he was afraid the strikers would be encouraged to prolong the strike. I submit that right there and then he had the greatest opportunity of his life, either to call the bluff of the strikers if he thought they were bluffing, or to settle the strike; but he failed to do so.

On May 26 General Kitchen reported the arrival of the 27th battalion in Winnipeg, and that he was conferring with General Hill that evening. He added:

> The machine gun section was in serviceable condition.

Now, Mr. Speaker, the ex-Minister of Labour in another place stated that on his honour as a minister of the crown there was not one soldier sent into Winnipeg. Well, there we have the acknowledgement of the arrival of the 27th battalion with twenty Lewis machine guns. I do not know how he harmonizes those two conflicting statements.

On May 26 General Kitchen communicated with the Prime Minister and others that after conferring with the ministers who were in Winnipeg — that is, Senator Robertson and Mr. Meighen — the only solution to his mind was to have the agitative leaders arrested for instigation and intimidation. He continued:

*The O.B.U. eventually did fail, but not without a tremendous assist from Senator Robertson who, in collusion with employers and US trade union officers, waged a bitter struggle to crush it.

If this was possible I consider the bottom would fall out of the movement to tie up the whole country by a sympathetic strike.

On May 27 Senator Robertson again wired council that labour leaders were frantically endeavouring to camouflage the issue by attempting to contend for the recognition of collective bargaining, and that "General Kitchen's arrangements were both adequate and admirable." In the first place, he had refused to make a declaration in favour of the principle of collective bargaining, and two or three days afterwards he pointed out that the strike leaders were camouflaging, yet he did not use enough horse sense to call their bluff. So I repeat my statement that had he used a little horse sense he could have settled the strike without one shot being fired and without any bloodshed.

On May 31 General Kitchen wrote to the Minister of Justice, that Mr. Meighen, and Senator Robertson had arrived in Winnipeg on May 22, and that Mr. Meighen had issued a proclamation to the postal service on strike warning them that all employees would be given until 11 a.m. on the 26th of May to return to duty, that after that date such as did not accept the offer would be dismissed and debarred from further employment in the postal service, and that the vacancies so caused would be immediately filled by the selection of suitable volunteers. During the last election, Mr. Speaker, the late Minister of Labour, Mr. Murdock, was very properly ridiculed for telling the post office employees at Toronto "They could stay out until hell froze over." This is a similar expression, in effect that if they did not accept the position by a certain date they could also stay out till the same place had frozen over.

Then there was a certain time which was apparently utilized to beat the strikers rather than to settle the strike. On June 5th, Senator Robertson wrote a letter giving permission for 44 porters to be brought in from the United States to take the place of the Canadian Pacific Railway men on strike. On June 7th, Mr. [A. J.] Andrews of Winnipeg, who was acting for the Justice department, wired Senator Robertson giving details of an offer of the metal employers to settle the strike. Here was an opportunity to settle the strike at the instance of the employers themselves.

On June 9th a message was sent by a gentleman who I understand was a member of this House at that time, Mr. Allan, interfering in the matter. He wired to a gentleman by the name of Nanton — I think we all knew Sir Augustus Nanton* — as follows:

Feel strongly company should adhere to refusal mediator's pro-

*One of the top industrialists and financiers in Winnipeg.

posal collective bargaining and that sympathetic strike should be called off before negotiations are resumed. Understand citizens' committee and companies agreed sympathy strike cannot be allowed wholly or partially to succeed.

In other words, they were more interested in breaking the strike than in settling the strike. Evidently the interference had some result, because on June 10th Sir Augustus Nanton answered Mr. Allan — and by the way, through the military sources here — to the effect that all sympathetic strikes must be called off as a preliminary to any further negotiations, and Senator Robertson was again called on to use all his influence in the matter.

On June 9th evidently there were some members of the government here at Ottawa who did not desire the strike should be called off, because I find here a message from Mr. Meighen to Mr. Andrews advising that certain legislation was likely to be introduced — we were discussing some of that legislation today — and it seemed to him — Mr. Meighen — that the settlement on the terms proposed would be a triumph for the strike leaders. In other words, members of the government here at Ottawa were not anxious that the strike should be settled or that the plans the employers had submitted should be accepted.

On June 15th, Senator Robertson wired the Prime Minister that owing to the failure of mediation proceedings and the strike extending to the train service men a clear-cut definition and declaration on the question of collective bargaining seemed to be justified, and that such was submitted to the metal trade employers and had been accepted. After he had refused to make this declaration on May 25th, he now considers, on June 15th, that this is the opportune time to make the statement he should have made long before. He advised further in that telegram that further action outlined in the telegram of the 13th was likely to be taken within the next twenty-four hours, "which we anticipate will result in speedy and satisfactory conclusion of the trouble here." In other words, he was advising that there would be arrests of some of the men within the next twenty-four hours, and within the next twenty-four hours ten men were arrested.

On June 17th, Senator Robertson wired the Prime Minister pointing out the importance of providing machinery for the deportation of undesirables, also advising him of ten arrests on the previous night, and that the Labour temple and several Labour halls had been searched for printed literature and records.

On June 17th, the day after the arrests, Mr. Meighen wired from Ottawa to Mr. Andrews in Winnipeg questioning the legality of the arrests, and pointing out that the arrests had been made without proper authorization, but that the proper authorization was being immediately despatched. In other words, the men had been arrested illegally, but once arrested the government was going to make their arrests legal. Mr. Andrews got a slight slap on the wrist there from (Mr. Meighen), and answering the Minister the next day he practically blamed the whole situation on Senator Robertson. He said:

> Everything I have done has been at the suggestion of Senator Robertson, but because it might weaken his position with Labour I have taken the full responsibility for the Justice department.

In other words, Senator Robertson was in politics, and if he had done anything along these lines it might have weakened his position with Labour if it had been found out, so they had in Winnipeg, acting for the Justice department, another gentleman, who was not in politics, and who took full responsibility in order to save Senator Robertson in a political way.

On June 17th, Mr. Meighen wired to Mr. Andrews that although he had himself questioned the legality of what had been done, it was all right anyway. He said:

> Notwithstanding any doubt I have as to the technical legality of the arrest and the detention at Stony Mountain, I feel that rapid deportation is the best course now that the arrests are made, and later we can consider ratification.

In other words, legal or not, the arrests had been made and the government were determined to get these men out of the country, and later ratify the action that had been taken. We were discussing a bill here this afternoon, in a camouflaged sort of way which does not go to the kernel of the matter, for the legislation was put there for no other purpose than to break the strike in 1919.

On June 17th Mr. Calder wired to the head of the mounted police in Winnipeg:

> You are hereby authorized under section 42 of the Immigration Act to take into custody and detain for examination for the purposes of deportation the several persons referred to in your telegram of the seventeenth.

In that he was authorizing the arrest and detention of men after they had already been arrested and detained in Stony Mountain.

Again, on the same day, Mr. Meighen wired to Senator Robertson advising delay in arrests, in which he said that the provincial government had so advised. "Authorization depends wholly on you." In other words, Senator Robertson was in Winnipeg with full authority in regard to the arrests, but in view of the fact that the provincial government advised against the arrests Mr. Meighen wired to Senator

Robertson that authorization depended wholly upon him, the Minister of Labour. On the same date Mr. Calder wired to Judge Robson as follows:

> Message received. If Senator Robertson has not left, please get in touch with him immediately as local representative was directed, to obtain his approval for any action contemplated.

Again putting the whole responsibility on Senator Robertson, the then Minister of Labour. On June 18th Senator Robertson wired the Prime Minister reporting: everything quiet in Winnipeg and that "our action has proved effective and satisfactory to citizens generally and will be wholly justified." He asked in the same message that certain amendments to the Criminal Code be hastened, as Commissioner Perry, of the northwest mounted police, might desire to take general action throughout western Canada at an early date. Having arrested ten men illegally and put them in Stony Mountain penitentiary, having conquered Winnipeg, as it were, he was now prepared to attack the whole of western Canada. He therefore asked for certain legislation to be hastened so that he could get out on the war path again. On June 19 the Prime Minister wired Senator Robertson as follows:

> Thanks for various messages and especially your telegram of yesterday. Pray accept warmest congratulations upon your masterly handling of a very difficult and complicated situation.

So that apparently the whole proceedings had the blessing of the Prime Minister and the government generally. But two days later something serious happened. I have led up to the point where a situation occurred that is deplorable to think of. On June 21st a message was received here in Ottawa to this effect:

> Serious riot started at 2:45 p.m. Mounted police turned out and now engaged with crowd. Mayor read Riot Act and called on militia. Turning out at once.

So it happened that the militia were used. On the same day there was a message from Mr. Andrews to Hon. Mr. Meighen in reference to the strike, in which he stated:

> I think, however, if we had not admitted to bail, riots would have been participated in by strike committee who I believe, did all in their power to prevent red soldiers parade which started riot.

I want to draw this to the attention of hon. members: The strike committee were blamed for causing a riot. The ex-Minister of Labour, speaking in another place on the 12th of May, went on to say that the committee of the strikers with whom he had been negotiating at an hotel left the hotel with the statement that they were going out to fight that afternoon, and one of them said, "No, we don't want anything to eat; we can fight better on an empty stomach." Nevertheless we find the general officer commanding in Winnipeg making this statement in a telegram to the Hon. Mr. Meighen: "I believe the strike committee did all in their power to prevent the red soldier parade which started the riot." On the other hand Senator Robertson is found declaring in another place that the strike committee were prepared to fight on empty stomachs.

Mr. MANION: In the riots the hon. member speaks of were any people killed?

Mr. HEENAN: Yes.

Mr. MANION: How many?

Mr. HEENAN: One.

Mr. MANION: Were there any others killed during the strike in addition to that one person?

Mr. HEENAN: Not that I know of. I do not mind any hon. gentlemam asking questions. May I just say at this point that I was in Winnipeg. I have been in the labour movement all my life, and have been at the head of every union with which I have been identified locally and I never was on strike one day in my life. I was more interested in an honourable settlement of this strike at that time than I was in anything else. But when it comes down to placing the responsibility for certain occurrences that took place at that time I am going to state the facts no matter who is injured by it.

Senator Robertson in another place made the assertion that I had made a false statement on the floor of this House knowing it to be false, and that I did so for a malicious purpose.

Mr. MANION: My hon. friend has invited questions; may I ask him one more? Was it the troops or the mounted police that did the killing?

Mr. HEENAN: If my hon. friend had been following me he would have gathered that a squadron of mounted police arriving from overseas had been demobilized in Winnipeg so that they would not be known as soldiers but as mounted police. They were the men that did the shooting. If my hon. friend will just give me time I will cover all those points as I go along.

Mr. SPENCE: What do you hope to accomplish by rehashing this matter of the Winnipeg strike? You are simply creating bad feeling in this country.

Mr. HEENAN: I hope to vindicate my honour in the face of the charges made against me.

Mr. SPENCE: It was nothing but an attempt at revolution, that is all it was.

Mr. HEENAN: On what do you base that opinion?

Mr. SPENCE: Everybody is of that opinion.

Mr. HEENAN: I will tell you what it was: A straw man was simply put up for the purpose of knocking it down. That is all it was. I never heard anything so ridiculous in my life as the suggestion that there was an attempt at revolution in Winnipeg. The 27th battalion with twenty machine guns were there, and yet the ex-Minister of Labour made the statement in another place that not one soldier was called upon. This is the gentleman who charged an hon. member of this House with making a malicious statement knowing it to be false. Do hon. gentlemen opposite think that I have no honour or self-respect?

The ex-Minister of Labour in another place made a statement to the effect that there were men on the tops of buildings and other very secluded places firing rifle or revolver shots at the mounted police. There is on record a report from one of his own men who states the circumstances under which the shots were fired. I cannot pronounce this man's name, no Irishman in this country could pronounce it. The initial of his Christian name is all right. It is "P." Whether that is "Patrick" or not, I do not know. The surname is spelled in the following manner — G-u-g-e-y-e-z-u-c-k.

Mr. JACOBS: Can you sneeze it?

Mr. HEENAN: The ex-Minister of Labour eulogizes this individual in another document as one who could be depended upon and recommends that he be given extra pay for his work during the trouble. This man had been reporting regularly. Two days after the strike, on the 23rd of May, he states:

> The authorities were well prepared to stop any disturbance. At 2:30 they began to gather around the market square. The Royal Northwest Mounted Police and special police came up to keep order and stop the parade. As soon as they were near the crowd many stones and bricks were thrown at them and yelling "boo-hoo." In reply to this the mounted police started shooting. There was one killed, thirty were injured and about one hundred arrested.

Instead of firing revolver shots from the tops of buildings, as the senator says, somebody shouted "boo-hoo." Then the mounted police started shooting and killed a man.

Mr. SPENCE: They did fire a revolver shot and threw two brickbats. I was there myself at the time.

Mr. HEENAN: What is the government doing in this connection? I ask the government to amend the act so that no soldiers can be sent into any strike area, except on the responsibility of the government. I do not believe we should allow orders to go round this country promiscuously, requiring soldiers to go into any of these areas. I think I have proved conclusively that the Minister of Labour did on a whim of his own, against the advice of some of his own colleagues, prolong the strike by refusing to declare in favour of collective bargaining. I think he says himself it was in the interests of the international unions. Speaking in another place the hon. minister said that the hon. member for Kenora-Rainy River, who was a young member in the House, should confess his indiscretion in making such statements, should admit the truth and thus apologize. In speaking to the House I have left out a lot of quotations from statements from the files because I think it is in the interest of the country not to use them.

In conclusion I have one apology to make, and that is that I was one of the men who was instrumental in recommending to the Prime Minister the appointment of Senator Robertson to represent Labour in the Senate of Canada. I have now to apologize and say that we appointed a man who became a misfit, and through his indifference actually caused the riots in Winnipeg. I repeat again that had he used a little common sense —

Some hon. MEMBERS: Order, order.

Mr. SPEAKER: I would remind the hon. member that the gentleman of whom he is speaking is a member of the Senate. According to our rules decorum must be observed and no expression imputing discredit on a member of the House of Commons or member of the Senate should be used. The hon. member used the expression ''misfit'' and applied it to a senator. I do not think the expression is parliamentary, and I ask the hon. member to withdraw it.

Mr. HEENAN: I withdraw it; I am sorry I used it if it is against the rules. But I think someone should communicate to the other chamber and inform them of the rule, so that the same order might prevail over there. I do not think a member of the House of Commons, who has to go before the electors, should be spoken about in the way I was spoken about by a member of the Senate who feels a certain amount of security, in that he does not have to face the electors.

I do not want to dictate to the Speaker, but I feel that in all fairness he should communicate to the Speaker of the Senate the ruling he has just given. I am perfectly willing to abide by it. The ruling is a proper one.

The strike we have been discussing should have been settled, but the whole negotiation leading up to the riot was carried on in a manner to prevent its being settled. I do not think anyone could rely on the information the commanding officer was receiving from different sources, because I find in the documents that he had secured a man to go amongst the labour unions as one of them, to find out what was going on and report to the officer. He was paid $75 a week on account of the danger of the job. But, hon. members will note that the officer had so little confidence in that man that he had to employ another man at $50 a week to check him up for fear he would be double-crossed. That is the report received from the general officer commanding at Winnipeg. If I had been an officer of the Crown receiving the reports here, I would have been afraid there was actually a revolution of some description in progress in Winnipeg. I say there was no sign of a revolution, and when the minister went up there for the purpose of settling the matter, if he had really attempted to settle it or was desirous of settling it, he could have done so without the delay that actually did occur in bringing about a settlement.

Excerpts from
W. A. Pritchard's
Address to the Jury
March 23-24, 1920

My Lord, and Gentlemen of the Jury:

You and I have sat here now for some nine weeks, eight of which have been taken up by the learned counsel for the Crown in an effort to build up a case. We have been interested — I am sure I have; and you have also been very patient. I am going to ask you to extend that patience, as I know you will, for just a little time longer.

As I stand here before you in this court, my mind travels to the 17th of February, in the year 1600, when Giordano Bruno offered his life, bound to the stake in the flower market of Rome, because of his scientific analysis of the then known world; because he followed his intellectual master Copernicus, and had declared in certain writings that the universe was not geocentric; that the earth was not the centre of this solar system, but the sun. Of course, he had taken these findings of his and levelled them against the superstition and ignorance of his day, and because of that fact we find him bound to a stake on the 17th February, in the year 1600, in the flower market at Rome.

On June 22nd, 1633, we find Galileo, because of his age and his infirmities, recanting in front of the authority of the State and the Church, from opinions which he knew to be perfectly correct. He had exploded the theory of Aristotle concerning falling bodies. He was master of physics at that time, not only from the mathematical standpoint, but by demonstration had proven his position to be correct. And the power of the Church and State was placed upon the neck of Galileo until he himself rebelled. Today the name of Galileo is given forth in our schools as a master of mathematics and physics, while the names of his prosecutors and his traducers are known only to a few who delve into history.

I am placed in the position where I have to defend the history and literature of two movements. When you look through the address given by the Crown, you will see that I do not have to offer a defense — I would not lower myself to give it such a name. But I have to explain to this Court the history of the Trades Union Movement and the history of the Socialist Movement. In the explanation of the history and literature of the Socialist Movement it will take you into a library which in all probability is the greatest library of any school of thought of any day in history.

Not only has the Socialist Movement in the course of its development produced itself one of the greatest volumes of literature, but it has at the same time in opposition to itself, created a library greater than its own. From the day when the Minister of Finance of Austria, Dr. Albert Schaffle wrote his "Quintessence of Social Democracy," the opponents of Socialism have been adding to the stock of literature given in opposition to the Socialist Movement.

Mr. Andrews drew a picture of work, sweet, beautiful, enjoyable work. Where was he? Not a hundred years back with his Law and Economics, but he was away on the village green in the old country, in merry England, dancing around the Maypole, when work was something which took man outside; when work was something which made men; not the hideous thing it is today in our modern factory hells, something which strangles and kills. Work, work! Let us listen to the song, a psalm of praise, to work, as it comes tripping from the lips of a corporation lawyer. Did he ever work in a coal mine? Does he know what it is to bend his back before the face of the rock, or push wagons from the drive to the bottom of the shaft? Does he know what it is to stand in a slicker and sou-wester and with the rain pouring down engage in painful and persistent perambulations behind a truck heavily laden with wet fish, for seventeen hours a stretch. If he did he wouldn't find so much annoyance in terms. There is a little work, which I haven't here with me, called: "Useful Work versus Useless Toil," which Mr. Andrews might well read to his advantage.

Propaganda! He said: "I think they go to bed at night and wake up saying: 'Strike, strike, strike.' " I don't know — the experience we have passed through — remember, gentlemen, it has been some strain upon you for the last two months. I have been under this strain for the last nine months. Yes, I wake up at night and say: "Strike, strike, strike!" I am entitled to say also, if I wanted to use that kind of language that he used respecting us, that he might wake up at night and say "The Citizens' Committee." That is more likely. Why were men rushed to Stony Mountain Penitentiary in the fashion you have heard? Warden Graham said it had never been done before. My learned friend is liable to retort that it was as a measure of safety for the men themselves. Perhaps. "A measure of safety!" Instead of putting them into gaol they took them to Stony Mountain as a measure of safety. I suppose they dragged me back from Calgary and put me in Stony Mountain, because Stony Mountain was much safer than the Calgary goal.

We have a despatch from London — showing that the story must have seeped through to the labor men in the Old Country — of how the Labor Congress in Southport, held in the early days of June of last year, passed a resolution asking the British Government to bring to the attention of the Canadian Government, and bring pressure to bear on the Canadian Government, to see that British-born citizens of Canada should not be deported without a jury trial. Counsel for the Citizens' Committee has told you that he wanted to be fair to me. Well and good, and yet I can see that in his fairness to me he would have been so fair as to have desired that you twelve gentlemen would not have been the tribunal to sit upon this matter. Why did these workers in Britain take the position they did?

We come to this pamphlet, "Canadian Socialist Party," which has been used against me. It appears to be a kind of manifesto issued by a certain group, as to their position. With that we are not concerned. But I must use it for myself, as it has been used against me. What says this pamphlet? I didn't know there was so much literature in the world until now. Page 17: "The present ruling power which is in the hands of the capitalist class is so powerful, that the working class in its present circumstances is unable to overthrow it. The fists of the working class, weakened by hunger, are too insignificant against the gatling guns in the hands of the capitalists. An armed revolution therefore is out of the question as long as the ruling power is in the hands of the capitalist class. The field for the class struggle is therefore in Parliament." Anything about the vote in that, gentlemen? Anything about the ballot; anything about constitutional practice? Anything about Parliament? "The field for the class struggle is therefore in Parliament."

Exhibit 208: Platform of the Socialist Party of Canada, together with the application for membership. The application for membership states: "The applicant recognizes that the struggle between the capitalist class and the working class is a struggle for political supremacy." In any organization you have the organization blank filled in to see whether the applicant is a fit and proper person for your society. It may be any kind of society, gentlemen — it may be the Elks, or the Bull Moose, or any other organization, and you put your questions short and pithy, not that the world might know, but that the applicant and the members of your organization might know.

Then I want you to look at this Exhibit 541, "The Slave of the Farm." This was evidently the first edition. A small one gotten out in the form of a complete article. The other one, "Slave of the Farm," which you will remember I read to you somewhat extensively, was gotten out later on, rather built upon this, so it would appear, and it was put in the form of letters, like a young romantic man would write to a dear lady. He always writes: "My Dear E." In the first

one, Exhibit 541, page 16, issued by the Dominion Executive Committee of the Socialist Party of Canada, put in as an Exhibit against
us, says: "Our work is plain before us, the masters hold their place
because they hold political power, they are few; we are many, we
must then join hands with our brothers of the factory. With our brothers
of the factory, mill or mine, and workers all, go to the ballot and
grasp political power; send our own men to Parliament to rule as
we shall dictate."

In the Western Clarion, of Oct. 15th, 1918, page 2, there is an
article — it may be strong language, "Nationalization of Industry":
"For as long as the Capitalist class remains in possession of the
reins of the Government, all the powers of the State would be used
to protect and defend their property rights in the means of wealth
production and their control of the products of labor." "National
ownership or control is only more and more a development of capitalism
and is generated by the commercial jealousy of one section of the
Capitalist class against another which holds a monopoly of some essential industry and in furtherance of their aims, they bamboozle the
workers at election times into voting for a so-called public ownership."

Then there is a historical article, which is continued evidently from
previous issues, "Capitalism in its latest stages in England."
Remember, counsel for the Crown said: "What do they mean by
political action." Right in here appears the meaning. I am going
to take the time, gentlemen, because I think you will bear with me
in doing this; you have a duty to perform — so have I. I owe a
duty to myself; I owe a duty to my wife and to my children in this
matter. I owe a duty also to my fellow-workers, and I do not propose
to shirk those duties in any particular.

"Any attempt on the part of the workers to improve their conditions
was regarded in the nature of a conspiracy and severely suppressed.
Until the early part of the 19th century, up to 1824, when the 'Combination Laws' were repealed, workmen could not even meet to discuss
or deliberate on the question of wages or hours. But, of course, it
was considered no offense for employers to organize for the purpose
of regulating working conditions to their own advantage."

Where are these articles taken from? From "Toynbee's Industrial
Revolution," and from the "Industrial History of Great Britain,"
by H. de B. Gibbon, Prizeman in political economy, Wadham College,
Oxford University.

"Lacking political power the workers were unable to help themselves." "But even had they possessed" — what? — political power?
What says the article? "Lacking political power the workers were
unable to help themselves, but even had they possessed" — political
power in practice — "even had they possessed a voice in the Govern-

ment they would certainly have accomplished nothing of permanent benefit to themselves, for they understood the fundamental causes of their misery even less than do the workers today."

To show you our viewpoint all along, not only at elections, but between elections, here is an article on "Women's Rights," by J. Harrington. The article is fairly philosophical in its way. He deals with the cry that is coming to the surface for rights for women. And he says: "The non-participation of women in active national affairs and the narrow sphere in which they have moved for so many centuries, naturally produced a narrow viewpoint. This sufficiently accounts for their undoubted conservatism." Here is the problem that this writer lays before the Government: "The balancing of the increasing radical slave vote" — may be strong language, perhaps we call ourselves slaves — perhaps we call one another wage slaves. If we go to a volume that was written by Robert W. Service, in his "Songs of a Sourdough," we find a poem on the "Wage Slave" — "The slave vote, with a number of Conservative votes, certainly cannot be overlooked by the master class, obviously apprehensive of a new post war slave psychology."

Harrington sees the problem here, that the politicians of today, in order to offset the increase in votes against them by the men, will grant the vote to the women. This was written in March of 1917, gentlemen, and in the Fall of that year, we had a number of politicians who fulfilled that prophecy to the very letter. They gave the vote to a certain number of women because they considered they could use that vote. There was a certain writer of note who said that the differences between politicians and statesmen was this: A statesman is a man who honestly desires to do something for his country, and a politician is a man who wants, in any way at all, his country to do something for him.

There were a bunch of these politicians who worked that franchise and they climbed into office by virtue of a War Times Election Act, and a number of women who have since repented.

You will remember how my learned colleague, Mr. Queen, pressed home the point that Arthur Meighen came down here with the Hon. Mr. Robertson. His was the fine Italian hand which drew the War Times Election Act, the same fine Italian hand which wrote the amendment to the Immigration Act that Mr. McMurray* brought to your notice, whereby a British subject can be deported from British possessions — that same Italian hand which fulfilled the prophecy made by Harrington months before in this Exhibit of the Crown's, No. 843. He is a politician, a gentleman of parts — I should say of

*E. J. McMurray: counsel for the defence.

several parts — a politician with a rather shady past and a very hazy future, and if I can read the signs of the times aright, a Machiavelli who will go down at the next election.*

Now, gentlemen, I stand here before you accused of conspiring and agreeing to carry into effect a seditious intent and that I am thereby guilty of seditious conspiracy. I am also accused of aiding, abetting, counselling, procuring and forming a common intention to commit a common nuisance. You have seen the indictment, I think. I won't offer you that indictment. I looked at it the way it reads when right side up, and then I turned it upside down and read it that way; I read it from the middle towards both ends, and I worked back again. There was a fellow — he may have been a little profane — who was reading this with me, and he said: "This is the devil's own indictment."

Let us see — there are two phrases which my learned friends of the legal profession use — one is "de jure" and the other is "de facto." Speaking briefly, as you know, gentlemen, "de jure" means in the Law — according to the Law; "de facto," according to the fact. When my learned friend pointed his finger at us and said: "The accused Pritchard; the accused Heaps; the accused Johns" — it ran in my mind, yes, the accused Pritchard "de jure" — according to the Law; but not the accused Pritchard "de facto." I stand here according to the Law the accused Pritchard; but according to the facts of life, according to the experiences of my fellow-workers in industry, according to my own experiences — some of them bitter and painful — I stand here "de facto" the accuser of malicious conspiracy; the accuser of men — not because I hate them — because I don't — not because I think anything vile about them. I don't. But I stand "de facto" the accuser of men, who have lent themselves to the most damnable piece of infamy that has ever been perpetrated in any part of the British Empire in the name of Law. I stand here today de facto the accuser of men who entered into a conspiracy to rob the constitution, to carve the vitals out of the privileges of British subjects; who knock the props from underneath free speech and free press. Everyone who lent themselves to that business, gentlemen, aided and abetted, counselled and procured, and assisted and formed the common intention to enter into a malicious conspiracy to do away with the entire British constitution.

Speaking as a student somewhat of constitutional history, I want to tell you it is in the realm of constitutional history that the working

*Pritchard's prophecy was fulfilled. Meighen went down to ignominious defeat in the general elections of 1921. He was defeated in his own riding of Portage La Prairie, and all his supporters in Western Canada met the same fate.

class stands supreme. The working class has nothing to lose, and everything to gain by working within the limits of the constitution. Where that constitution gives an ever-extending franchise to the people as they grow and develop, the movement can take place peacefully. When that constitution is throttled; when that constitution is violated, when that constitution has been raped, gentlemen, there is bound to be a clash somewhere, sometime.

I am giving this to you because after lunch I want to go into one or two things dealing with political action, dealing with the constitutional character of the organizations to which I belong. I want to show you that men who could frame the War Times Election Act; who could write — I don't care what the situation was — the amendment to the Immigration Act, such as was rushed through both houses of Parliament in about forty minutes, can do anything. Nothing can ever be given as a pretext for passing that kind of legislation. But to deal with the history of this thing as it is, I have got to show you why, in a Labor Convention, I stood right behind certain resolutions. I have got to show you why it was we objected to a Government by Order-in-Council, professedly being a Government of the people, by the people and for the people. I have got to show you when that Government — first of all I trust it is plain that I will use the Crown Exhibits — I am going to show you, to the best of my ability how that Government in its very inception was a conspiracy; how it bought up every newspaper of any standing in Canada.

My Lord and Gentlemen of the Jury: Discussing the matter of the position of the Socialist Party of Canada, I would like to give you a text, which can be found in Exhibit 492, "Red Flag," May 24, 1919. All through this trial the thought expressed in this text seems to me to have been hammered home. It is an utterance, an epigram by one of the finest men of letters of Britain today. You may disagree with him, but any man of standing in the world of literature will tell you, if you ask for the names of the three men in Britain who stand out pre-eminently in the world of letters: George Bernard Shaw, Gilbert Chesterton, and Hillaire Belloc. Shaw says this: "Nothing is so terrifying to the Socialists of today as the folly of their opponents."

You have been troubled a little about Plato's "Republic," as to whether Plato's "Republic" had not been forbidden under an Order-in-Council. I find, however, gentlemen of the jury, right from the Exhibits put in by the Crown, that Shaw's "Unsocial Socialist," the "Mikado" and other plays by W. S. Gilbert, were banned. "Mademoiselle Fifi," by de Maupassant, one of the finest of the French story writers, was banned. "First Principles of Sociology," by Herbert Spencer, was banned. "The Origin of the Species," of

Charles Darwin, and I could give you a whole lot more of the same
kind that were banned. To understand my position, you must understand the position of the censor. What is the position he then took.
I am not claiming, gentlemen, when the censor under Orders-
in-Council passed a blanket order to a certain publishing house that
he was acting maliciously. I would not for a moment think so. I
don't think so now, but I can come to no other conclusion than that
he was acting absolutely from pure ignorance. But, however, discussion of politics brings me to the Manifesto of the Socialist Party
of Canada. Before I touch that there is something else I want to
say first. Making request of the Crown for further particulars as to
how the bottle of medicine came to be mixed we were furnished
with a number of them. I had to use the microscope again. And
this is what I find about myself in the particulars: "The accused
Pritchard was a party to the said conspiracy long prior to the Western
Labor Conference in March, 1919, which he attended as a delegate."
Now, really it would be amusing, gentlemen, were it not so sad.
My particular objection to this set of particulars is to be found in
the fact that they lack particularity. You have heard something about
fairness. I think I can look beyond the personalities, and look into
those great causes which produce economic and political movements,
but I must say this that personally I am not suffering from any heavy
sense of that fairness.

Under the heading "Politics," in the Manifesto of the Socialist
Party of Canada, there is an excerpt from the Communist Manifesto.
I am going to read to you that excerpt as it was read· to you by
counsel for the Crown: "Free man and slave, patrician and plebian,
lord and serf, guild master and journeyman, in a word, oppressor
and oppressed stand in constant opposition to one another . . ." Do
you notice any difference? Did you notice the difference between
the past tense and the present tense — that is how it was presented
to you, and yet, immediately before that paragraph is the key which
explains that this is treating the matter historically. "The history of
all hitherto existing society (that is, all written history) is the history
of class struggles." Written history takes us back to the hardy pioneers
on the shores of the Mediterranean, the Phoenicians. It must be dug
out of the records of the past, as it can be found in tools and instruments
used by primitive man in various stages of development. You see
how a small thing will give it an entirely different complexion: "Free
man and slave, patrician and plebian, lord and serf, guild master
and journeyman, in a word, oppressor and oppressed, **stood** in constant
opposition" — twisted into "stand" in constant opposition.

Dealing with this matter of the ballot, and with the matter of the
Socialist Party of Canada and Parliamentary action, they read to you

from the first paragraphs of the section on politics. I had already read this to you some time ago, and I also read concerning the rise of the different slave empires, the prelude to feudalism, then the institution of feudalism, the rise of the merchant class, the destruction of feudalism. Then I went into the section on "Economics," showing our definition of value, what we mean by the Law of surplus value, what we mean by price, by exchange, and all the other terms that are used in the science of economics. Why did I do that? To give you an idea of the work in its entirety, to show you, that while it was the Manifesto of the Socialist Party of Canada — which fought in every election up to the present time — it was nevertheless a disquisition on the history of movements throughout the world; it was a work explaining world movements. The wheat that you produce on your land ties you up to every other country in the world. The ships that I load and unload connect me, maybe, with the labors of the Chinese coolies of Shanghai, Hong Kong and other oriental ports; and brother Johns, as he works with the micrometer and the lathe in the machine shops, his labor is connected with the slaves of the American rolling mills. That is why I read specifically from this work, which deals with the movements throughout the world. "For one country it may be the ballot, in another the mass strike, in a third insurrection." And they try to read the thing upside down.

I will refer to Exhibit 577, No. 20 in the circle, in the Socialist column of the Western Labor News. "The Dictatorship of the Proletariat." It says, signed "Local No. 3, Winnipeg, Socialist Party of Canada." Yet, in the article itself, right in the commencement, gentlemen, it says: "The Law of the great and free Canada informs me that the literature of Kerr,* of Chicago, is banned," and so on. Now, it indicates it was written by one man — "informs me" — and counsel for the Crown gloated over that and also — that there were some quotations from the Communist Manifesto. And this writer who states: "The Law of this great and free Canada informs me" — goes on with the quotation: "In one country the ballot, in another the mass strike, in a third insurrection." The point that he was making in the definition of political action was the fact that this Manifesto is addressed to the International Working Class, and that there is implied therein that political action can take various forms in different countries, according to the conditions of those countries. And then he says — and this was emphasized strongly by the Crown — "At one time we thought that the constitution of Canada allowed us to come under the first category, but now-a-days we are in doubt."

*Charles H. Kerr Co. of Chicago was the North American publisher of Marx's work, as well as other socialist literature.

Written in January, 1919. I feel almost like saying, "Perhaps so."
Thousands of Orders-in-Council put forward in lieu of statutes. Now
we are in doubt. We could hardly blame him when we see what
has been enacted in the name of Legislation down at Ottawa, and
when we further bring to mind the fact that they have so bolstered
up themselves that they could declare to the world at large that they
were going to hang on until 1923.

Gentlemen, you have heard something of Marx. I have got to
introduce you to Marx. The "Communist Manifesto" has been thrown
around and quoted from quite a lot. Who was Marx? It is not
a matter of any hero-worship. My learned friend said that in his
young and romantic days he, too, was a Socialist, but he had heard
nothing of this Marxian Socialism. Marx's father was a Jewish
lawyer, who, in 1824, went over to Christianity. The whole family
were baptised as Christian Protestants. Karl Marx went to the High
Grammar School at Treves, and afterwards, in 1835, to the Universities
of Bonn and Berlin. He studied first Law, and then history and
philosophy, and in 1841 he took the degree of Doctor of Philosophy.
In Berlin he had close intimacy with the most prominent representatives
of the Young Hegelians, the Brothers Bruno and Edgar Bauer and
their circle, the so-called "Freien."

After a while he became editor of a certain paper, the Journal
of the Rhine, and while it is not necessary to the argument, it may
be interesting to tell you that he married the daughter of a Government
official, Jenny von Westphalen.

In contradistinction to most of the Socialists of the day, Marx laid
stress upon the political struggle as the lever of social emancipation.
In some letters which formed part of a correspondence between Marx,
Ruge, Ludwig Feuerbach, and Mikhail Bakunin, published as an introduction to The Review, this opposition of Marx to socialistic dog-
matism was enunciated in a still more pronounced form. "Nothing
prevents us," he said, "from combining our criticism with the criticism
of politics, from participating in politics, and consequently, in real
struggles. We will not then oppose the world like doctrinarians with
a new principle; here is truth; kneel down here. We expose new
principles to the world out of the principles of the world itself. We
don't tell it, 'Give up your struggles, they are rubbish, we will show
you the true war-cry.' We explain to it only the real object for which
it struggles, and consciousness is a thing it must acquire even if
it objects to it."

In Paris, Marx met Friedrich Engels. Friedrich Engels became,
as C. P. Scott, Editor of the Manchester Guardian, says, "The letters
that passed between Marx and Engels" — but this is a historical

sketch and has nothing to do with this case. We are prepared to admit, if it will help my learned friend, that Karl Marx may have written many books, but they say only the Communist Manifesto was distributed, and therefore we cannot consider these interesting letters to Engels. Like the flowers that bloom in the Spring, my Lord, they have nothing to do with the case.

There came a time when Marx came to London, after being buffeted from pillar to post, and was invited to write letters to the New York Tribune, of which Horace Greeley was editor. Some of these letters have been published under the title, "Revolution and Counter-Revolution in Germany in 1848." They constitute a great analysis of the political conditions of that day. He also wrote letters to the New York Tribune, for a living, on the Eastern question, and they were published under that title. Part of these letters dealing with the Eastern question and the Crimean war were published in 1897, in London, and somewhat later reprinted in pamphlet form.

It was in 1859, that he published his first real work on economics, "A Critique of Political Economy." This was the first part of a larger work planned to cover the whole ground of political economy. But Marx found that the arrangement of his materials did not fully answer his purpose, and that many details had still to be worked out. He consequently altered the whole plan and sat down to rewrite the book, of which, in 1867, he published the first volume under the title of "Das Capital," and the economic theories that are in that work have been reduced and embodied in that little work to which I referred.

This argument proceeds — gentlemen, that he has been justly compared with Darwin, it is in these respects that he ranks with that great genius, not through his value theory, ingenious though it may be. With the great theorist of biological transformation he had also in common the indefatigable way in which he made painstaking studies of the minutest details connected with his researches. In the same year as Darwin's epoch-making work, the "Origin of Species," there appeared also Marx's work, "A Critique of Political Economy." The Crown told you the Communist Manifesto was drawn up in Germany. The preface of the work, written in 1888, by Friedrich Engels, tells us that though drawn up in Germany in 1848, the manuscript was sent to a publisher in London a few weeks before the French Revolution. A French translation was brought out in Paris, shortly before the insurrection of June, 1848, and the first English translation, by Miss Helen Macfarlane, appeared in George Julian Harney's "Red Republican," London, 1850.

It is in this work, about which they have made so much; this work from which they have taken one or two points, I would like to show you, gentlemen of the jury, that it was in this work first of all that

Marx developed his concept of historical development, that men do not produce movements, but that movements produce men; that it was not so much Napoleon that made the conditions of Europe of his time, but that the very conditions of Europe themselves called out for Napoleon to appear. You may not agree with this view of history, gentlemen, but I must put it before you — that we look not on the passing of feudalism as an incident in the Lutheran reformation, but we look upon the Lutheran reformation itself as an incident in the passing of feudalism and the coming into existence of capitalism, and this preface was written in London, by Frederick Engels, on the 30th of January, in 1888, and so far as I know, is still circulated among the Labor and Socialist Movements of Britain.

In Manitoba, for the first time in the history of the Labor Movement in any part of the British Empire, so far as I know, it has been dragged in as evidence of a seditious conspiracy. I know if the learned counsel of the Crown were as conversant with the tools of my occupation as he is with his own, and if I were as conversant with his occupation as I am with my own, we might make a better legal argument out of it, but I have got to get the facts before you as best I can, to the best of my little ability. We are driven into this position, that throughout the length and breadth of the British Empire, it is left to a province in the Middle West of the Dominion of Canada, to say, "this is poison," "this is seditious" — and shall we say it, gentlemen, merely because learned counsel for the Citizens' Committee come forward and tell us that it is so?

Take that preface, what does it tell us? Dealing with the work itself, in this preface, Engels says: "Yet when it was written, we could not have called it a Socialist Manifesto." Why? Because the term Socialism was used by Robert Owen, by Fourier, who built Utopias in the way Bellamy did. Why does Engels say this in the preface? He says: "An Armenian translation, which was to be published in Constantinople some months ago, did not see the light, I am told, because the publisher was afraid of bringing out a book with the name of Marx on it." Well, we might understand that in the land of Turkey. "Thus the history of the Manifesto reflects, to a great extent, the history of the modern working class movement; at present it is undoubtedly the most widespread, the most international production of all Socialist literature, the common platform acknowledged by millions of working men from Siberia to California. Yet, when it was written we could not have called it a Socialist Manifesto. By Socialism, in 1847, were understood, on the one hand, the adherents of the various Utopian systems; the Owenites in England, Fourierists in France, both of them already reduced to the position of mere sects, and gradually dying out; on the other hand, the most multifarious social quacks, who, by all manner of tinkering, professed to redress, without any danger to capital or profit, all sorts of social grievances; in both cases men outside the working class movement, and looking rather to the 'educated' classes for support.''

Then he gives a quotation from his preface to the German edition of 1872: "However much the state of things may have altered during the last 25 years, the general principles laid down in this Manifesto, are, on the whole, as correct today as ever. Here and there some detail might be improved. The practical application of the principles, will depend, as the Manifesto itself states, everywhere and at all times, on the historical conditions for the time being existing, and, for that reason, no special stress is laid on the revolutionary measures proposed at the end of Section II. That passage would, in many respects, be very differently worded today. In view of the gigantic strides of modern industry since 1848, and of the accompanying improved and extended organization of the working class, in view of the practical experience gained first in the February revolution, and then, still more in the Paris Commune, where the proletariat for the first time held political power for two whole months, this programme has in some details become antiquated.'' Further on he tells us: "Also, that the remarks on the relation of the Communists to the various opposition parties, Section IV., although in principle still correct, yet in practice are antiquated because the political situation has become entirely changed, and the progress of history has swept from off the earth the greater portion of the political parties there enumerated.''

Why did I take you into that preface, gentlemen? Because the end of Section II., and the end of Section IV., were the particular portions of this Manifesto that were brought to your attention by the learned counsel for the Crown.

I read before, when I had the opportunity, showing you how this deals with the development of industry from the Middle Ages to the present time, dealing with the changing of political conditions. Remember this, gentlemen, written in 1847, applying to the political conditions in Europe, around the time of the Chartist Movement in the Old Country, long before the working class were ever given a chance to express themselves by the franchise. What does he tell us: "That portion would, in many respects, be worded very differently today ... because the political situation has been changed, and the progress of history has swept from off the earth the greater portion of the political parties there enumerated.''

I wanted to deal with that Communist Manifesto at greater length, but I think I have told you something about it. I have made it clear from the book itself that it has an extensive circulation in the mother country. You will remember the outburst of righteous indignation from the lips of counsel for the Crown: "Would you like your children to read that?" Who was it, gentlemen, who said: "When I was a child, I spoke as a child, but when I became a man I put away childish things." Some people, evidently long after they become men, do not put away childish things.

I am going to break off there, gentlemen, and I am going to bring to your attention the witness in the box — Zaneth.* You will remember I asked: "Is this what I said — Production is not undertaken for the sake of consumption but for profit, so that the man who believes that he has a good chance of improving his condition goes to work and produces without asking himself whether there is need of his product or whether he can meet the required conditions; is that what was said?" He said, "Yes, you were always talking like that." Wouldn't it be surprising, gentlemen, if you find that is a quotation taken word for word by myself not very long ago in this court room from Dr. Bonger's work on Criminology and Economic Conditions? He was sure that was what I said. "This then is what freedom of labor means, a freedom that the slave never knows, freedom to die of hunger. No one guarantees to the workman or his family the means of subsistence, if for any reason, he is not able to sell his labor. The slave owner had an interest in taking care of a sick slave, for the slave represented value which he did not care to see diminished. But if a workman is sick he is discarded and replaced by another. The sickness and death of the laborer do not harm the capitalist at all." That is what Dr. Bonger said, the most eminent criminologist of the present day. What more does he say, gentlemen: "At length the workers have perceived that the interests of the employer are opposed to their own, that the cause of their poverty lies in his luxury. They have begun to set up opposition when they learn that by organizing themselves into labor unions they gain a power by which they can ameliorate their lot. The work no longer being done separately, as in the time of the guilds, but together, there has been this consequence for the workmen, that being now in the same position with regard to the capitalist, and in the same social condition, they have gained in the feeling of solidarity and in discipline, two conditions which are essential to victory in the struggle. Little by little the workers have learned that their enemy is not their own employer, simply, but the whole capitalist class. The strife has become a strife of classes." You remember what my learned colleague Mr. Queen had to say about that? His argument will suffice for me, gentlemen.

"The means by which the working class attempt to better their

*An undercover agent of the RNWMP (now the RCMP) whose testimony was heavily used by the Crown.

position are of various kinds. First, there are the unions, which undertake the contest for the shorter day and higher wages. Then there
is co-operation and finally, and above all, politics. The movement
for unions, which could not exist without liberty of the press, of
meeting, and of forming associations, forces the working man to
take part in politics. At first when they still had no clear idea of
the position they occupied in society, the working men permitted
other political parties to make use of them. But coming to understand
that the laborers form a class apart, whose interests are different from
those of other classes, they formed an independent working man's
party. Finally, the contest of the working class could not limit itself
to improvements brought about within the framework of the existing
economic system; if they wished to free themselves permanently,
they saw themselves obliged to combat capitalism itself. Thus modern
Socialism was born; on one side from an ardent desire of the working
class to free itself from the poverty caused by capitalism; on the
other side from the development in the manner of capitalistic production, in which small capital is always conquered by large capital.
The conviction becomes more and more general that capitalism has
fulfilled its historic task — the increase of the productive forces —
and that the means of production must belong to all if we are effectively
to deliver humanity from the material and intellectual miseries which
result from capitalism. The Labor movement blends itself with Socialism, then, and thus social democracy becomes the political organization
of the working class.''

Why do I belong to a Trades Union? Because working at a certain
job, and finding that the workers on that job are organized for their
collective betterment, I join that organization. In fact, I might tell
you that I could not work on that water-front in Vancouver had I
not been a member of that organization. But in any case, there is
the situation. Why do I come together with my fellows into a Trades
Union? Now then there are, in a Trades Union, all kinds of men.
I suppose — in fact, I was going to say I know — I know some
of the farmers of Alberta — however, you know your own position,
but in the United Farmers' of Alberta there will be even Socialists,
Conservatives, Liberals, men of all political faiths, and some with
no political faith at all. But what is it that binds them together in
that Farmers' Organization? Common interest. The same with the
Trades Unions. In Trades Unions there are men of all political faiths,
and some without political beliefs at all. I might be a member of
a political party — a Socialist, and I might be president of the International Longshoreman's Association in Vancouver; and the Business
Agent, being a capable man in doing his work, might be high in

the circles of the Conservative Party, and yet we are bound together
with a common tie in the Trades Union. He works at the job; I
work at the job, and despite our different political beliefs we are
both bound together by this one thing, that is, the conditions of work,
the hours of labor, and the rates of pay on that job. However much
I might differ with him on other matters, I fight the best I know
how for the betterment of conditions and for the maintenance of our
wage schedule. I have done that right along. At the same time, on
the floor of this Union, when some hair-brained, loose-tongued
anarchist gets up and presents his views, I can get up on the floor
of that Union and tell him they are entirely wrong in their premises,
and that all this ranting and roaring about things will not accrue with
any benefit to themselves; they must get down and understand what
they are talking about.

Now, from what I have briefly given you as to the industrial working
conditions, the circumstances under which the modern workers are
brought up, you will have got the idea of how anarchists are made
sometimes, and the conditions, particularly in the Western portion
of North America, which produce large numbers of modern workers,
who, becoming disgusted with things as they see them, moving around
from one job to another, engaged in such jobs that they cannot get
an organization of their own, in various camps, in different works,
where the worker has to move on from one point to another, and
he cannot very well better the conditions except he is on the job.
I trust you follow me, gentlemen, because when you have such jobs
as these lasting four or five or six months, either you must take
the conditions as you find them, or else you must fight to better
those conditions, and by the time you have accomplished something,
you have to go somewhere else. That is the reason why possibly
so many of the workers in the places where I have mentioned have
been driven, from their lack of knowledge of the character of the
conditions which they face, toward what I would call the violent
anarchist school. I want to tell you, gentlemen, sincerely, that knowing
that they are being produced by a combination of those circumstances,
their own quarrels, and the nature of the conditions, I am pleased
to be able to say I am taking my little part in trying to rid them
of their ignorance. The man who is ignorant is oftentimes dangerous,
and when such a one appears it is better to deal with him and attempt
to give him such little knowledge as you possess yourself.

I have pointed out one or two things about the working class movement, and in this movement, in attempting to give the working class
education, the hardest fight that the scientific Socialist has — Mr.
Ivens used that expression, I don't want to go to work to explain
it — just accept it as it stands — the scientific Socialist has to wage

is against the violent type of anarchist, and the element that turns to sabotage, represented by the I.W.W. On the one hand, you have these individuals who are driven through a combination of their own ignorance and the conditions under which they work, into the school of sabotage and anarchy; on the other hand, you have individuals who form, I would call, the idealist anarchist school.

Perhaps it is not the place to say so, but I would put Mr. Ivens in that school of idealists. The school to which I belong is one which tries to explain the nature of conditions to the idealist, and at the same time rob the violent anarchist of his nonsensical ideas of attempting to make progress by a policy merely of ranting and destruction. But if we get these men into our organizations, what can we do with them? Take the organization like that one I have spoken of, with 1,500 members. You can easily see that all kinds of men get into organizations like that. You would have at least two or three anarchists in a group of 1,500 workers. When I say anarchist, I mean those who are anarchist in thought. You will have a number belonging to the Socialist Party, and so on all along the line. What are you going to do? My position is to obey the regulations in the organization of which I am a member, which circumstances compel me to be a member of. Take the Socialist Party, you saw the application form I gave you this morning. Men like Beattie drift into your membership at times. Then there would be some of the other school drift into that party, and realizing the policy, they honestly state their lack of working class education. What would be your position, gentlemen? The position that I take is that we should welcome them if they show a desire to educate themselves. I might state that of such was this man Beattie. Of course, the necessity of circumstances finds us unwillingly in the company of men of these different schools, just as in travelling in a railroad train, and taking a quiet smoke in the smoker, you might find yourself mixed up with a number of card sharpers and artists of that kind.

However, I pointed out that the counsel for the Crown have made or have tried to make quite a lot of the anarchistic remarks in Beattie's letters, where he talks about "riots and petty revolutions." I am going to deal with these things because the Crown may come back and say Pritchard never touched upon them when he was showing to the jury how the Socialist Party of Canada had contested such elections as their finances would permit, all along the line. What does he say, this man who says he knows very little about Socialism and who wants someone to come and tell him something; that if they only had somebody who knew something they might be able to make more progress with the study class. "The remedy we all know of, capture the reins of Government, but how, certainly not by the ballot." "The only way we will get anywhere is by using force," and so on. And the Crown tried to gain a point by stating that these sentiments were not combatted by Stephenson, whom they claim to be the Dominion Secretary of the Socialist Party of Canada. I have pointed out why such men should not be combatted; I have pointed out that when we meet men with energy of this kind it is a matter of grave consideration to turn that energy in proper channels, not oppose them to such an extent that they will make use of that energy in a false direction. When we find men who desire to work, not only for their own education, but for the education of those surrounding them, is it, gentlemen, good policy to hit those men over the head with a club? For if you can get such an one with so much energy to study at all, even if it take a year or two years, if finally you get a proper scientific concept into that man's mind, what have you done? You have taken a man who had given every promise of being a violent anarchist and by your careful handling of such a person, and by the methods you have adopted in educating him, you have made of him another educator, who can turn around and deal with other anarchists in a somewhat similar fashion.

Mr. Andrews said the son of the boot-black can become Premier of Canada if he be worthy. I don't know. During these last two or three years, in the Province of Manitoba, it seems to me that his father would have to have a good stand-in with Arthur Meighen before he would have any show at all of becoming Premier of Canada. "Any man can become what he likes." I am not fighting my learned friend over this. I am just arguing. I am just telling him as I am telling you. I believe he will be a better man and know a little more possibly when this is over than he did before, because I could not bring myself to the point of thinking that he was only talking with his tongue in his cheek, but — "any man can become what he likes, anything at all." Just think for a moment; just let that sink in. Gentlemen, take it home to yourselves. How many farmers on this bald prairie, raising grain, does it take to make a coupon-clipper in the wheat pit of Chicago? Every man that goes into the British army has a chance to become field marshall — how many generals, colonels, majors, captains, right away down the line to "buck" privates does it take to make a field marshall? You point to the initiative of the millionaire, who became great by his own integrity and brains. He is a millionaire in what? In copper. A copper king on Wall Street. How many toiling slaves in the hills of British Columbia and Montana are necessary to make a copper king? How many workers in the Southern States in the cotton fields does it take to make a cotton king? How many farmers with mortgages on their farms and collection bills from the machinery companies against them does it take to make a wheat king? — a man who may not be able to tell a grain of wheat from a grain of barley, but who is content to gamble upon wheat, upon the wheat exchange of Chicago, New York, Manchester. And as you belong to that vast army of toilers who produce wheat, I belong to that other vast army of industrial workers whose every energy makes possible the existence of some clever, marvellous individual, who has become king in a certain realm by virtue of his own effort? I know if I were John D. Rockefeller I could only hold my position as such so long as there were crowds beneath me toiling in my mines, and toiling in my mills.

In the English language the term "Revolution" is used for all kinds of things. What we mean by it will be shewn when I deal with the history of the term revolution. The daily motion of the earth we call a revolution; the movement of the earth around the sun we call a revolution. It was considered that William Morris, the Socialist writer, who loved the beautiful for the sake of the beautiful, made a revolutionary change in the art of printing.

Revolution means a change which comes at the end of a line of growth or evolution, and the scientist, insofar as I can see, when he looks into the world of material things around him, does not distinguish evolution from revolution. That is growth from change. He sees them as parts, one of another. Even in the article which has been given here as an Exhibit, "By which means — evolution or revolution," you will see the same thought expressed and made clear. And keeping in your mind what I said before, that Marx and Engels, as students in the early days, could see even then — when the working class had obtained only a partial franchise — because of the nature of the conditions in Britain, because of the traditions of the British working class, this revolution which they looked forward to would come about peacefully in Britain. I referred to that revolution when I got into controversy with His Lordship about whether James II abdicated or just ran away — a glorious revolution — no one hurt. James II just rowed himself across the river Thames in a boat.

That word "Revolution" has been taken as though it meant violence, bloodshed, anarchy, chaos; as though it meant everything that could be combed together from the calendar of crime, and you are asked to believe that that is what we mean by the term "Revolution." It has been used by historians all along the line to indicate certain great political changes or certain great industrial changes. That is the sense in which we make use of that term.

I stated that I have been placed in a position where I had to defend, as it were, the history and literature of the two movements — the Trades Union Movement and the Socialist Movement. I tried to explain as well as I could some of the terms that are used in Socialist literature, terms that are used on the Socialist platform, terms which are used even today, gentlemen, in the literature and on the platforms of the Socialist Parties in Britain — exactly similar language.

In one of the Exhibits I noticed the Platform of the Socialist Party of Great Britain, almost identical with the platform of the Socialist Party of Canada; so with the other parties, the terms used — used for half a century — are dragged into a court in Manitoba to be given a twisted meaning.

My learned friend goes back a hundred years. He does well. He goes back to the time, gentlemen, when British workmen met in their Trades Unions and kept the books of their organizations concealed upon the moors of the North Country and of Scotland, and when, between the years 1819 and 1823, a most horrible oath was exacted from the members of a certain Scotch Union, in order to escape, if possible, the application of that particular Law. However, March 1, 1823, the repeal of these Laws was moved by Peter Moore. The campaign was renewed the following year, resulting in the Law of 1824.

I might go from one point to another and consider them in detail as legal instruments, but at the moment I am interested only as to the interests that brought these Laws upon the Statute Books, and as to the fight the working men put up in order to maintain themselves and their organizations.

The history of the fight for the ten-hour day in Britain makes remarkable reading. I have not time to go into that. I just want to show you that whatever position is held today, gentlemen of the jury, by a Trades Union here or in Britain, is the result of ceaseless fighting on the part of individuals comprising these unions; that every so-called concession and privilege has been wrenched, if I may use that word, from the opposition. What we are now concerned with is the result. Mr. Queen told you of the ceaseless fighting on the part of those who have gone before for the right of working men to combine. In those fights that occurred we could, had we time, show you how the British privilege of free speech and free press was not something that came on a silver platter for the working men to use, and that all along the line they had to keep their eyes open and watch that these dearly bought liberties were not filched from them. The fight raged before the passing of the Act of 1871, and was carried on until the framing of the Law of 1875, a fight that culminated in the Taff Vale decision and then we have the passing of The Trades

Union Act of 1906. How was it brought about? By leaving it to the gentlemen of the legal fraternity to look down upon the experiences of working men and then telling what they thought was good for the workers? No; it was by carrying the fight into the ranks of the opposition; letting these people see something of the conditions of the working class, and by that ceaseless vigilance of the workers in Britain, free speech, free press and free assembly as we had it was maintained for others.

The gentlemen of the Crown see great danger in the One Big Union. They see a danger, they say, in the Socialist Party — a danger to their commercial system.

Gentlemen, this brings me to the Western Calgary Convention. The Crown take this up from Quebec. I was not at Quebec, at least the Crown did not say so. Gentlemen, from evidence given by Percy, the Crown sought to show that there was something sinister, something seditious, in the fact that resolutions put to the Congress asking for this breaking down of craft divisions and of the organization upon industrial lines, that this came from machinist organizations, and the learned counsel for the Crown stated that this is significant. Russell and Johns were both members of the machinists' organization. Let me tell you, in my humble opinion, these resolutions came from the machinists, in spite of, and not because of Russell and Johns. Possibly the machinist is the one man in the workshop today who has felt that skill being taken from him by an ever developing and extending use of machinery, consequently he wants a closer affiliation with his fellow-workers. He does not want jealousies pounded back and forth with the boilermaker, he wants to join the boilermaker in the fight to maintain a standard of living to which they have been accustomed.

Quite a story was unfolded in the calling of the Western Calgary Convention. Then the evidence of Percy and from the statements made from time to time by the counsel for the Crown — these things appear clearly to you, gentlemen. First — dissatisfaction by the Western members with the machine politics of Congress. Of course, in P. M. Draper, as Secretary of the Canadian Trades Congress — why was it pointed out? — Why did they not come along and say that he had held that job for some 15 years, and had been away from his trade and lost touch with the workers; or that he held a job under the Government, which may actually, if not nominally, have been that of King's Printer? Dissatisfaction in the machine politics of Congress!

Disparity in the representations between East and West because of holding this Congress down in the East — I think Winnipeg is about the third largest city in the Dominion — I do not know when the Congress was held in Winnipeg last — there is no evidence to show us; I cannot tell you. The Congress is always flooded with International officers who sit there by virtue of their office that I have told you about. And in addition to the development of the machine which was breaking down these craft divisions there has been growing, particularly in Western Canada, in the ranks of organized labor, a resentment against the red tape and the cast iron formula of the American Federation of Labor.

I know well enough this country cannot be bound by the Laws of a foreign organization. Nevertheless, we have in this country taken into the Government of this country, a man who boasts of his connection with that same foreign organization — the American Federation of Labor.

THE COURT: I am not bound by what the Government does, but what is on the Statutes, and the jury are not bound by them.

Mr. PRITCHARD: I will not proceed with that.

THE COURT: If the members of the Government were to come into the court and attempt to tell us what the Law was, I would probably send them to jail.

Mr. PRITCHARD: A member of the Cabinet did come into this court in the closing days of the Russell trial —

THE COURT: Yes; but he did not attempt to tell me what to do. He has the right of every citizen to come into court.

Mr. PRITCHARD: I understand that, My Lord.

THE COURT: The jury is not bound by any member of the Cabinet, and under our constitution, as it is, nobody but myself can tell the jury what to do.

Mr. ANDREWS: I also object to the accused saying the Minister of Labor boasts of being a member of the American Federation — there is no evidence of that kind here, and I think the accused may as well know now. He has not been particularly offending up to date, but he thinks he may tell the jury anything that is not before the court, stating facts before the jury we cannot meet — that the Machinists' preamble is the same as the O.B.U. — we cannot deny it.

THE COURT: There is no evidence of that. I will have to tell the jury there is no evidence that Gideon Robertson is a member of that institution.

Mr. PRITCHARD: I did not say that; my learned friend gets up to say something; I did not say the Minister of Labor — I said a member of the Government, and he came along and made it specific —

THE COURT: I hope you are not referring to the Minister of Justice.

Mr. ANDREWS: This may be very funny and suit the crowd at the rear, but every one knows when the reference is made to a member of the Government being a member of the Federation of Labor, he means the Minister of Labor. It is not funny — it is quite improper.

Mr. PRITCHARD: It is not funny at all. I have known a man rise from the workshop bench and go into the legal profession. I think there are men of that description who have left their tools and gone into the legal profession.

THE COURT: What has that to do with it?

Mr. PRITCHARD: They might become Minister of Justice and then boast of the American Federation of Labor (laughter).

My Lord and Gentlemen of the Jury: I want you to take a look now with me at the Western Labor Convention, of Calgary. I want you to keep in mind that the accusation of our learned enemies is that this was an ingredient and a substantial part of the seditious conspiracy, and that they attempted to persuade you that they have discovered this. They contended that at that convention we were against parliamentary action, and there seems to be, at least to my mind, an endeavor to confuse this particular issue by interchanging the term parliamentary with the term constitutional. It seems to me there has been a great anxiety to labor a false point, namely, that the only constitutional action permitted to the British people is to go along once in five or seven years and mark a ballot and drop it in the box. If that is the sum total of the activities of the people at large in the affairs of the country, what kind of a pass should we come to? Something infinitely worse even than what we have at the present time.

There are other ways, in the course of history, whereby man can attempt to redress grievances, and my experience, and the experience of my fellow-workers has been that, generally speaking, they have been driven into a corner before they take any kind of action. They are always the first to suffer, and they suffer all the time. Possibly it is for this very reason that our opponents shout when the action of the working men may bring a little inconvenience to them. Inconvenience, suffering, and hardship are the lot of the workers on such occasions, nothing new to them, and consequently they are victims of that familiarity which breeds contempt. The other man gets excited.

He is not used to it.

There may have been some in the Calgary Convention, some two of the delegates, as I remember, who wanted the Convention to ignore Parliaments altogether. Some were at the other end of the plank and wanted that Convention to start and make a new political party. There were others, myself included, who tried to point out that we had already some political parties of the working class, and that a man might join these if he so desired, according to his light and opinion — that he could join the Labor Party by paying a dollar for admission fee; that he could join the Socialist Party if he considered that to be the best political expression of working class needs; that he might, if he so desired, join the Social Democratic Party.

The logic of the situation was this: If there are already certain political parties in existence, why is this Convention composed of representatives of certain Trades Unions talking about forming a political party? What business have they to do so, especially when it was discovered that not a man on the floor had any instructions along that line?

It has been pointed out by learned counsel for the Crown that I was there representing Vancouver Trades and Labor Council. How did that happen? We will suppose, gentlemen, that I was a member of a Trades Union in Vancouver; we will suppose it is the International Longshoremen's Association, and that I had been sent by the votes of the members of that Trades Union as a delegate to the Trades and Labor Council at an election, which is held, we will say once every three months — and that is a democratic election, to my mind — once every three months. The Trades and Labor Council of Vancouver is affiliated with the B. C. Federation of Labor; affiliated with the Trades Congress of Canada; affiliated with all the different International Unions in the different cities of the United States, and the American Federation of Labor. Because of the reasons that I have enumerated, the Western delegates down at the Trades Congress, as a result of those accumulations of disgust over a period of years, had decided to send out a call, which would be voted on, as to the Western delegates holding a Convention of their own before the next Congress met. I am not sure, but in this correspondence you may find that at the Western Caucus down at Quebec it was resolved that a meeting be held for the Western delegates a week prior to the next Congress. However, the Western Convention was called.

This is what I want to make clear to you. It seems to me that counsel for the Crown were trying, by inference, to make something out of the fact that first of all you get at a certain date the Alberta Federation of Labor Convention, then right on the heels of that you get the United Mine Workers of America Convention, District 18

— that takes in the coal mines of British Columbia in the Crows Nest Pass, on the Main Line, Canmore, Bankhead, and away up to Drumheller, and those points up to the Yellowhead Pass — that these were all held together, and the very fact that these Conventions were held in that fashion, close together, would in itself suggest some master-mind, or a number of master-minds running these Conventions, with seditious intent.

At these Conventions, as you may know, the delegates strike off their various committees. And every one of the resolutions brought in by every delegate from their own unions goes to the Resolution Committee, and the Chairman of the Resolution Committee gives those resolutions to the meeting.

This is resolution No. 1: "Realizing that the aims and objects of the Labor Movement should be the improving of the social and economic condition of society in general, and the working class in particular; AND WHEREAS the present system of production for profit and the institutions resulting therefrom, prevent this being achieved; BE IT RESOLVED, that the aims of Labor as represented by this Convention are the abolition of the present system of production for.profit, and the substituting therefor, production for use, and that a system of propaganda to this end be carried on."

If that be seditious, gentlemen, let me say this, that it is a late day in the world's history to find it so, and it is a funny place in the British Empire to declare it so — in the Province of Manitoba.

There is something in those Exhibits about the Rochdale Co-operative Movement, whose motto is: "All for each and each for all." "To every man according to his needs — from every man according to his ability." What is that, gentlemen, but production for use instead of production for profit? Many, many moons have come and gone since the Rochdale pioneers launched the Co-operative Movement.

Then there came the resolution that was made so much of, and which I have dealt with last night and this morning: "WHEREAS, great and drastic changes have taken place in the industrial world; AND WHEREAS, in the past the policy of organized labor of this country in sending their Provincial and Dominion Executives to the Legislative Assemblies, pleading for the passage of Legislation which is rarely passed, and which would be futile if it were, is now obsolete. THEREFORE BE IT RESOLVED, that this Conference of Western Workers lay down as its policy the building up of organizations of workers on industrial lines for the purpose of enforcing — —" How that word rankles in the legal mind. Amongst the workingmen, generally speaking, there are no very fine distinctions in language. There are very few of them, gentlemen, suffer from a university "degradation" — but they are educated — I WANT TO TELL YOU THAT, GENTLEMEN. Education is not something which proceeds from reputed halls of learning; education is the realization of the problems that stand in front of you and me. That is education. And the school of real education is the school of experience in the material world. There is a big difference between education and instruction — I am not going to develop that — I may have time later on, when the mists have blown away, to tell the people in Winnipeg the difference between instruction and education, but I must pass on.

RESOLUTION No. 5: "WHEREAS, holding the belief in the ultimate supremacy of the working class in matters economic and political and that the light of modern developments have proved that the legitimate aspirations of the Labor Movement are repeatedly obstructed by the existing political forms, clearly showing the capitalistic nature of the Parliamentary machinery.

"This Convention expresses its open conviction that the system of industrial Soviet control by selection of representatives from industries is more efficient and of greater political value than the present system of Government by selection from district.

"This Convention declares its full acceptance of the principle of "Proletarian Dictatorship," as being absolute and efficient for the transformation of capitalist private property to communal wealth." That was made a lot of, gentlemen, and I will have to deal with it at length. This was also made a lot of: "The Convention sends fraternal greetings to the Russian Soviet Government, the Spartacans in Germany, and all definite working class movements in Europe and the world, recognizing they have won first place in the history of the class struggle."

This Convention, you will recall, gentlemen, was held in March, 1919. From these Exhibits we could show you that working class political parties in their Conventions, and the Trades Unions in their Conferences in Britain, both before our own Calgary Convention and after that Calgary Convention, had sent similar greetings, what decision will you come to? That working men's Congresses throughout the length and breadth of the Mother Country can send greetings of this kind, but it must not be in Calgary, it must not be in Manitoba. It is all right in Nottingham; all right in Southport; all right in London; all right in Glasgow; all right in Manchester, but, gentlemen, a horrible crime in Calgary; a horrible crime in Winnipeg. Are you going to take that position? It is for you to decide. As I have told you, I am not worrying a great deal about it, because, as I develop these points, I am going to show you that it is not a matter merely of Pritchard's personal liberty — it will be a matter of history, history that I am sure will defend us in that respect. I told you how the name of Galileo today is respected, and the names of his persecutors and traducers almost forgotten. What are the learned gentlemen for the crown doing, gentlemen? What are they doing? They do not know. They learn nothing. They forget nothing. Why are they building up a case, gentlemen, in this year 1920 in the City of Winnipeg?

There is the resolution, passed at Calgary, on dictatorship, the suppression of the dictatorship of the bourgeoisie — that is all it means — in other words, to put it in good, simple language so that you may understand — the suppression of the dictatorship of the financiers, the suppression of the dictatorship of what is known in popular parlance as the profiteer; the suppression of the dictatorship of the bourgeoisie; the suppression of the dictatorship of the Pattons, the Flavelles, the Rosses and the Allisons; the suppression of the dictatorship of the bourgeoisie. The suppression of the untrammeled dictatorship of the financiers of foreign lands in Canada; the suppression of the dictatorship of the unscrupulous Wall Street financiers as they operate the copper mines in British Columbia, without any regard for the workmen in any respect — only for profit for the Guggenheims and Rockefeller's Standard Oil Company. Go out into the pockets of the hills where they pick copper. Who are the owners? The suppression of the dictatorship of the bourgeoisie. Backus, at Fort Francis, would let Canada go without daily newspapers so that his investments be maintained, and profits flow from the production of pulp down at Fort Francis into the coffers of, as far as we are concerned, gentlemen, unknown persons that adorn Wall Street in the United States. I know, in the Law, we have nothing to do with the United States, but I know that you cannot touch an industry in Canada of any account without touching United States capital.

There is a different tradition behind the Labor Movement of Britain than there is behind the Labor Movement of America. Some of the greatest struggles have been fought out between capital and labor in the last few years. You will get a 2 x 4 strike in someone's backyard in the States, and immediately you get gunmen and hired thugs to break it. There is a difference between the history of the Labor Movement in British countries and the Labor Movement in America. So we have something to do with America after all.

You will remember, I told you, in dealing with the Socialist Party's position, in regard to political action, yesterday, how this fellow Kavanagh had stated that it was: "None of our business at this Convention." This is from the Western Labor Conference minutes, page 107: "Delegate Sinclair (Vancouver): 'Do I understand there is no political action at all?' "

"Delegate Kavanagh (Vancouver, Chairman of Committee): 'Not

this Convention; not within the scope of this Conference; it is purely an industrial organization, founded along industrial lines. Either going in favor or going against is not within the scope of this Conference, and as such we lay it on the table; it is our duty at this moment.' ''

An economic organization of the workers cannot pretend to lay down political lines of action for these workers — that is purely within the province of those workers themselves.

"Delegate Sinclair (Vancouver): 'If it comes to elect representatives of our own calibre at all, there will have to be political action taken some time sooner or later, and it would be through the workmen; it doesn't matter how it comes, it has got to come some time, and until we have men of our own calibre, you will never get what you want; never will. Now, what I want to be clear on is this; practically at no time have labor men been united for to take political action.' ''

"By the Chairman: 'That matter has not been decided or stated definitely by this Convention.' ''

So you see the charge that that Convention repudiated political action, in its proper place, falls to the ground both in substance and in fact.

But in this regard, fortunately, I do not have to depend altogether upon my own words and thoughts, as to the theories I may hold concerning Governmental action. Gentlemen, it is the right of a British subject to hold any theory of government that he desires, and even to promulgate those theories, provided he does it without violence and without inciting to disaffection. It is possible for well known Republicans like H. G. Wells and Bernard Shaw to defend their theories, as they do. It is my right and your right to proclaim the virtues or denounce the shortcomings of any particular form of government, providing it be done in a manner that is not malicious. After all, when you take this case and pull it to pieces and expose it to the winds, the real matter at issue is the intent or the maliciousness; that is all, as far as I can see, it amounts to — whether there was a criminal intent or maliciousness.

We were discussing, gentlemen of the jury, the British subject's right of holding any theory of government that he so desires. As I look over the history of the British Constitution, I see where that constitution itself holds all the possibilities for any change in its structure. By virtue of that constitution, properly considered, you could constitutionally abolish the constitution. I hold these theories — that is my right and my privilege. If there be any merit in them I contend that as education goes amongst the people they will accept them. If there be no merit in them, then the same people will reject them.

Did you ever consider, gentlemen of the jury, that you cannot kill ideas with a club? You cannot drive theories into oblivion by machine guns. If an idea be healthy, if a theory be correct, drag it out into the open and let us look at it. If it be healthy, sunshine will help it to grow; if it be not healthy, sunshine will help to kill it. That is my position. I may be wrong, or I may be correct in many of the views that I hold. It is to my benefit, if I am incorrect, to have those things pointed out to me. If it can be demonstrated to my satisfaction that I am incorrect, then it is to my advantage to accept the conclusions thus brought to me. What is the use of going through life in a position which is manifestly false, if it has been so demonstrated to you?

With the modern spirit of individualism, the widely diffused consciousness of individual freedom and individual worth, and the right of everyone alike to life, liberty and the pursuit of happiness, no tyranny can be very grinding, no autocracy can press very hardly and very obviously on the masses of any nation. On the other hand, a modern popular movement can be exceedingly corrupt and almost inconceivably inefficient. So it comes about that, while an hereditary monarchy of the autocratic type must, by the very conditions of its existence, maintain a certain high level of efficiency, and has little or no temptation or tendency to corruption, in so-called democratic countries, on the other hand the people are very often badly cheated and almost invariably very badly served.

I go on with my argument — it does not necessarily follow from a perception of these truths that democracy, as a form of society, is bound to perish, or that autocracy, as a form of government, is likely to persist. But on the other hand it has become very obvious that if those countries whose social construction is democratic are to continue to exist as national entities, it is becoming increasingly imperative for them to adopt some different institutions of governance than those embodied in the party system.

So-called popular government has become as great a tyrant as any autocracy. Indeed, in some ways it is worse. The ultimate sum of its activities may be even more deadly and destructive than those of an absolutist monarch, just as the ravages of a swarm of locusts is more harmful than the occasional incursion of a larger beast of prey.

The main point of distinction lies in the fact that its depredations are usually spread over a larger area, and are accomplished, as far as possible, in secret; and also that it relies more on corruption than on open violence. Its ravages are therefore more insidious because less noticeable.

No one can doubt that a democratic structure of society is most calculated to secure the happiness of the greatest number. Possibly most men will agree that a Socialistic structure of society is the ideal of human progress; the persistent effort after social reform, which has been so characteristic of the last decade and a half, marks a dim apprehension of this goal of human effort.

I would like to continue with my argument, gentlemen, if you will bear with me. Quite recently the evil I have been speaking of has attained alarming proportions. Popular government has altogether ceased to perform the functions for which it was instituted. It has become merely a means for the existence of politicians, for the enrichment of the leaders of the dominant party and the livelihood of the rank and file. In addition to the ordinary expenses of the administration, the nation has to provide for those who guide and those who support the political parties. Politics has become a recognized means of earning a living. Politicians have become a professional class. A new burden of taxation has been imposed on the people, the more dangerous, as it cannot be controlled; the more insidious, as it is unavowed. Large parts of the public revenue are secretly and fradulently diverted to serve the needs of party politics. A whole host of parasites fatten on the public wealth.

This portentous phenomenon has been brought about by a skilful misuse of the representative system, and the regimentation and rigid control of the parties. The public has become familiar with "machine" government without paying much attention to all that is latent and implied in the conception. The political machine, as it is called, that is the party organization, would be more aptly compared to the nervous system of the animal body. It consists of a flexible network of agencies, ramifying into all the structures of the social organism. The forces at its disposal are bribery and persecution. The elements of political power, the votes of the electors must be combined, and this necessary work is accomplished by the hierarchy of political agents by means of a system of rewards and punishments. All the levers of temporal interests by which men's activities are largely determined are utilized by the "ward-heelers" of modern political life. The sinister influence of the politicians is brought to bear upon the mass of the people through the means by which they earn their living. The merchant's market, the tradesman's custom, the professional man's clientele, the parson's congregation, are all influenced by the activities of the party organization. The political boss has become ubiquitous. Men like G. B. Cox, in Cincinnati, dominate whole cities and districts and extend the ramifications of their powerful influence into the domain of national policy. Nations are governed in the interests of particular classes. All this political organization, all these party activities, need copious supplies of money; and those who pay the piper feel justified in calling the tune. Every organ of public life becomes corrupted. The newspapers are bought or run to advance the interests of particular groups of society, and this species of corruption is perhaps more dangerous than the grosser methods of debauchment, for material advantage is sought under the guise of the advocacy of moral advancement. The world has become familiar with the "cocoa press"; immense campaigns have been fought, in the pretended championship of temperance, really for the profit of the manufacturers of non-alcoholic liquor. The great evil springing from this venality of the public press lies in the debasement of public opinion. The masses of the nations have become readers of newspapers, and are daily fed on lies. The unveracity of the daily paper is only equalled by its ignorance, its illiteracy, and its impudent scurrility. It fabricates news which may tend to the advantage of its masters, it suppresses everything which it dislikes, it venomously attacks all those whom it fears or disapproves of. Gentlemen, I have met coal miners from the face of the rock, who could argue on points in philosophy and political economy as well as anybody I ever heard. I think, honestly in my own mind that some of these scarred, black-faced toilers from the depths of the mines could write better editorials with their picks, possibly, than the editor of the "Free Press" with his pen. Its readers, occupied with their own several cares and concerns, have little inclination or means to investigate the truth of what is read, and lose all possibility of forming a correct judgment on the questions of the time.

By these means a political party is built upon the foundations of the material interests of certain social classes, and affords scope for the criminal activities of the professional politician. All the strings of the organization are held in the hands of a few men who, by superior improbity and craft, have succeeded in dominating the party. In the hands of these men rest the destinies of the countries. They exercise almost despotic power. To attack them means usually to imperil the interests of the party. Over their followers they maintain their hold by a similar system of rewards and punishments. The faithful are rewarded by employment for themselves and their relatives in the public service.

If I put that forward as an indictment against the present system, it is my constitutional privilege to do so. And if I hold that greater efficiency and greater good to the greatest number can be made possible in the nation by holding and advocating another system of government, it is my constitutional right to do so. This is true of Britain, and, in a sense, it is true of other countries.

This party system is not bound by the English channel and the Irish sea. The Dominion of Canada has felt the curse throughout its length and breadth. From the Atlantic to the Pacific has rolled the tide of corruption, inefficiency, waste and mismanagement which flows from the mimic strife for place and power. New Brunswick, Manitoba, Saskatchewan, British Columbia, have each added their melancholy tale of political immorality, gross dishonesty and squandering of the public wealth. Nor does the Federal arena display any brighter scene; for, to the ordinary peculations of politicians has been added the new and attractive pursuit of making illicit profits out of the preparations for the war.

I continue this argument. If anything had been wanting to make party politics stink in the nostrils of all honest men, the conduct of Canada's military business would assuredly have supplied the lack. The greedy crowd of politicians and political adherents rushed to share the spoil, like a cloud of noisome flies flattening on a carcass. Everything that the soldier needed was sold to the Government, at prices ranging from twice to two hundred times what the article was worth; and not seldom the things which did reach the man in the field were useless and even dangerous.

The binoculars cost the country anywhere from twice to six times their real value, but they could be used, and they were not actively dangerous. But what of the boots which were condemned by ninety odd regimental boards of inquiry, which were so well made and so well inspected that "the men had to tie shingles and bits of board and pieces of bags across the bottom of their boots to keep their feet off the ground."

Mr. ANDREWS: There is no evidence of all this. There is evidence that the Canadian troops were the best provided for troops at the front. I do not think, in this court of Law, we are here to discuss supplies furnished, and criticisms by the accused of the administration of the army.

Mr. PRITCHARD: My Lord, I was developing my argument. It is my right to hold any theory of government I desire, and I can put forward, in a perfectly constitutional way, my views on any theory of government.

THE COURT: Is it your view that the soldiers were not provided with proper shoes?

Mr. PRITCHARD: It was, My Lord, and it is. I was showing that if this inefficiency occurs because of the character of the administrative machinery, then I can put forward my own theories as a means for a more efficient administration for the benefit of the people of this country.

Mr. ANDREWS: The accused was stating these things as if they were facts. They are not in evidence, and not in issue.

THE COURT: I have already told the jury that they cannot consider these hypothetical arguments put forward, as making any facts or evidence. "If the moon is green cheese." If the sun is just a mile or two away from this earth, and if this and if that ... They should pay no attention to those hypothetical matters. But I am somewhat interested in Mr. Pritchard's view that our soldiers had no shoes, and thereby the Government ought to be interned. I am somewhat interested in that. Go on, Mr. Pritchard.

Mr. PRITCHARD: My Lord, do I then understand that supposing it to be common knowledge, from our understanding of the term, that there have been appointed in this country commission after commission to look into these very things, that I cannot refer to them, and mention it to the jury?

THE COURT: No, you may be able to present your side of the facts, but you are coming up against what I told you when you came to address the jury; you must keep to the facts that are in and not go afield.

Mr. PRITCHARD: I watched my learned friend, Mr. Andrews, very carefully, and let him run along, and I thought I might be allowed to travel in somewhat the same direction. However, I will have to pass that.

THE COURT: Mr. Andrews was not giving evidence. I have frequently told him and you, too, that when counsel was going too far afield the jury were to pay no attention to him. There are a lot of things you say are common knowledge that do not seem to be known to me at all. However, as to whether the soldiers were well shod or badly shod is not material to the issue. There is nothing there that will justify sedition. If the jury arrives at a view of sedition which will be contrary to your interests, you cannot show that because the soldiers were not well shod you had a justification. The whole thing will turn on whether what was said was or was not seditious.

Mr. PRITCHARD: My Lord, that is not my argument; and if that is to be made my argument I will refuse to proceed with it.

THE COURT: Then I wish you would not go into those things, because you may get into the position that that might be taken from your argument. Go on.

Mr. PRITCHARD: Gentlemen of the jury, we will pass on. We

come now to Resolution No. 4, at the Calgary Convention, page 45. This deals with the question of free speech and free assembly. This is the original resolution: "WHEREAS certain scientific and religious literature has been placed on the prohibited list, owing to regulations imposed under the War Measures Act of the Dominion of Canada; AND WHEREAS, the war has to all intents and purposes ceased, the armies being in process of demobilization. THEREFORE, be it resolved that this Convention demand full freedom of speech, press, and assembly, and advocate united action by organized labor to enforce these demands. And be it further resolved that this Convention demand the release of all political prisoners and the removal of all disabilities and restrictions now upon working class organizations, and that we favor united action by organized labor to enforce these demands."

They took the position, just as the workers in Britain took, the position that oftentimes it is necessary to speak in no uncertain way.

Dealing with the War Measures Act I want you to get in your minds what it was we were protesting against. Shortly after Canada became engaged in the recent European war there was passed through Parliament an Act known as the War Measures Act, 1914, Chapter 2 of 5 George V, and entitled: "An Act to confer certain powers upon the Governor-in-Council and to amend the Immigration Act."

Section 6 of this Act is the section defining the special powers given thereby to the Governor-in-Council, which you will notice made the Governor-in-Council practically an autocrat, over all the matters mentioned in this section. I want you to follow me and see the amount of power placed in the hands of an individual, because we must come to that censorship and the powers of the censor. I may be wrong, gentlemen, but I have always held, since I came to years of understanding, that under the British Constitution, legislative power could not be delegated. I may be wrong in that, and if I am, well, it is not too late in the day for me to be put right.

Section 6 of the War Measures Act says: "The Governor-in-Council shall have power to do and authorize such acts and things, and to make from time to time such orders and regulations as he may by reason of the existence of real or apprehended war, invasion or insurrection deem necessary or advisable for the security, defense, peace, order and welfare of Canada; and for greater certainty, but not so as to restrict the generality of the foregoing terms, it is hereby declared that the powers of the Governor-in-Council shall extend to all matters coming within the classes of subjects hereinafter enumerated, that is to say:

"(a) Censorship and the control and suppression of publications, writings, maps, plans, photographs, communications and means of communications;

"(b) Arrest, detention, exclusion and deportation;

"(c) Control of the harbors, ports and territorial waters of Canada and the movement of vessels;

"(d) Transportation by land, air, or water and the control of the transport of persons and things;

"(e) Trading, exportation, importation, production and manufacture;

"(f) Appropriation, control, forfeiture and disposition of property and of the use thereof.

"(2) All orders and regulations made under this section shall have the force of Law, and shall be enforced in such manner and by such courts, officers and authorities as the Governor-in-Council may prescribe and may be varied, extended or revoked by any subsequent order or regulation; but if any order or regulation is varied, extended or revoked, neither the previous operation thereof nor anything duly done thereunder, shall be affected thereby, nor shall any right, privilege, obligation or liability, acquired, accrued, accruing or incurred thereunder be affected by such variation, extension or revocation."

Now, section 5 declares that the state of war existed from the 4th day of August, 1914, and shall be considered to exist until it pleases the Governor-in-Council to say that it exists no longer. So that, legally speaking, gentlemen — "de jure" — I understand we are still at war, and this section 5 reads as follows:

"Section 5. It is hereby declared that war has continuously existed since the fourth day of August, 1914, and shall be deemed to exist until the Governor-in-Council, by proclamation published in the 'Canada Gazette,' declares that it no longer exists; but any and all proceedings instituted or commenced by or under the authority of the Governor-in-Council before the issues of such last mentioned proclamation, the continuance of which he may authorize, may be carried on and concluded as if the said proclamation had not been issued."

Section 3 states that: "The provisions of Sections 6, 10, 11, and 13 of this Act shall only be in force during war, invasion, or insurrection, real or apprehended."

Now, under the powers vested in the Governor-in-Council by this Act, hundreds, yes, I think I may say thousands of Orders-in-Council were issued. It is totally impossible for the man in the street to keep track of them all. They were passed at Ottawa, and became the Law of the land, and had the force and authority of Acts of Parliament, as far as the ordinary man was concerned.

Here is the pith and substance of my argument. If a man had

plenty of money and could afford to employ eminent legal counsel, he could probably put up a fight against some of these Orders-in-Council, so as to test their constitutionality. That is a luxury that the ordinary working man cannot afford. And that ordinary working man went to gaol, by the scores, by the virtue of what I consider these arbitrary orders.

In the matter of banned literature, "Fragments from Science," by Tyndal; "First Principles of Sociology," by Herbert Spencer; "Theory of Banking," by Howe; "Ancient Society," by Professor L. H. Morgan.

THE COURT: Are these Exhibits?

Mr. PRITCHARD: They are all mentioned in Exhibits. They are covered by a blanket Order-in-Council, put in here as an Exhibit by the Crown, the one I argued against — you remember the Order-in-Council which reads: "A post card and other publications."

It might be interesting to run through a list of all those books that are thereby banned from entry into Canada. There has been only one man in America who has been recognized by the Universities of Europe as a real scientist, Professor Lewis H. Morgan, author of epoch-making works on ethnology, who lived for a quarter of a century amongst the Iroquois Indians, gathered all their customs and habits and presented them scientifically to the world. Gentlemen, I had to take that book off the shelves of my library because of the Order-in-Council passed at Ottawa — the only really comprehensive work on the science of ethnology in the English language. I told you yesterday that I objected to that procedure, not because I considered the censor had acted maliciously, but I could come to no other conclusion than that he had acted out of pure ignorance.

In the matter of banned literature, these orders were published, as it were, overnight, and even before many lawyers in the country were aware of the ban — without taking into consideration the ordinary man — the secret police were raiding houses and stores belonging to anybody whom they considered suspect, with general warrants to search for banned literature. We have had a little recital of such proceedings.

I am going to argue, gentlemen, that possibly while engaged in war, under the then existing conditions, such things had to be tolerated, but you will remember, gentlemen, I don't know that it is in as evidence, but I think I can tell you this, that the armistice was signed on November 11, 1918. My position is that Parliament, when passing this Act, at least it appears to me from the reading of it, intended that Section 3 should terminate the autocratic powers of the Governor-in-Council upon the conclusion of active hostilities, that is, providing

Parliament gave the matter any consideration at all, and did not blindly vote for the measure simply because it was a Government measure.

Our Convention was held on March 13th, 14th, and 15th, 1919, just four months after the conclusion of hostilities, and these arrests were still going on and the country still being ruled by the Governor-in-Council under powers given him by this War Measures Act. Do you wonder, gentlemen, we were against the banning of literature necessary for keeping the working class movement straight, clear, scientific and orderly? Do you wonder that we protested against those censorship regulations? And new censorship notices covering more books and papers were being issued every day or so; no one seemed to be safe. Protests seemed to have little effect, and the workers talked strike, as Mr. Andrews said — they talked strike. Mr. Andrews urged that we should have waited until the next election, waited until the crowd at Ottawa got ready to hold an election which, we notice, they are staving off until 1923.

Exhibit 513. This man Berg writes to Russell* and says: "I have been asked by some of the railroad men here if it is possible to bring you West to address a meeting of the railroad organization" — evidently Russell was a member of a railroad organization — "If you can do this, let me know. The Provincial Committee will stand all the expenses. I just got a shipment of Bolshevik funds for this purpose. One Miners' Union sends $250, and tell me they will send more."** The term "Bolshevik" there is used in a facetious sense, the letter carrying on the face of it its own meaning. When I was speaking of prejudice, yesterday, gentlemen, I had this particular thing in mind, part of the barricade that has been erected around we men of the working class as we stand here today on trial. I can understand that prejudice, and I do not hate anybody for it. Neither do I contend that the term prejudice carries with it the meaning of something malicious, but it arises from being a total stranger to the situation and the circumstances.

This fellow Berg writes to Thom — something, Prince George, B.C., Exhibit 527, and he says: "Well, I see by today's paper that the powers that be have raided the offices in Vancouver, wonder who is next? I also notice that they got a letter that I wrote to Russell in Winnipeg, where I said to Russell that I had just gotten in some Bolsheviki funds (you know the saying, we are supposed to have all kinds of Bolsheviki moneys) and they printed this, but they were

*Carl Berg, Calgary trade unionist and R. B. Russell, one of the accused strike leaders.

**The RNWMP with a straight face released this story to the press, which carried screaming headlines to the effect that a "document" had fallen into the hands of the police, proving without a shadow of doubt that the strike was being financed from Moscow! The "document" turned out to be this letter of Berg's.

careful not to print the following sentence, which would have explained the whole thing, as I stated that one Miners' Local just sent in $250.00 with the promise of more to get speakers and literature in the field; a man does not even dare to think these days ...'' Gentlemen, if this man away out there in Northern Alberta could read from the press that they had given so garbled an account out to the public at large, don't you think that the rest of the people in Winnipeg, where we had to come on trial, would be to some extent influenced by that? If I were to tell you that that letter did appear in the newspapers in Winnipeg, garbled to that extent that a comma had been taken and changed to a full stop, and that the qualifying portion of a sentence had been entirely obliterated, what would you say concerning the fairness of the tactics used against us, and if I were to tell you, gentlemen, that the letter was put into the newspapers in that fashion by a responsible minister of the Crown, what would you say to that?

Gentlemen of the jury, I have gone at some length, and possibly even to the point of exhausting your patience, into this question of the attitude of the workers here in Western Canada to the Russian situation. I have done so, gentlemen, for the reason that the contention of the Crown is, that at the Walker Theatre meeting, and meetings in Calgary, in Vancouver, and it may be in other places, similar resolutions were being passed dealing with this question, and asking for the withdrawal of troops from Russia, and by that process of reasoning, the Crown contends further, that since the acts of this Conference and the acts of that and the other Conferences all look alike, the conclusion to be drawn is, as Mr. Ivens said, that there was a conspiracy amongst the hens. And in making our position clear for demanding the withdrawal of troops from Russia, I have gone to some pains in order to put before you, if I could, our general viewpoint; and to show you that what we workmen in this part of the Dominion were doing, was identical with the position taken by some of the leading men of the day; identical with the position of Senator Johnson of the United States of America; identical with the position taken by the workers in the I.L.P. Conference held in Huddersfield, Yorkshire, in April, 1919; identical with their Conventions in Glasgow and Southport; identical with the position taken by the Triple Alliance, the organization of the Railway Workers, the Miners, and the Transport Workers of Great Britain. The workers in all these organizations were against prosecuting a war against a country and a people when war had not been declared upon them.

And at the very same time when we were sending greetings to the workers of Russia, concerning which the Crown has made so much fuss, the same thing was being done all over Great Britain by the workers in that country, and they had even taken the position that if necessary drastic action be taken with respect to this particular question.

I have developed my argument also, to show you that the resolutions passed, concerning the political prisoners, the withdrawal of troops from Russia, and the removal of the censorship on certain scientific and religious works in this country, were similar to resolutions passed by the workers in the Old Land; and whatever language had been used, and whatever sentiments were expressed at these different times and places, that on no occasion was the language half so strong, half so forceful, half so incisive, as the language used in the editorials of the "Manchester Guardian" upon the same questions.

I have not dealt very much at all, gentlemen, with the Winnipeg strike. Mr. Andrews, in his address, said that I did not appear here myself until after June 10th, and the evidence has shown that these men were arrested in the early morning of June 17th. I was arrested afterwards so that I must have left Winnipeg before June 17th. You can please yourselves as to how long you think I was there. There is the evidence, came into Winnipeg some time after June 10th and left Winnipeg some time before June 17th. The evidence shows that I addressed a meeting of the so-called Labor Church along with the Rev. A. E. Smith, of Brandon, and J. S. Woodsworth, of Vancouver.

Now, gentlemen of the jury, I have tried to give you, in a more or less haphazard fashion, some of my views. I have tried to explain to you some of my actions; have tried to show you a little of the history of the Trades Union and the Socialist Movements; I have tried to deal, to some extent, with certain parts of the literature; I have gone into points in connection with the Socialist Party of Canada; I have taken you over the charter application form for new locals, where the men signing that form (or the women) subscribed to a pledge by which they said they would maintain and enter into no relations with any other political party, that they would support by voice, vote and all other legitimate means the ticket and programme of the Socialist Party of Canada; I have gone through various parts of this evidence to show our standing with respect to parliamentary action and that it surely is not our fault, gentlemen of the jury, if we have not put up any candidates since the last election. I have tried to show as clearly as I can what we mean by the words, "Class Struggle," the fight that goes on all the time; what we mean by the term, "Revolution," and you might recall the quotation that I gave to you from Ingersoll: "To teach the alphabet is to inaugurate a revolution."

We have come before you, gentlemen; we have tried to show you a little of what kind of men we are; we have tried to go into some of this literature; we have tried to explain some of the terms; we have dealt with resolutions passed in different places and explained them; we have shown that those resolutions were similar to resolutions passed in other places and passed by the workers in Britain; we have shown you that the stand that the workers took regarding intervention or non-intervention in Russia was similar to the stand being taken by the workers in the Old Country, by other people in different walks of life and I have tried to show you in my humble way as a workingman, with the task before me of finding bread and butter for a wife and family, a hard enough task, that at the same time, honestly, sincerely, I have tried to do my little bit in the education of my fellows.

Gentlemen, I have done my little bit in attempting to make for working class advancement; I must leave it with you to judge whether or not in my actions amongst my fellow-workers, whether it be on the job, in the Trades Union Hall, or on the floor of a Convention, wherever it may be, as a Trades Unionist, I have sought to advance the interests of myself and my fellows along perfectly peaceable and constitutional lines; whether I have been actuated by criminal motives; whether or not in my work as a member of a political party the same holds good; whether in doing that I have honestly set before myself — making mistakes, perhaps, and the man that never made a mistake never made anything! — set before myself the task of honestly seeking to explain to my fellows the cause of those things in human society, explain to them the nature of these admitted evils, of these social problems, to show them whether or not there is a solution.

You have heard Mr. Queen; you have heard Mr. Ivens; you have seen us all for the last eight weeks; you have seen us, possibly, gentlemen, with a little spirit of'fire, temper, upon occasions, but I think you have been able to judge the character of the men who are now before you. The Crown may contend all it likes; we contend the opposite, gentlemen.

Mr. Ivens told you that he was staggered when he found conditions as they exist in working class homes. Gentlemen, I am going to ask you right in the close of my address to assume something more than those conditions which staggered Mr. Ivens, as he says, when he found them; to assume that somewhere between the end of the battle of Waterloo and the declaring of war between Russia and Japan I appeared upon the scene of human activity. I cannot give evidence, but I am going to ask you to assume that somewhere between those two dates I came along, and gentlemen, Mr. Ivens was staggered. But I staggered into those conditions — I do not think it is a matter of giving evidence — in the year, 1888, in the industrial section of South-east Lancashire. You might not know much of the conditions there. I do. We talk of fathers in this court whether we have fathers or not. An explosion takes place in a coal mine, 1885 or 1886, in the Clifton Hall Colliery, in Pendlebury, Lancashire, two or three years before I was born. My father was one of the last men to come out alive. Why? Coal Mines' Regulations Act violated because of greed for profit. But I will be done with that, gentlemen, and give you the summary of my position in these words; my position honestly. I have held and accepted for some years the position I have briefly attempted to outline to you and shall I now shrink from the possible consequences of such acceptation? Perhaps, I, even as Bruno, can look my prosecutor in the face and say: ''Perhaps you are more afraid of me as you pass sentence than I am of you in receiving it.''

No more industrial rivalries — this is what I am honestly striving for, gentlemen, ''no more industrial rivalries, no more wars; work and peace. Whether we wish it or no, the hour has come when we must be citizens of the world or see all civilization perish. My friends, permit me to utter a most ardent wish,'' said Anatole France to the teachers, ''a wish which it is necessary for me to express too rapidly and incompletely, but whose primary idea seems to me calculated to appeal to all generous natures. I wish, I wish with all my heart that a delegation of the teachers of all nations might soon join the Workers Internationale in order to prepare in common a universal form of education and advise as to methods of sowing in young minds ideas from which would spring the peace of the world and the union of people.''

Reason, wisdom, intelligence, forces of the mind and heart, whom I have always devoutly invoked, come to me, aid me, sustain my feeble voice, carry it, if that may be, to all the peoples of the world and diffuse it everywhere where there are men of good-will to hear the beneficent truth. A new order of things is born, the powers of evil die poisoned by their crime. The greedy and the cruel, the devourers of people, are bursting with an indigestion of blood. However, sorely stricken by the sins of their blind or corrupt masters, mutilated, decimated, the proletarians remain erect; they will unite to form one universal proletariat and we shall see fulfilled the great Socialist prophecy, ''The union of the workers will be the peace of the world.''

Gentlemen, if I have erred, I have erred in good company. If I have erred, I am glad, gentlemen, to have erred in company with Anatole France, with Bernard Shaw, and with any other of those bright minds who are seeking to use such talents as they possess to bring about the day when the sword in reality shall be beaten into the ploughshare. I do not want to afflict you with memories that have seared my mind from childhood. One thing I desire —

for myself I am not making a plea — but, gentlemen, if any suffering can be passed on to my carcass and in its passing my children can be saved from what I passed through as a child, I am satisfied. Look at all that is in this case now; take it to pieces in your own mind; use your own judgment. I shall be satisfied, gentlemen. I am satisfied.

And standing before you now, on the threshold of the parting of the ways, one path leading, maybe, to the concrete-bound and iron-clad obscurity of the penitentiary and the other leading out to life, to comparative liberty, to wife and children and such home as a working-man may possess, I want to tell you, gentlemen, standing at that point, with a mind clear to myself and before my fellows, I can say truthfully: "I have done nothing of which I am ashamed; I have said nothing for which I feel I need apologize." Gentlemen, in so far as my poor self is concerned, this case is in your hands. I am satisfied. And in parting, let me tell you that what I have done, I have done, and in stating that I want you to carry this with you as coming from the innermost recesses of my being. What I have done, I have done in good faith, in sincerity, and, from my own standpoint, from the purest of motives. I thank you, gentlemen, for the patience you have shown in listening to me for these last two days.

Bibliography

Books and pamphlets

Balawyder, A. *The Winnipeg General Strike*.
Toronto: Copp Clark, 1967.

Heaps, Leo. *The Rebel in the House*.
London: Niccolo, 1970.

Kidd, Peter, ed. *The Winnipeg General Strike*.
Toronto: Clarke Irwin, Jackdaw series C29, 1971.

Lipton, Charles. *The Trade Union Movement in Canada 1827-1959*.
Montreal, 1966, chapters 10 and 11.

Logan, Harold A. *Trade Unions in Canada*.
Toronto: Macmillan, 1948, chapter 12.

Magder, Beatrice. *Winnipeg General Strike*.
Toronto: Maclean-Hunter, Canadian Issues, 1969.

Masters, D. C. *The Winnipeg General Strike*.
Toronto: University of Toronto Press, 1950. (Now
available in the Scholarly Reprint Service from
the publisher.)

McNaught, Kenneth. *A Prophet in Politics*.
Toronto: University of Toronto Press, 1963.

Robin, Martin. *Radical Labour in Canadian Politics*.
Kingston: Queens University Press, 1968, chapters 11 and 12.

Smith, Rev. A. E. *All My Life*.
Toronto: Progress Books, 1949.

Articles and essays

Bercuson, David J. "The Winnipeg General Strike, Collective
Bargaining, and the One Big Union Issue," *Canadian
Historical Review* (June 1970), pp. 164-76.

Canadian Dimension. *Winnipeg General Strike: Looking
Back* 6, no. 2 (July 1969).
   Interview with Fred Lange.
   Interview with Fred Tipping.

Pentland, H. C. "Fifty Years After."

Penner, Ald. J. "The Winnipeg General Strike," *National Affairs Monthly* (October 1950).

Rea, J. E. "The Politics of Conscience: Winnipeg after the Strike," *Canadian Historical Association Reports* (1971), pp. 276-88.

Woodsworth, J. S. "The Labour Movement in the West," *Selections from the Canadian Forum* (Toronto: University of Toronto Press, 1972) pp. 16-18. In addition to the above, extended references to the Winnipeg General Strike can be found in biographies of Dafoe, Meighen and in Manitoba histories.

In addition to the above, extended references to the Winnipeg General Strike can be found in biographies of Dafoe, Mieghen and in Manitoba histories.

Reference

Bercuson, David J. "Labour in Winnipeg: The Great War and the General Strike." Unpublished Ph.D. thesis, University of Toronto, 1971.

Dixon, F. J. *Address to the Jury in Defence of Freedom of Speech.* Winnipeg: Defence Committee, 1920.

Pritchard, W. A. *Address to the Jury.* Winnipeg: Defence Committee, 1920.

Trueman, W. H., KC, *Russell Trial and Labour's Rights.* Winnipeg: Wallingford Press, 1920.

Index

287